A TRANSNATIONAL POETICS * *Jahan Ramazani*

D0814980

The University of Chicago Press   Chicago and London

The University of Chicago Press, Chicago 60637
The University of Chicago Press, Ltd., London
© 2009 by The University of Chicago
All rights reserved. Published 2009.
Paperback edition 2015
Printed in the United States of America

24 23 22 21 20 19 18 17 16 15   2 3 4 5 6

ISBN-13: 978-0-226-70344-2 (cloth)
ISBN-13: 978-0-226-33497-4 (paper)
ISBN-13: 978-0-226-70337-4 (e-book)
10.7208/chicago/9780226703374.001.0001

Library of Congress Cataloging-in-Publication Data

Ramazani, Jahan, 1960–
A transnational poetics / Jahan Ramazani.
       p.   cm.
   Includes bibliographical references and index.
   ISBN-13: 978-0-226-70344-2 (cloth: alk. paper)
   ISBN-10: 0-226-70344-4 (cloth: alk. paper) 1. Poetry—History and
criticism. 2. Poetics. 3. Literature and globalization. 4. Transnation-
alism in literature. 5. Postcolonialism in literature. I. Title.
   PN1111.R36   2009
   809.1'93581—dc22

                                                        2008041464

♾ This paper meets the requirements of ANSI/NISO Z39.48-1992
(Permanence of Paper).

For Cyrus & Gabriel

CONTENTS

Preface ix

Acknowledgments xv

1 Poetry, Modernity,
   and Globalization 1

2 A Transnational Poetics 23

3 Traveling Poetry 51

4 Nationalism, Transnationalism, and
   the Poetry of Mourning 71

5 Modernist Bricolage,
   Postcolonial Hybridity 95

6 Caliban's Modernities,
   Postcolonial Poetries 117

7 Poetry and Decolonization 141

8 Poetry and the Translocal:
   Blackening Britain 163

Notes 181   Index 211

PREFACE

Editing the third edition of *The Norton Anthology of Modern and Contemporary Poetry,* I was reminded of Captain MacMorris's question in *Henry V:* "What ish my nation?" Though working on a cosmopolitan anthology, I soon discovered I hadn't escaped the riddles of national identity. Glossing the phrase "Eliotic bones" in Melvin Tolson's *Harlem Gallery,* I was perplexed when a copy editor asked me to name T. S. Eliot's nationality. By standard editorial practice, nationality is, along with dates and occupation, one of three identificatory matrices, or miniature hermeneutic triangles, that also interlock in *Webster's Dictionary* or *The Encyclopaedia Britannica*. But Eliot, whose transatlanticism is hardly a surprise, and a variety of other poets, whose cross-nationality is less frequently considered, brought this sensible institutional practice into collision with the transnationalism of modern and contemporary poetry in English. Should Eliot and his writing be tagged "American" since he grew up in the United States and wrote "Prufrock" and "Preludes" there? Or "Brit. (Am.-born) poet and critic," as *Webster's* puts it, since he published these and other poems only after settling in England in 1915, and in 1927 he became a British subject? Or perhaps "European poet," since he aspired to write out of "the mind of Europe," or even "global poet," given his poetic uses of South Asian religions and languages? Working on a gloss to another of Tolson's allusions, to Gertrude Stein as "the High Priestess of 27 rue de Fleurus," I again had to ask, is "American poet" adequate to a writing career spent in France? Another footnote raised the less obvious question whether W. B. Yeats, who lived much of his life in England, is adequately understood as "Irish," for all his English, European, South Asian, and East Asian affiliations. Reluctantly adopting tags such as "American-born modernist," "Irish poet," or (in another context, for Picasso) "Spanish-born expatriate painter," I continued to feel that these formulated phrases, though useful and even unavoidable, were inadequate to their transnational subjects. That this issue came to a head for me when I was working on notes to Tolson's *Harlem Gallery* was no mere coincidence: his poem of polyglot hybridity and pan-cultural allusiveness, like many other modern and contemporary poems, explodes mononationalist conceptions of culture and pushes toward the transnational and perhaps even the global, ranging as it does from Greece and Ethiopia to Harlem, from Demosthenes and Eliot to Louis Armstrong, from African American "folk" forms such as the blues to elite European poetic genres such as the Pindaric ode.

Though trivial in itself, this small-scale abrasion between a normative editorial practice and the transnationalism of much poetry in English has broader implications for how we conceptualize, analyze, and institutionalize twentieth- and twenty-first-century literary texts — implications I explore in this book. My sense of the need to reconsider poetry's cosmopolitan bearings, particularly in the twentieth century and beyond, grew in part out of the experience of editing a global anthology of poetry in English and, with Jon Stallworthy, the twentieth-century volume in *The Norton Anthology of English Literature*. Collecting, selecting, and presenting poetry in English on a worldwide scale, I was alerted to transnational circuits and convergences that seemed to me ill served by nationalist and regionalist paradigms. Books often develop, of course, out of questions left unresolved by one's previous work, and the present book came in part out of a desire to knit together my initial and subsequent areas of interest: the Irish, American, and British poetry interpreted in *Yeats and the Poetry of Death* and in *Poetry of Mourning: The Modern Elegy from Hardy to Heaney*, on the one hand, and, on the other, the Caribbean, African, and South Asian poetry featured, along with Yeats, in *The Hybrid Muse: Postcolonial Poetry in English*. The cross-cultural dynamics illuminated by postcolonial studies seemed to me to promise a fresh angle of vision on other modern and contemporary texts, just as the premium on form and style in modernist studies might shed light on undervalued aspects of postcolonial and other nonmodernist texts.

A Transnational Poetics argues for a reconceptualization of twentieth- and twenty-first-century poetry studies. Straddling not only the transatlantic divide but also the vast historical and cultural divisions between global North and South, East and West, it proposes various ways of vivifying circuits of poetic connection and dialogue across political and geographic borders and even hemispheres, of examining cross-cultural and cross-national exchanges, influences, and confluences in poetry. It deploys, in approximate order of their appearance, a variety of transnational templates — globalization, migration, travel, genre, influence, modernity, decolonization, and diaspora — to indicate the many ways in which modern and contemporary poetry in English overflows national borders, exceeding the scope of national literary paradigms.

Drawing on transnational studies of modern culture by James Clifford, Arjun Appadurai, Kwame Anthony Appiah, and others, this book also builds on and hopes to encourage the post- and transnational critical work emerging in different areas, including the newly globalized fields of modernist and American studies, as well as the always already transnational frameworks of black Atlantic and postcolonial studies. Because of poetry studies' genre-based cross-nationalism, I seek to indicate how poetic analysis in particular — attentive to figure, rhythm, allusion, stanza, line, image, genre, and other such resources — can foster an aesthetically attuned transnational literary criticism.

Although national narratives of poetry in English as "American" or "British" or "Irish" remain dominant and are unlikely to disappear, a remapping of the field, I propose in the first two chapters, can help show how globalization, cross-national migration, and modernity's geospatial stretch have affected and been reimagined by a range of modern and contemporary poets, from T. S. Eliot, H.D., and Claude McKay to Derek Walcott, Christopher Okigbo, and Marilyn Chin. While sketching the broad contours of the argument, chapter 1 asks what we can learn about globalization from poetry and from poetry about globalization; and chapter 2 asks what the formal, historical, and disciplinary consequences are of cross-national influence and interstitial migrancy for English-language poetry in the twentieth and twenty-first centuries. In the third chapter, I consider what specific poetic devices enable extraterritorial imaginative travel, and what their implications are for a poetics of transnational identity. This chapter looks at the formal means by which the poetry of writers as diverse as Langston Hughes, Elizabeth Bishop, Frank O'Hara, Sylvia Plath, and Dionisio D. Martínez imaginatively travels — in its metaphorical leaps and rapid transitions — across enormous geographic distances. Turning from rhyme, rhythm, lineation, and other such techniques to genre, I ask in the fourth chapter how, why, and to what extent nationalism, antinationalism, and transnationalism intersect in poetry of mourning, and how the elegy might help in developing a taxonomy of the various forms of literary transnationalism. Although poetry in general and poetic mourning in particular are frequently put to nationalist purposes, as this chapter concedes, transnational analysis reveals intercultural microcommunities of grief between mourner and mourned, as well as nation-crossing figurations of death and mourning, in elegies by Yeats, Wilfred Owen, W. H. Auden, Denise Levertov, Wallace Stevens, Kamau Brathwaite, and others.

In the book's second half, this global approach to modern and contemporary poetry in English allows analysis of the largely unexplored connections between Western modernism, both black and white, and poetry of the global South, without eliding their differences. Despite modernism's vaunted internationalism, disciplinary boundaries between postcolonial and modernist studies have tended to veil the overlap, circulation, and friction between postcolonialism and modernism. How and why do poets indigenize and hybridize cultural materials from different parts of the world — postcolonials in relation to Euromodernism, Euromodernists in relation to Asia — and what is the place of such cross-cultural bricolage and hybridity in literary history? Contrary to the commonplace that postcolonial writers rebut Western modernism, chapter 5 argues that poets such as Lorna Goodison, Okigbo, Brathwaite, and Agha Shahid Ali put to use the modernist bricolage of Eliot, Yeats, and Ezra Pound in exploring their own still more complexly hybrid experience — a connection that can prompt, in turn, a reconsideration of modernist cross-culturalism. How does poetry typically defined not as "modernist" but as "postcolonial," asks chapter 6, respond to the technology, alienation, and other features of global modernity, in comparison to more canonically modernist poetries of the Euro-American metropole and of the Harlem Renaissance? Taking up this perhaps surprising area of convergence, the chapter examines the shared alienation and mutually ambivalent response to the shock and creative potential of modernity on the part of canonical modernists (e.g., Eliot and Hart Crane), Harlem Renaissance poets (McKay, Hughes, Jean Toomer), and postcolonial poets (Wole Soyinka and Louise Bennett), whose association of modernity with the West often intensifies their ambivalence. What are the poetic effects of another global change, the decolonization of the British Empire, particularly given the hemisphere-crossing affiliations forged by poets? Bringing Edward Said's ideas of cross-national affiliation and decolonizing cultural resistance to the analysis of poetry, chapter 7 explores how a defining historical feature of the last century — the massive rupture of decolonization — looks on opposite sides of the colonial divide, for postcolonial poets such as Bennett, Walcott, and Okot p'Bitek, in comparison with British poets such as Philip Larkin sity; Namita Goswami for the symposium "How to Practice Postcolonial Theory in a Secular Way: In Memory of Edward Said," Philosophy Department, DePaul University; Laurie Shannon and Michael Valdez Moses for the English Department, Duke University; Pete Monacell for the "Literature of the Margins" graduate conference, English Department, University of Missouri–Columbia; Jay Clayton for the English Department, Vanderbilt University; Anne Goodwyn Jones and David Leverenz for the American Cultures Series, University of Florida, Gainesville; and Janet Gezari for the Lorna F. McGuire Lecture, English Department, Connecticut College.

Finally, I thank editors and publishers for their editorial suggestions and for their permission to reprint material of mine, though in some cases significantly changed for this book, that appeared in earlier form as "A Transnational Poetics," in "Transnational Citizenship and the Humanities," ed. Wai Chee Dimock, special issue of *American Literary History* 18, no. 2 (2006): 332–59; "Modernist Bricolage, Postcolonial Hybridity," in *Modernism and Colonialism: British and Irish Literature, 1889–1939*, ed. Richard Begam and Michael Valdez Moses (Durham: Duke University Press, 2007), 287–313, and in "Modernism and Transnationalisms," ed. Simon Gikandi, special issue of *Modernism/Modernity* 13, no. 3 (2006): 445–63; "Traveling Poetry," in "Globalism on the Move," special issue of *Modern Language Quarterly* 68, no. 2 (2007): 281–303; "Caliban's Modernity: Postcolonial Poetry of Africa, South Asia, and the Caribbean," in *The Cambridge Companion to Modernist Poetry*, ed. Alex Davis and Lee M. Jenkins (Cambridge: Cambridge University Press, 2007), 207–21; "Black British Poetry and the Translocal," in *The Cambridge Companion to Twentieth-Century English Poetry*, ed. Neil Corcoran (Cambridge: Cambridge University Press, 2007), 200–214; "Poetry and Decolonization," in *A Concise Companion to Post-War British and Irish Poetry*, ed. Nigel Alderman and C. D. Blanton (Oxford: Blackwell, 2009); and "Edward Said and the Poetry of Decolonization," in *Edward Said: Emancipation and Representation*, ed. Adel Iskandar and Hakem Rustom (Berkeley: University of California Press, 2009).

CHAPTER 1

POETRY, MODERNITY, AND GLOBALIZATION

The narrator of Derek Walcott's "The Schooner *Flight*," a sailor nick-named Shabine in West Indian patois because of his light black skin, memorably declares his cross-regional allegiances and inheritances:

> I'm just a red nigger who love the sea,
> I had a sound colonial education,
> I have Dutch, nigger, and English in me,
> and either I'm nobody, or I'm a nation.[1]

Shabine would be a "nobody," if to be somebody one had to belong to a single cultural or ethnic group, if a literary voice were recognizable only when it could be slotted into a national category, or if the nineteenth-century British historian James Anthony Froude were right to say of the culturally and racially mixed Caribbean, "no people there in the true sense of the word."[2] But in Walcott's twist on a moniker adopted by wily Odysseus, as by Emily Dickinson and Sylvia Plath, and so suggestive of the cipher of the poetic "I," this supposed "nobody" is teeming with bodies—the bodies genetically deposited in his fictive body by Dutch, African, and English ancestors, the bodies of various national and ethnic literatures incorporated in this literary character.[3] This nobody contains multitudes. If a "nation," he is so as an irreducibly plural aggregate, not in the sense of a people united by common descent and language living in the same territory, as in the Dutch or English nation, or even—in extended usage—the pan-African nation. A character of cross-cultural as well as cross-racial heterogeneity, he announces his plural attachments, to the Caribbean Sea and to a British education imposed from overseas; his odyssey, set in the Caribbean basin, is told in Standard English iambic pentameter in alternating rhyme, inflected by vernacular triple speech rhythms and West Indian verb forms ("who love the sea"). The difference between the racist slur used for his African inheritances, though proudly transvalued, and the Standard English terms for his European inheritances marks the painful discrepancies of power between the cultural spheres soldered in his diction, grammar, and body. Learning that he fits the identitarian preconceptions of neither white settlers nor black nationalists, Shabine remarks, "I had no nation now but the imagination."[4] As indicated by this wordplay, Walcott, like many other modern and contemporary poets, conceives the poetic imagination as transnational, a nation-crossing force that exceeds the limits of the territorial and juridical norm.[5]

Walcott's Shabine is hardly the first or last such "compound" figure in twentieth-century poems written in English, to recall T. S. Eliot's "compound familiar ghost" whose spectral address not incidentally compounds elements at once English and American, Italian (terza rima), and Irish (over half a dozen echoes of Yeats).[6] In Mina Loy's semiautobiographical "Anglo-Mongrels and the Rose," the narrator witnesses the comically awkward sexual union of a Hungarian Jewish father and a Protestant English mother that will eventually issue in her "mongrel" birth — and the birth of her "mongrel" poem.[7] The school composition anticipated in Langston Hughes's "Theme for English B" will interfuse African American student and European American instructor across inequities of power; it will likely be as cross-cultural as the student's bilabially entwined list of favorite "records — Bessie, bop, or Bach."[8] "*Am I a slave or a slave-owner? / Am I a Londinio or a Nubian?*" asks the self-dramatizing "composite" character Zuleika — the Afro-Roman, black British protagonist of Bernardine Evaristo's *The Emperor's Babe*.[9] The very name Marilyn Chin — "Marilyn" a starstruck, immigrant Chinese American father's transliteration of "Mei Ling" — becomes a trope for transhemispherically splayed identity in "How I Got That Name," a Pacific Rim poem plaited out of Chinese, Euromodernist, confessional, and black feminist strands.[10] These and a host of other cross-cultural figures personify the variegated transnational poetries of the twentieth century and beyond that are the subject of this book, from the modernism of W. B. Yeats, T. S. Eliot, Ezra Pound, Mina Loy, and W. H. Auden and the Harlem Renaissance of Claude McKay, Jean Toomer, and Langston Hughes, to post–World War II North American poets Elizabeth Bishop and Sylvia Plath, North Atlantic poets Seamus Heaney, Tony Harrison, and Paul Muldoon, contemporary "ethnic American" poets Dionisio D.

Martínez and Li-Young Lee, "black British" poets Linton Kwesi John-son and Bernardine Evaristo, and postcolonial African, Caribbean, and South Asian poets Wole Soyinka, Lorna Goodison, and Agha Shahid Ali. Although creolization, hybridization, and the like are often regarded as exotic or multicultural sideshows to literary histories of formal advance-ment or the growth of discrete national poetries, these cross-cultural dynamics are arguably among the engines of modern and contemporary poetic development and innovation.

Poetry may seem an improbable genre to consider within transna-tional contexts. The global mobility of other cultural forms, such as digital media and cinema, is more immediately visible, and most com-mentary on literary cosmopolitanism has been on prose fiction, one scholar theorizing cosmopolitan fellow feeling as the "narrative imagi-nation."[11] Poetry is more often seen as local, regional, or "stubbornly national," in T. S. Eliot's phrase, "the most provincial of the arts," in W. H. Auden's.[12] In another critic's summation, it is understood as "the expression and preservation of local attachment," "the vehicle of par-ticular attachments, to mother, home, and native place."[13] While prose fiction's interdiscursive and intercultural porosity is frequently re-hearsed, lyric poetry especially is seen as a genre of culturally and psy-chologically inward turns and returns, formally embodied in canoni-cal attributes such as brevity, self-reflexivity, sonic density, repetition, affectivity, and subtlety.

Mikhail Bakhtin famously distinguished between the "centripetal," "singular," "unitary, monologically sealed-off" qualities of poetry and the dialogic and double-voiced, heteroglot and centrifugal structure of the novel.[14] It would be easy to subvert his distinctions on the ba-sis of counterexamples; even Bakhtin conceded that his classifications blurred, especially in the twentieth century, when he saw poetry as be-ing radically prosaicized.[15] The intercultural congress within postcolo-nial and ethnic minority poetries and the anti-Romanticism of modern-ist and Language poetries obviously challenge Bakhtin's definitions of poetry as unitary, subjective, and monologic. But perhaps more produc-tive than dissolving these theoretical antitheses altogether would be an effort to examine how transnational poems such as Walcott's "Schooner *Flight*" twist together the polarities. These are poems of heteroglossia, but often internalized (e.g., the intersection of standard and dialectal discourses in Shabine's self-reflections), of psycho-cultural inwardness, perhaps, but shot through with cross-cultural heterogeneity (Shabine as self-obsessed poet and Caribbean collectivity). They display Bakhtin's centripetal intentionality (the poet's self-recasting as Shabine), but are torqued by the centrifugal counterforce of cosmopolitan experience, allusion, and travel. The paradigm of a continuum between transnational poetry's centripetal and centrifugal tendencies avoids the Scylla of strictly poststructuralist models, in which the poem as discursive collage is evacuated of subjectivity, and the Charybdis of overly intentional models, in which the poem as personal utterance is reduced to authorial speech act. Although many transnational poems are "lyric" in being compressed, self-aware, and sonically rich, they also evince Bakhtin's dialogism, heteroglossia, and hybridization — the latter a term Bakhtin uses for the literary mixture of "utterances, styles, languages, belief systems."[16] From Eliot and Sterling Brown to Brathwaite, Muldoon, and Grace Nichols, cross-cultural poems cannot be reduced to Bakhtin's putative lyric homogeneity: instead, they switch codes between dialect and standard, cross between the oral and the literary, interanimate foreign and indigenous genres, span distances among far-flung locales, frame discourses within one another, and indigenize borrowed forms to serve antithetical ends. Because poetic compression demands that discrepant idioms and soundscapes, tropes and subgenres, be forced together with intensity, poetry—pressured and fractured by this convergence — allows us to examine at close hand how global modernity's cross-cultural vectors sometimes fuse, sometimes jangle, sometimes vertiginously counterpoint one another. Bringing poetry into critical conversations about globalization can thus help focus attention on the creolized texture of transnational experience as it is formally and imaginatively embodied.

A lyric from the 1960s that suggests poetry's grounding in "mother, home, and native place" is Christopher Okigbo's invocation of a local river goddess of eastern Nigeria in his sequence *Heavensgate*:

> Before you, mother Idoto
>   naked I stand;
> before your watery presence,
>   a prodigal
>
> leaning on an oilbean,
> lost in your legend.[17]

This poem enacts a longed-for communion with the ancestral goddess of the village stream, near where Okigbo grew up, in Ojoto, part of the

Biafra for which he died fighting in the Nigerian Civil War in 1967. Its devices for bringing together supplicant and goddess, he leaning on her totemic, West African oilbean tree, include an imagery of watery reflection, the "I-Thou" formation of second-person lyric address, the symmetry between the first two and the last two stanzas, the epanalepsis in the line "watchman for the watchword," and the alliterations of "leaning on an oilbean, / lost in your legend." The resources of poetry enseam the speaker and his toponymically and botanically localized world. The poem could be seen as acting out a role Okigbo was to have taken up in life, as the inheritor of his grandfather's priestly responsibilities to Idoto's shrine.

Yet, ironically, the poet's mythologization of his return to indigenous roots is routed through the detours of Western modernist syncretism and free verse, the Christian story of the prodigal son and — in the last two lines — the language of the psalms:[18]

> Under your power wait I
>   on barefoot,
> watchman for the watchword
>   at *Heavensgate;*
>
> out of the depths my cry:
> give ear and hearken . . .[19]

With its deep formal and allusive memory, lyric both locates and dislocates the speaker. Even as he elects a native return, he superimposes the language of monotheistic prayer on Igbo polytheism, redeploys Latinate syntactic inversions, and Africanizes the modernist concept of poetry as a personal verbal rite. A priestly offering to a local goddess, the sequence is also, according to Okigbo's introductory comments, an Orphic exploration of the poetic creativity that results, implicitly, in the very poem we read.[20] If the speaker is at one and the same time the prodigal son, a psalmist, an Orphic poet, and an Igbo supplicant, the goddess he invokes, later appearing in the guises of lioness and watermaid, is an Igbo river deity, earth mother, muse, maternal culture, Eurydice, the Madonna, and the beloved. Okigbo holds in a rich poetic solution his Igbo, Christian, classical, and high modernist sources. Whereas Walcott's Shabine emphasizes the jarring discordances between the unlike spheres compacted in his being, this speaker melds a cross-hemispheric range of local and distant references in his poetry's musical resonances, alliterations, and fluid syntax, in accordance with Okigbo's avowed sense that there was no contradiction between his European, African, and other inheritances.[21] Still, for all these differences, poetry functions for both Walcott and Okigbo, as for a host of other writers, as a language that can mediate seemingly irresolvable contradictions between the local and global, native and foreign, suspending the sometimes exclusivist truth claims of the discrepant religious and cultural systems it puts into play, systems forced together by colonialism and modernity.

If modernity is "inherently globalising," as Anthony Giddens puts it, then twentieth- and twenty-first-century poetry 's participation in the processes threading across geographic and political boundaries should be axiomatic.[22] An Igbo Catholic, or a Catholic Igbo, with a classical education and an African upbringing, who read manuscripts in Nigeria for Cambridge University Press, Okigbo lived a life and built a body of work on various global and ex-colonial criss-crossings; so too, in different ways, transnational poets have done, from Pound to Walcott, Loy to Chin. Under modernity, to summarize baldly, global space and time have contracted; ever more people have traveled and migrated; technology and communication systems have circulated ideas, images, and voices across distant locales; empires have transferred armies, religions, goods, canons, and artifacts; militaries have unleashed destruction worldwide; and capitalism has "glocalized" products and services across national borders. Globalization — understood here as having a long prehistory in empire and trade but having been dramatically sped up by modernity, especially in the twentieth century[23] — is the large, amorphous term that lumps together these and other distinct but entangled processes, different aspects of which are highlighted by different models.

Often globalization is represented as the one-way homogenization and westernization of the world, a model that accentuates the persisting asymmetries of economic and political power, in the wake of formal decolonization. Indeed, in defiance of the erasure of their cultural worlds, some poets champion poetry as a tool of resistance to the ravages of (neo)colonialism and modernity, as will be seen in chapter 6. Already in Okot p'Bitek's 1966 book-length poem *Song of Lawino*, an Acoli village woman named Lawino, anticipating antiglobalization discourse, rails against the displacement of rural African practices by Western technologies, foods, dances, religions, and beauty ideals. To her Mercedes-driving, whiteness-adoring, Africa-denying husband, she protests:

> Listen, Ocol, my old friend,
> The ways of your ancestors
> Are good,
> Their customs are solid
> And not hollow. . . .
> . . . .
> I do not understand
> The ways of foreigners
> But I do not despise their customs.
> Why should you despise yours?[24]

But Ocol is a lost cause, having thoroughly internalized imperial attitudes toward African rural culture as primitive and backward. He and others like him, reports Lawino, dress

> As if they are in the white man's country.
> At the height of the hot season
> The progressive and civilized ones
> Put on blanket suits
> And woollen socks from Europe,
> Long under-pants
> And woollen vests,
> White shirts;
> They wear dark glasses
> And neck-ties from Europe.
> Their waterlogged suits
> Drip like the tears
> Of the *kituba* tree
> After a heavy storm.[25]

Lawino's comparison of the sweat-dripping suits to "the *kituba* tree / After a heavy storm" wryly indigenizes her husband's infatuation with everything Western. A resolute defender of African cultures against Western assimilation, Okot records in loving ethnographic detail the songs and dances, medicinal and religious practices, of the rural Acoli.

Even so, the form, structure, and language of his long poem complicate the notion of poetry as local or national resistance to a hegemonic modernity, since *Song of Lawino,* though hardly woolen suited, combines the long Western dramatic monologue in free verse with the repetitions and oral urgency of Acoli songs; its diction intertwines Acoli words and semi-translated proverbs with a robustly Africanized English; and its anti-Western localism is informed, ironically, by Okot's Western anthropological training.[26] The poem's literary transnationalism dialogically interanimates the one-way thrust of Western homogenization, on the one hand, and, on the other, of nativist assertion. In language, form, and subject matter, such poems articulate and imaginatively remake the contending forces of globalization and localization, alien influx and indigenizing resistance. In *Omeros*, a later long poem that grapples with economic globalization, Walcott places in a volcanic hell the "traitors," or local government officials, who "saw the land as views / for hotels" and so abetted the tourist industry's despoliation of his natal Saint Lucia.[27] Yet Walcott also acknowledges his book's complicity in the tourist exploitation of his island, its picturesque poverty, and its violent history; the poet is like his character Philoctete, who "smiles for the tourists" at the opening of the book, and for extra money, "shows them a scar," emblematic of the ancestral wounds of slavery.[28] The poem works both within and against the globalizing circuits that simultaneously stamp touristic sameness on the poet's cherished island locality and yet help give rise to the unique synthesis of Walcott's cross-cultural epic. Like other poems criss-crossing unequal and discrepant worlds, it carves out what Homi Bhabha calls an "interstitial" or "third space," born of the imaginative "negotiation of incommensurable differences."[29]

As the complex texture of these poems reveals, the homogenizing model of globalization is inadequate for the analysis of specifically poetic transnationalism. Applied to poetry and other cultural forms, moreover, it risks replicating methodologically the totalization it is meant to critique. Poetry indicates the oversimplification in believing, as Andreas Huyssen writes, that "the local opposes the global as authentic cultural tradition, whereas the global functions as . . . a force of alienation, domination and dissolution," "that only local culture or culture *as* local is good, authentic and resistant, whereas global cultural forms must be condemned as manifestations of cultural imperialism."[30] To the extent that this nondialogic paradigm represents "each national culture" as what Fredric Jameson calls "a seamless web of habits and habitual practices which form a totality or a system," threatened by a "singular modernity," it can be of little help in analyzing the dynamic cross-currents and exchanges in poetic forms, genres, and vocabularies, whether across even or uneven terrain.[31] The nuances of cultural influx and efflux are lost when non-Western poetry and other forms are assumed to be irreparably "destroyed" or diluted by Western influences: in one of the few critical works on poetry and globalization, Stephen Owen bemoans modernism's degradation of an authentically "local" and "national" Chinese poetry into a homogenized "world poetry."[32] Similarly, the authors of *Toward the Decolonization of African Literature* complain that the influence of modernism on poets such as Okigbo is an imperial imposition that derails African oral literature into privatist and obscurantist writing.[33]

Yet a close look at transnational poetry reveals more complex patterns of assimilation and resistance. If criticism is to be alert to both globalization and to any particular poem as text in its literal meaning of a woven thing, with sometimes contending and overlapping discourses, forms, techniques, and ideologies, it might look instead to dialogic or enmeshment models, attuned to the "growing *extensity*, *intensity*, and *velocity* of global interactions" and the "deepening enmeshment of the local and global."[34] Such models involve both homogenization and heterogenization, both standardization and resistant diversification. Stuart Hall highlights the coexistence of pressures of "homogenization and absorption" and "forms of local opposition and resistance" at "exactly the same moment."[35] A poem such as *Song of Lawino* exemplifies both local defiance and, in its formal and conceptual hybridity, a measure of accommodation with, and remaking of, the hegemonic impositions it resists. According to Arjun Appadurai, for whom the "central problem of today's global interactions is the tension between cultural homogenization and cultural heterogenization," to overemphasize homogenization is to fail to consider "that at least as rapidly as forces from various metropolises are brought into new societies they tend to become indigenized in one or another way: this is true of music and housing styles as much as it is true of science and terrorism, spectacles and constitutions."[36] Okigbo indigenizes Western poetic forms to pay homage to the Igbo river goddess dwelling near his home village, and Okot refashions Western ethnographic monologue to give literary voice to the rural Acoli. Such poets demonstrate what the anthropologist Ulf Hannerz calls Third World cultural entrepreneurs' "tampering and tinkering" with alien forms to create new ones responsive to their experience, akin to what Janet Abu-Lughod terms the "orientalization" of Western cultural influences.[37] Inflected by postcolonial studies, this model of globalization sees culture not as simply transferring "in a unilinear way," in Revathi Krishnaswamy's summary, "because movement between cultural/geographical areas always involves selection, interpretation, translation, mutation, and adaptation — processes designated by terms such as *indigenization* and *vernacularization* — with the receiving culture bringing its own cultural resources to bear, in dialectical fashion, upon cultural imports."[38] While globalization produces homogeneity, writes Kwame Anthony Appiah, it "is, equally, a threat to homogeneity," since people "are constantly inventing new forms of difference: new hairstyles, new slang, even, from time to time, new religions," and, we might add, new kinds of poetry.[39] Without losing sight of the losses inflicted by a globalizing modernity, we can explore how poets, working in a genre with especially abundant formal and linguistic traces, have also imaginatively transvalued and creolized these global forces to bring into expression their specific experiences of globalized locality and localized globality.

In contrast to the one-way, homogenizing model, poetry's transnational flows can be seen as moving in multiple directions, or in leaps and loops, or in what creolization theorist Édouard Glissant styles as returns and detours (*le retour et le détour*).[40] Kamau Brathwaite describes West Indian writers as being given access for the first time to their local speech rhythms as materia poetica, ironically, through the detour of none other than T. S. Eliot's voice transmitted to Barbados by the British Council, the Caribbean writer becoming more "indigenous" by virtue of becoming at the same time more "modernist." In another transhemispheric detour analyzed in chapter 5 below, Ezra Pound discovers in haiku and other East Asian cultural forms possibilities for breaking through the impasse of European symbolism to an imagist poetics of the natural image, though perhaps predicated on a creatively naïve misreading of East Asian poetry as nonsymbolic.[41] Not that the global circuits of Brathwaite's northward- and Pound's eastward-detouring transnationalisms are the same: Brathwaite hears a recorded voice from the "frozen Nawth" by way of a propaganda arm of the British Empire, while Pound's arrogation of minimalist Asian technique may not be innocent of American expansionism.[42] Despite these geopolitical discrepancies, both poets fashion a locally responsive poetics, paradoxically, by virtue of a bypass through the global. Nourished by poetry's cross-national and ever-mutating storage house of forms, techniques, genres, and images, individual poems give expression to locality at the same time that they turn formally, linguistically, allusively in other directions. Perhaps the most vivid twentieth-century poetic testimony to East African experience, Okot's *Song of Lawino* mediates Acoli village life in part through the reterritorialization of Longfellow's ethnographic *Song of Hiawatha* and the biblical Song of Solomon.[43] Even when poets hark back to local or regional precedents, the imagistic, linguistic, and formal building blocks of their poetry, especially in the context of a globalizing modernity, are shot through with transnational ingredients.

In efforts to theorize the cross-cultural on a global scale, orientalism — the concept that the East is discursively a subordinate and exoticist product of the West — has helped foreground an important part of the story of interactions between East and West, or global North and South.[44] Yet Edward Said's early paradigm for transhemispheric studies is sometimes deployed in ways that ironically limit the boundary-traversing power of poetry and harden rather than complicate identitarian boundaries. Criticism that reduces high modernist and later cross-regional "appropriations" to orientalist theft or primitivist exoticism may risk circumscribing instead of opening up possibilities for global and transnational analysis.[45] The conceptual framework of a closed, nonporous discursive system, determinative of Western interactions with the orient, is inadequate, I argue in chapter 5, to the counterdiscursive frictions within Western modernism, as suggested by poems by Yeats, Eliot, and Pound, in which "alien" cultural materials are sometimes assimilated incompletely and disjunctively, and so retain at least some capacity to interrogate and disrupt the cultural episteme of their host texts. As Dennis Porter writes, such "only partially silenced counter-hegemonic voices" and "counter-hegemonic energies" call into question a "monolithic" orientalism.[46] Nor is the orientalist model sufficient, I venture in chapter 7, to the cross-national affiliations that Said, later countering the limitations of his earlier paradigm, analyzed in the poetry of decolonization. These solidarities are often South–South, but they also traverse the global divide, including alliances forged by such Northern hemispheric poets as Yeats, Allen Ginsberg, Tony Harrison, and Joy Harjo when they have threaded their experience through the literatures and cultures of the South.

Perhaps the most famous and controversial example of artistic appropriation across the North/South divide is Pablo Picasso's incorporation of African masks and forms in *Les Demoiselles d'Avignon* (1907), a work that notoriously echoes primitivist views and may aesthetically reenact colonial importation.[47] At the same time, however, the painting disrupts binaries of Western high art and African folk art, of advanced one-point perspective and backward nonrepresentational handicraft, making possible new transcontinental forms without prior existence in either European or African aesthetics. If one standard against which to gauge such transnational engagements across uneven global terrain is whether they reflect dominant ideologies, another perhaps more aesthetically calibrated measure is whether they afford fresh imaginative possibilities that generate new cultural work, either locally or globally. Poetry's still more intricate enmeshments — contrapuntal rhythms and layered landscapes, creolized idioms and vernacularized forms in a poem by Yeats or Toomer, Lorna Goodison or Agha Shahid Ali — belie not only criticism's no-escape discursive models but also less sophisticated if more popular cultural models of the world as divisible into irreconcilable units, as proposed by Samuel Huntington among others. Poetry's cross-cultural knotting, dramatized by Shabine's self-description as multivectored, transhemispheric subject, or Okigbo's invocation as Igbo-classical-modernist supplicant, provides a vastly more nuanced and cross-hatched picture of intercultural borrowings, affinities, and flows than does Huntington's dichotomizing and crudely cloisonné vision of the "great divisions among humankind" and "clash of civilizations."[48] For global and transnational studies of poetry, we need, in short, dialogic alternatives to monologic models that represent the artifact as synecdoche for a local or national culture imperiled by global standardization, a monolithic orientalist epistemology closed to alterities within and without, or a self-contained civilizational unit in perpetual conflict with others.

This is not to suggest that the nation will vanish from modern and contemporary poetry studies, any more than the flows of global capital will render the state obsolete in the analysis of world political history. To imagine and articulate identities at a national (e.g., Jamaican or Irish), subnational (e.g., Biafran or East Asian American), or cross-national (e.g., pan-African or West Indian) regional scale is a powerful impetus of twentieth- and twenty-first-century poetry. Though questioning the sufficiency of the nation-state as telos of the decolonizing project, Louise Bennett uses poetry to champion Creole as the very tissue of Jamaican cultural identity. And though richly and self-consciously hybridized and cross-national in its origins and its effects, Yeats's poetry also labors to rename and remythologize a nation emerging from colonial rule. As Pascale Casanova states, many a writer's position can be understood as "a double one, twice defined," "inextricably national and international" (though her Eurocentric framework for world literature may concede too much to the national paradigm).[49] Brathwaite's poetics is centered in the Caribbean, Okot's in East Africa, Yeats's in Ireland, at the same time that these and other poets also participate through poetic, ideological, and other global circuits in transnational imaginaries. Even "world texts," as Simon Gikandi writes, though perhaps "exemplars of globalization," reflect "the persistence of the nation-state in the very literary works that were supposed to gesture toward a transcendental global culture."[50] The effacement of newly articulated minoritarian and postcolonial identities under the all-flattening sign of an undifferentiated globality would be particularly unfortunate — hence my emphasis on the muddy footprints of the *trans*national and the *trans*local.[51] As Said's work helps me argue in chapter 7, partly through Yeats's example, poetry and decolonization can be seen as intimately interlinked, and chapter 4's discussion of elegy shows how poetry's sonic structures and mourning conventions can be put in the service of nationalism. The irony is, however, that because poetry is such a long-memoried form, it is enmeshed — even when stridently nationalist in ideology — by a complexly cross-national weave in its rhythms and tropes, stanza patterns and generic adaptations. Under globalization, poetry extends its imaginative reach ever farther along a horizontal spatial axis, but unlike more evanescent and short-tentacled global media, it simultaneously activates the vertical, temporal axis of tropes, etymologies, and forms embedded in the nation-crossing language it reshapes. Because of the interconnecting cultural traces wound into the DNA of poetic forms and poetic language, poetry's cross-national molecular structure betrays the national imaginary on behalf of which it is sometimes made to speak.

Poetic genres such as epic, ghazal, and pastoral elegy, let alone stanza forms and rhetorical figures, have long been circulated and adapted transnationally, but modernity-fueled globalization has accelerated and intensified this process. Under modernity, writes Giddens in *The Consequences of Modernity*, the level of interaction across distant regions "is much higher than in any previous period, and the relations between local and distant social forms and events becomes correspondingly 'stretched.'" Elaborating this explanatory metaphor, he continues: "Globalisation refers essentially to that stretching process, in so far as the modes of connection between different social contexts or regions become networked across the earth's surfaces as a whole," and "local happenings are shaped by events occurring many miles away and vice versa."[52] Globalization can thus be seen as perpetuating and multiplying the bipolar "spatial disjunction" of empire, since, as Jameson remarks, "It is Empire which stretches the roads out to infinity, beyond the bounds and borders of the national state," with globalization's webs spinning out and tightening these interconnections still further.[53] In Jameson's words, "colonialism means that a significant structural segment of the economic system as a whole is now located elsewhere," a disjunctiveness that leaves its formal mark on literature's "cognitive mapping."[54]

Modernists, postcolonials, and other writers have put poetry's resources to work in figuring this incompletely graspable geospatial stretch. Indeed, in a suggestive coincidence, poetic uses of language are also often regarded as "a stretch": the elasticity of poetry—its figural and allusive traversals of space, its rhythmic and sonic coordinations of distances, its associative suspension of rational boundaries—is well suited to evoking global modernity's interlinking of widely separated sites, from Eliot's *Waste Land* and Hughes's "The Negro Speaks of Rivers," to Elizabeth Bishop's "In the Waiting Room" and Dionisio D. Martínez's "Hysteria," as will be seen in chapter 3. Grabbed from a roof and turning the speaker's body (and the poem) into a switchboard, the electric wires in Les Murray's "The Powerline Incarnation" could be seen as both exemplifying and figuring the stretch of poetry. In the poem's on-rushing, unpunctuated, geography-spanning lines, mountains connect with plains, Australian farms with towns, European classical music with American country tunes:

> I make a hit in towns
> I've never visited: smoke curls lightbulbs pop grey
> discs hitch and slow   I plough the face of Mozart
> and Johnny Cash   I bury and smooth their song. . . .[55]

Murray's border-crashing syntax and grammatical elisions evoke the place-enjambing potentialities of both poetry and modernity.

Poetry's translocal stretch is easily seen in Eliot's intermapping of the River Thames with sites in the Mediterranean and South Asia, Evaristo's of Londonium with parts of the global South later colonized by Great Britain, Heaney's of Ireland with Jutland, Goodison's of Jamaica with Ireland; but it is also discernible in poetry that may seem unambiguously local in its grounding. Printed during World War II in Jamaica, Louise Bennett's "South Parade Peddler" firmly situates its higgler by the use of Creole and a Kingston street name. But under modernity, even a "national poet" turns out, on closer inspection, to also be a transnational poet. In this instance, the global reach of modern warfare, as of the communication systems reporting it, distends the scope of even such autochthonous poetry. Puffing herself up by deploying a vocabulary of military aggression, Bennett's female petty trader cautions one passerby to spend money lest she "bus up like Graf Spee," a German battleship recently blown up by its captain in Montevideo, Uruguay; she punningly berates another spendthrift, "yuh / Dah suffer from hair raid!" and asks yet another, "Dem torpedo yuh teet, sah, or / Yuh female lick dem out?"[56] This is more than a question of topical references that are extrinsic or incidental to the poem. In the stretched fabric of Bennett's translocal puns, metaphors, and allusions, the poem formally embodies the interpenetration of Jamaican space, both imaginative and real, with the so-called theater of global war. So too, its conjoined ballad stanzas creolize a poetic structure from the British Isles with Jamaican diction, orthography, and rhythms, inverting the earlier penetration of Jamaican space by European colonialism. In the twentieth century, even localist poems evince the contracted space and time of transnational flows and imaginaries.

Although the editors of the generative collection *Geomodernisms* call for a "locational approach to modernism," these and other examples of modernity's literary stretch suggest that what may be needed is a *co*-locational or *trans*locational approach to modernism, as also to post-colonialism, alert to how such art and literature interlace localities and nationalities with one another in a globally imagined space — Bennett's Kingston extending, for example, to Uruguay, Germany, and Scotland.[57] Poets and singers of the African diaspora, from Claude McKay to Wole Soyinka and Grace Nichols, as will be seen in chapter 8, have creolized metropolitan Britain with African and Caribbean spaces and styles, remaking London, in the words of Lord Kitchener's buoyant calypso, as "the place for me."[58] Colonial interpenetration and postcolonial migration anticipate the ever more enmeshed localities of subsequent globalization. Highlighting what he calls "situatedness-in-displacement," Bruce Robbins states: "If our supposed distances are really localities, as we piously repeat, it is also true that there are distances *within* what we thought were *merely* localities."[59] In Langston Hughes's exactly situated "Theme for English B" ("I cross St. Nicholas, / Eighth Avenue, Seventh, and I come to the Y, / the Harlem Branch Y"), a student studying at the predominantly white City College of the City University of New York pronominally and sonically intertwines himself with an apostrophized Harlem as if to insist, in a bebop-inspired riff, on their mirror relation: "hear you, hear me — we two — you, me, talk on this page."[60] As in Okigbo's invocation, poetry enables the speaker to rhyme himself with a top-onymically localized environment. Even so, the ensuing line, complicating this microlocational poetics, widens the geographic and cultural scope of the identity-shaping place to the larger city: "(I hear New York, too.) Me — who?" And subsequent lines open out still further to thematize identity as both discretely located and thoroughly enmeshed, networked, cross-racialized. Insofar as his composition is mediated by a white teacher ("it will be / a part of you, instructor"), preexisting racialized power structures ("you're older — and white — / and somewhat more free"), and self-reflexive lyric conventions ("This is my theme for English B"), the speaker cannot define himself in the immediate locational present ("I'm what / I feel and see and hear") without detouring through these various pasts that simultaneously root him in Harlem and relocate him elsewhere. Stretched in scale between the microcosmic ("the Harlem branch Y") and the macrocosmic (New York, the United States, interpenetrating human races), this and other poems also extend from the now through the long-echoing histories encoded in the literary and oral conventions they remake. By virtue of its extraordinary compression, poetry readily evinces the "time-space compression" of globalization.[61]

The reverse of verses such as Bennett's and Hughes's seemingly localist forms and topographies — Kingston, Harlem — planetary poems such as Auden's "Prologue at Sixty," Walcott's "The Fortunate Traveller," and Heaney's "Alphabets" peer down on the Earth from beyond its surface and figure the world as "O," or maybe "zero."[62] "It is striking that one of the effects of the process of globalization," writes Mike Featherstone, "has been to make us aware that the world itself is a locality, a singular place."[63] In the ontogenetic poem "Alphabets," Heaney returns repeatedly to the trope of the globe as "O":

> As from his small window
> The astronaut sees all that he has sprung from,
> The risen, aqueous, singular, lucent O
> Like a magnified and buoyant ovum . . .[64]

Borrowing the astronaut's literally *cosmo*politan perspective, his awareness through having temporarily left the world that he is a citizen of its global locality, the poet — aided by the split consciousness of poetry as a densely metaphoric and defamiliarizing genre — views the world from afar as his finite and fragile home. In the tradition of lyric self-reflexivity, he traces himself back through the multiple languages — English, Latin, Irish — that are the origins, the ground, as it were, from which his poetry has sprung. The "O" of which he is born is the planet and a maternal

ovum, yet it is also language, the fabricated "wooden O" of literary artifice, the apostrophic "O" of poetry, spoken as if in an echo of the round-
ness of a wonder-inspiring world.

Whereas the localist poem requires one kind of critical attention to
tease out its cross-culturalism in borrowed verse forms, sea-traversing
allusions, or subterranean influences that establish unexpected lines of
cross-cultural relationality,[65] the planetary poem, viewing the Earth from
the extraterritorial perspective of Heaney's astronaut, Auden's orbiting
dog, or Walcott's air traveler, requires another kind of critical pressure,
to specify its local, regional, and national bearings. In between these
poles are most of the poems I explore under the local-global-mediating
rubric of a transnational and translocal poetics. "In this emphasis we
avoid, at least," according to James Clifford, "the excessive localism of
particularist cultural relativism, as well as the overly global vision of a
capitalist or technocratic monoculture."[66] Even Heaney's brief imaginative glimpse of his planetary origins from a spaceship window quickly
pivots to a recognition of his more immediate, if unhomely, origins — the
family name inscribed on a gable, written with the plasterer's "trowel
point, letter by strange letter."[67] To borrow Gayatri Spivak's distinction
between the abstract geometry of the global and the lived history of
the planetary, transnational poems are written from the perspective of
"planetary subjects rather than global agents, planetary creatures rather
than global entities."[68] Although Spivak limits her definition of globalization to a uniformly imposed system of exchange in what she concedes
is an overly "neat contrast" with the planetary,[69] globalization, understood broadly as "the widening, deepening and speeding up of worldwide interconnectedness," both "real and perceived," is the necessary
condition for the lived experience of the planetary.[70]

The figure of the astronaut or airborne traveler might suggest an
older model of cosmopolitanism, a claim to universality and detachment
from bonds that Robbins styles the "luxuriously free-floating view from
above"; but more useful for understanding this and other such poems
may be concepts of a "located and embodied" cosmopolitanism that
aesthetically enacts multiple attachments rather than none.[71] As seen
in our initial examples of the sometimes contending, sometimes melding, allegiances in poems by Walcott, Eliot, Loy, Hughes, Evaristo, and
Chin, interstitial poetries — whether ethnic American, postcolonial, or
black British, Harlem Renaissance or high modernist — articulate a verbal space that resembles a "cosmopolitan public sphere": limited and
located, such translocal cosmopolitanisms intersect with national and

subnational public spheres but, unlike ethnic and state nationalisms, foster transnational engagement, dialogic encounter, and civil contestation.[72] Indonesian-born, Chinese American poet Li-Young Lee's "Persimmons," for example, conjoins American confessionalism (painful personal memories of being slapped by a teacher) with a Chinese father's ars poetica of calligraphic precision, memory, and texture — a painterly emphasis that the poem transmutes into the son's feel for the sensuous texture of persimmons and of words: *"the feel of the wolftail on the silk, / the strength, the tense / precision in the wrist."*[73] Not that the poem effaces intercultural conflict or dominance. The American teacher's belligerently ignorant blindness toward her Chinese immigrant student, her slapping him for not being able to pronounce the difference between "persimmon" and "precision," produces the friction out of which the speaker retrospectively leverages a poetic mastery of English, developing poetic connections between words that he was once punished for conflating:

> Other words
> that got me into trouble were
> *fight* and *fright*, *wren* and *yarn*.
> Fight was what I did when I was frightened,
> fright was what I felt when I was fighting.
> Wrens are small, plain birds,
> yarn is what one knits with.
> Wrens are soft as yarn.
> My mother made birds out of yarn.
> I loved to watch her tie the stuff;
> a bird, a rabbit, a wee man.

Even as it recalls violent intercultural collision, the poem explores, in its hybridizing mediation of Chinese and American stylistic elements, the possibilities of reconciliation at the aesthetic level that were unavailable in the schoolboy's lived experience. As Lee's poem indicates, transnational and intercultural poetry imaginatively reconfigures the relations among the ingredients drawn from disparate cultural worlds and fused within its verbal and formal space.

This poem's interweaving of English with Chinese — words both remembered and forgotten — might lead readers to ask, why limit my study to poetry written primarily in English? After all, many such poems, whether by Pound and Eliot or Lee and Lorna Dee Cervantes, interlace English with other languages — German and Sanskrit, Chinese and Spanish — or reflect in their diction, syntax, and sound the pressure of other languages, as in Ali's Urdu-haunted, Okot's Acoli-shadowed, or Alberto Ríos's Spanish-inflected English. From Pound to W. S. Merwin, Ali, and Lyn Hejinian, poets have been influenced by the languages and literatures they have translated into English. By limiting a study to English-language poetry, doesn't one risk following and perhaps even reinforcing what Spivak calls "the lines of the old imperialisms," including what she wryly terms "Anglophony," or what Jonathan Arac calls "Anglo-Globalism"?[74] The spread of English worldwide to its use by nearly a third of the world's population (though the mother tongue of a much smaller fraction) is indeed rooted in the might of the British Empire and has been perpetuated by the military and economic power of the United States.[75] Literary criticism on English- and other imperial-language literatures must coexist with studies of writing in local and regional languages of the global South. Even so, one way to complicate an imperial "Anglophony" from within criticism on English-language poetry is to explore the multiplicity of Englishes in which poetry is written, some of which, such as the Jamaican Creole of Claude McKay, Louise Bennett, and Linton Kwesi Johnson, was once seen as unworthy of poetry.[76] Another is to widen the geographic scope of anglophone poetry studies, so that poems from the United States, Britain, and Ireland are read alongside poetries from English-speaking dominions, territories, and ex-colonies.

Still, a primary reason for drawing a somewhat artificial boundary around poems in English is that, simply put, in poetry, more than perhaps in any other literary genre, the specificities of language matter. Horace's use of the flexibilities of Latin syntax to create pictographic framing ("Quis multa gracilis te puer in rosa," Odes 1.5), Hafez's deployment of monorhyme, assonance, repeated long vowel sounds, and bunched stresses for the euphony of a Persian ghazal, and Baudelaire's rhythmic and sonic simulation of place ("tout n'est qu'ordre et beauté, / Luxe, calme et volupté") exemplify how poetry, especially in its lyric mode, cannot be adequately studied in translation in the same way that drama, epic, and the novel can be studied within their generic frameworks even when translated into another language.[77] The heuristic corollary of this observation is that poems are best taught in the original, and in an English department in a predominantly English-speaking country, the teacher devising a poetry syllabus cannot usually presume student competence in multiple languages. Moreover, although poetic influences continually cross linguistic lines, the language specificity of poetry often grants the inheritances in a poet's working language(s) special weight. Usually, the language field out of which a poem is carved, and upon which it exerts the greatest pressure, is the language in which it is written. When Auden calls poetry "the most provincial of the arts" and claims that "in poetry . . . there cannot be an 'International Style,'" he highlights its language specificity ("Due to the Curse of Babel"), not its geographic boundedness, as indicated by his own nation-spanning poems and career.[78] The global spread of English and the rise of English-language literatures in Asia, Africa, the Caribbean, the Pacific Rim, and elsewhere are cultural realities that need to be studied and are unlikely to be thwarted or slowed by English departments or literary critics turning away from the language specificity of anglophone poetries. However diversified by region and nation, imaginative constructs in a shared language can be animated across vast distances, and so the English language — once conceived as the stuff of English national identity — is a world language for poets, or at least a semiglobal conduit through which poets encounter, advance, and redirect cross-cultural flows of tropes and words, ideas and images.

English-language poems, poets, and poetries of the twentieth and twenty-first centuries can no longer be seen, in Wai Chee Dimock's terms, as "the product of one nation and one nation alone, analyzable within its confines."[79] This is not to suggest that all these poetries are transnational in the same way. They differ, for example, in how they configure the relations among their cross-cultural ingredients. What we might call disjunctive poetic transnationalisms, as we've already seen, emphasize the intercultural discontinuities and conflicts between the materials they force together, while others — call them organic poetic transnationalisms — integrate these materials without playing up their unlikenesses.[80] They differ along lines of race. Some poetic transnationalisms, such as the black British and African Caribbean, are diasporic and thus emphasize a long, shared racial or ethnic history, whereas others radiate still more multinationally and multiethnically, drawing on materials with little or no shared cultural past. They differ geographically. The transnationalism of Eliot's "mind of Europe" is continentally bound, unlike his and later poets' imaginative traversals of intercontinental spaces.[81] They differ in their global positionings. Transatlantic and other First World poetic transnationalisms — say, of Euro-American modernism or the avant-garde in the United States, the United Kingdom, Canada, Australia, and New Zealand — traverse less culturally and socially disjunctive spaces than poetic transnationalisms that cross between First and Third worlds, ex-colonizer and ex-colonized. Accordingly, in chapters 5 and 6, distinctions between postcolonial and Western modernist transnationalisms will emerge ever more forcefully. Still, while I grant these lines of demarcation, we cannot be so fearful of blurring them that we retreat to understanding transnational poetries only within formal, national, or regional boundaries, and so I read poems within, across, and against these groupings. Although I investigate questions of poetic transnationalism from a variety of angles, the ramifications for poetry of global migrations and diasporas, of cross-national influences and genres, of modernization and decolonization, of travels both real and imagined, will remain to be worked out, so long as poets ask what it means to be neither a nobody nor a nation.

CHAPTER 2

A TRANSNATIONAL POETICS

"America is my country," remarked Gertrude Stein, only to fracture this apparently nationalist claim by adding, "and Paris is my home town."[1] Stein's translocal claim of identity — splaying herself between the spectral context of one nation and the lived metropolis of another — accords with the transnational affiliations and identities of many other modern and contemporary poets, though she is often absorbed into nationalist narratives of "American" literature. Studies in cultural transnationalism have recently proliferated in a variety of humanistic subfields, but in studies of modern and contemporary poetry in English, single-nation genealogies remain surprisingly entrenched: an army of anthologies, job descriptions, library catalogs, books, articles, and annotations reterritorializes the cross-national mobility of modern and contemporary poetry under the single-nation banner. If Stein were an exception among twentieth-century poets, this disciplinary paradigm — which goes back to Johann Gottfried von Herder's pre-Romantic concept of literature as an expression of national identity and rigidified in the cold-war American academy — could surely accommodate her. After all, humanistic disciplines must draw artificial boundaries to delimit their object of study — nation, language, period, genre, and such — and so must allow for anomalies. But the "exceptions" to mononational narratives — principally modern "American," "British," "Irish" poetry — are so abundant that they should spur a reconsideration of the conceptual structure of much critical production in the field. Globe-traversing influences, energies, and resistances, far from being minor deviations from nation-based fundamentals, have arguably styled and shaped poetry in English, from the modernist era to the present.

Although literary scholarship is not a branch of the Bureau of

Immigration and Citizenship Services, as the INS has recently been re-named, critics co-construct the national and ethnic identities of writer-citizens, routinely issuing passports to T. S. Eliot, Mina Loy, W. H. Auden, Denise Levertov, and Sylvia Plath, for example, in the shape of foot-notes, literary histories, and anthologies that claim them as "American" or "British." Because these national labels are made to serve disciplin-ary, ideological, and pedagogical functions, they often blur the distinc-tion encapsulated by Étienne Balibar between "*ethnos*, the 'people' as an imagined community of membership and filiation, and *dēmos*, the 'people' as the collective subject of representation, decision making, and rights."[2] While literature, as Benedict Anderson shows, helps fash-ion "imagined community,"[3] or *ethnos*, the boundaries of national and re-gional community are also confounded by poets, novelists, playwrights, and readers as they forge alliances of style and sensibility across vast dis-tances of geography, history, and culture.

How would modern and contemporary poetry studies in English — an area now largely subdivided along national lines — look if this trans-nationalism were taken to be primary rather than incidental? If poetic transnationalism were understood as being by no means confined to the post-Steinian avant-garde but far more pervasive?[4] How might the field seem different if the nationalities and ethnicities of poets and poems, of-ten reified by nation-based histories, anthologies, and syllabi, were gen-uinely regarded as hybrid, interstitial, and fluid imaginative constructs, not "natural, real, eternal, stable, and static units," in Werner Sollors's phrase?[5] And what are the methodological and even political implica-tions of reshaping a humanistic subdiscipline to reflect the intercultural energies and mobilities of cross-national literary citizenship? Although a full remapping of modern and contemporary poetry in English is be-yond the scope of this book, my hope is that an inevitably synoptic and scattershot redescription of it can help advance the field beyond the-oretical and piecemeal acknowledgment of this cross-culturalism to a more thoroughgoing internationalization of its disciplinary practices.

1.

The main reasons why mononational constructions of modern and contemporary poetry do not suffice should be obvious. That many of the key modernists were expatriates is frequently rehearsed. "Modern Western culture," summarizes Edward Said, "is in large part the work of exiles, émigrés, refugees."[6] Yet the implications of such human displacement for nation-based literary histories have not been fully absorbed within institutions of literary instruction, dissemination, and criticism, which remain largely nation-centric. Whether these migrant writers left home compelled by politics or lured by economics, whether in search of cultural traditions or freedom from the burden of such traditions, whether for publishing opportunities, educational advancement, or new cultural horizons, they produced works that cannot always be read as emblematic of single national cultures. "The most important general element of the innovations in form," as Raymond Williams says of the modernists, "is the fact of immigration to the metropolis, and it cannot too often be emphasized how many of the major innovators were, in this precise sense, immigrants. At the level of theme, this underlies, in an obvious way, the elements of strangeness and distance, indeed of alienation, which so regularly form part of the repertory."[7] Terry Eagleton also cites the "highly creative tension" for exiles and émigrés between the home cultures they remember and the metropolitan cultures they adopt.[8] The modernists translated their frequent geographic displacement and transcultural alienation into a poetics of dissonance and defamiliarization, and this hybrid and strange-making art also defies the national literary genealogies into which it is often pressed. The citizenship of a poem by the migrants W. B. Yeats, Gertrude Stein, Amy Lowell, Mina Loy, D. H. Lawrence, Ezra Pound, H.D., T. S. Eliot, Claude McKay, Robert Graves, Laura Riding, Langston Hughes, C. Day Lewis, William Empson, W. H. Auden, or Louis MacNeice, to mention only some of the most prominent examples before World War II, should not always be presupposed as "American," "British," "Irish," or "Jamaican."

Along with the increasing numbers of poets on the move, the cross-national reading practices of the twentieth century also impair the mononational literary model. The massive number of cross-national influences upon and appropriations by the modernists disrupt the usual dynastic narratives of compatriot X begetting compatriot Y begetting compatriot Z. "The first step of a renaissance, or awakening," Pound wrote in 1914, "is the importation of models for painting, sculpture or writing"—a remark that surely holds for the modernist literary revolution.[9] Reworking remote formal models, these poets intensify what Susan Stewart calls poetry's "processes of cultural catachresis and transformation."[10]

Further thwarting mononational narratives were the proliferation of geography-traversing technologies such as the telephone, cinema, and radio; the increasing ease of travel by ship and by air; the massive migration of black North Americans from the rural South to the urban North; the circulation of avant-garde art and translations among European and North American cities; the rapid global movement of capital; the researches of globe-trotting anthropologists; the dramatic expansion of the British Empire across a quarter of the land's surface by World War I; the emergence at the same time of the United States as a new political and economic world power. Even poets "at home" in America or Britain were coming into contact with images, peoples, arts, cultures, and ideas from across continents and hemispheres. Modernist-era poets experienced their environments within the context of the space-time contraction, the transnational flows and circuits, of global experience and imaginaries. As Michael North writes, building on Williams's analysis, "the effects of that global mobility" and "mediation" were so far-reaching that "even the sedentary might be mobilized."[11]

Yet a large number of the critical books and anthologies published in recent decades bearing on modern and contemporary poetry in English have been nationally or regionally focused rather than cross-cultural, as if literary critics have been elegiacally recathecting the national at a time when the globalizing processes of a century ago have multiplied and accelerated.[12] As the "world has become deterritorialized . . . , diasporic, and transnational" (Arjun Appadurai),[13] critics have increasingly attacked, in the words of the editors of *Locations of Literary Modernism: Region and Nation in British and American Modernist Poetry*, "the construction of modernism as an international, urban and yet placeless, phenomenon."[14] In U.S. studies, a critic who dismisses the "international character of modernism" as little more than a "critical commonplace" believes "American literary modernism as a whole," including poetry, should be "understood primarily as a response to the felt needs of the nation."[15] Another offers *A New Theory for American Poetry* (2004) after Whitman, according to which, as if updating Montesquieu's theory of national character, America's poetic forms are seen as expressing its natural environment.[16] Still another, while partly excepting Pound, characterizes most "major American texts" after World War I—including poems by William Carlos Williams, Langston Hughes, Jean Toomer, and others—in terms of a "structural intimacy between modernism and nativism."[17]

If we turn from North America to the British Isles, perhaps the single most searching and influential critique of the emphasis on modernism's "cosmopolitanism and internationalism" is Robert Crawford's book *Devolving English Literature* (1992, 2000), which argues: "Modernism was an essentially provincial phenomenon."[18] Revaluing especially Scottish writing, which he persuasively shows to have been too "smoothly absorbed or repressed" within the hegemonic designation "English Literature" (302), Crawford claims that modernist writers, like their heirs, wrote deliberately provincial poetry, at odds with the normative values and Standard English of the English metropolitan center, and thus "devolved" cultural authority to the margins of the former British Empire. But to resist Anglocentric imperialism, Crawford ironically contributes to a more recent imperial narrative, decentering one literary empire at the cost of reinforcing another. His discussion of twentieth-century literature is anchored in an effort to establish T. S. Eliot's "un-Englishness" and thus "persistent American-ness" (220). He traces Eliot's literary roots to the "very American" writer Henry James and, before him, to Walt Whitman (226), eclipsing such English precursors as the metaphysical poets and the English Romantics. Indications of a more ambiguous cultural identity are converted into their opposite: Eliot's concept of "the mind of Europe" exhibits a "quintessentially American" longing for European identity; as for Eliot's declaration of his classicism, royalism, and Anglo-Catholicism, "no normal Englishman would have made such a public declaration, for England is a country in which individuals, like governments, prefer to avoid a written constitution" (232).

Devolving English Literature takes a similar approach to Ezra Pound, even though he was the central figure of the London avant-garde in the 1910s, forged his imagist aesthetic partly out of an encounter with Japanese haiku and Chinese poetry, and layered Chinese, Italian, and Greek in *The Cantos*—and even though the London "vortex" that helped stimulate Pound's innovations included T. E. Hulme, Ford Madox Ford, Wyndham Lewis, Henri Gaudier-Brzeska, and other non-American writers and artists. As with Eliot's South Asian explorations, Pound's interest in East Asia is deemed "fundamentally American" because it relies on the work of the American Ernest Fenollosa and is mediated through Whistler's interest in Japanese art. Arguing for Pound's "essential American-ness" (235), Crawford even reads Pound's rejection of Vachel Lindsay, Edgar Lee Masters, and other overtly provincial American poets as indicative of his "deepest American-ness" (259). Pound's and Eliot's American backgrounds are surely crucial to their art, as Crawford usefully demonstrates, but identitarian tags such as "the poet from St. Louis," "fundamentally American," "quintessentially American," "distinctively American," "very American grain," and "solidly American" risk draining modernism of its cross-national complexity.

The modernism Crawford sees as "essentially provincial" (270) is instead profoundly cross-cultural, translocal, and transnational. Pound's and Eliot's achievements are incomprehensible without taking seriously the global reach of a modernism that, polyglot and jaggedly transcultural, interweaves Euro-classicism and Chinese ideograms, cockney gossip and Sanskrit parable, Confucius and Thomas Jefferson, the thunderous God of the Hebrew Bible and a Brahmin creator god. Riding the back of European imperial and anthropological incursion, this poetry was profoundly shaped not only by transatlantic migration but also by the encounter with East and South Asian cultural materials; Pound's imagism is no less indebted to East Asian models than is Picasso's cubism to African masks; and *The Waste Land*, though surely altering Eastern materials in assimilating them to a Western crisis narrative,[19] reconceives Christianity by seeing it through the lens of Sanskrit parable, the teachings of Augustine by associating them with those of the Buddha. Although these poets' cultures of origin can help clarify how, why, and to what effect they assimilate "foreign" materials, such attention should not obscure the interstitial affiliations and ambiguous identifications, the imaginative globalism and lived transnationalism, that shape their work.

Poetry criticism has often defined writers as "essentially American" or "Scottish" or "Irish," assigning each to a closed, organic group of traits and behaviors in accordance with early anthropological models of culture. But more consonant with the cultural and national ambiguities and global mobilities of much modern and contemporary poetry than these "localizing strategies in the construction and representation of 'cultures'" are what James Clifford calls the "emerging transnational cultural studies" and "multi-locale ethnography" of such anthropologists as Arjun Appadurai, Kirin Narayan, and Clifford himself, who describe affiliations and identities that are overlapping and conflicted, multiple and fluid.[20] "Practices of displacement might emerge," Clifford notes incisively, "as *constitutive* of cultural meanings rather than as their simple transfer or extension."[21] Central modernist strategies — transnational collage, polyglossia, syncretic allusiveness — are "practices of displacement" that instance this cross-cultural generation of meanings. Interstitial concepts of culture — hybridization and creolization, contact zones and diaspora identities — are well suited to modern and contemporary poetry's translocal conjunctures and intercultural circuits. More generally, the mononational paradigm runs the danger of reinforcing, in post-cold-war U.S. classrooms and criticism, ideologies of American exceptionalism; in this context, a transnational poetics can help define an alternative to nationalist and even to civilizational ideologies.[22] Such an alternative may be especially urgent in an era when monoculturalist assumptions have sometimes underwritten violent confrontations between the United States and its supposed civilizational "others."

Numerous individual poets pose obstacles for the monocultural ethnographer, and not only the exilic "high modernists" Stein, Eliot, and Pound. Though Claude McKay is usually assimilated into narratives of the Harlem Renaissance as the author of a book that partly helped inaugurate it, *Harlem Shadows* (1922), he wrote his first two books in Jamaican English before emigrating to the United States; he then spent over a decade (1919–21, 1923–33) in Europe, the Soviet Union, and North Africa, barred from the United States and the British colonies after his enthusiastic 1923 Soviet trip;[23] in 1934 he finally returned to the United States and in 1940 became an American citizen; still later, he was posthumously claimed as a national poet of Jamaica. His so-called dialect verses may seem authentically "Jamaican," but McKay's use of Creole was ironically encouraged, as Michael North and Charles Bernstein note, by the English linguist and folklorist Walter Jekyll, and the primary formal structure of McKay's Jamaican English poetry is the ballad stanza inspired by Robert Burns.[24] But if these poems do not belong to a local, pristine "folk" culture, neither are they merely caught within metropolitan norms and expectations; to represent them as such is to risk muting their transnational dynamics of ambivalent resistance and adhesion. McKay's "A Midnight Woman to the Bobby," for example, stages a challenge to McKay's own complicity with British colonial authority: the speaker-prostitute accuses the bobby, recently come from Jamaica's backwoods, of being a mere tool of the white colonial government in Jamaica: "You lef' you' district, big an' coarse, / An' come join buccra [white] Police Force."[25] The poem thus dramatizes McKay's self-division: his youthful Jamaican self, gendered female and associated with prostitution, and his constable self, the policeman-poet who ethnographically records Jamaican speech and character for display to the British authorities. Footnoted and framed, prefaced and published by Jekyll, the poem connives in British colonial rule, and yet its oppositional "Jamaican" voice also forcefully talks back. In the preface to McKay's *Songs of Jamaica,* Jekyll tries to contain Jamaican speech as lisping, lazy, and effeminate: "It shortens, softens, rejects the harder sounds alike of consonants and vowels; I might almost say, refines. In its soft tones we have an expression of the languorous sweetness of the

South: it is a feminine version of masculine English; pre-eminently a language of love. . . ."[26] But in this poem McKay's language is sonically explosive: "No palm me up, you dutty brute, / You' jam mout' mash like ripe bread-fruit." Anticipating Édouard Glissant, David Dabydeen, and other theorists of West Indian speech,[27] McKay emphasizes the harshness and noisiness, the vivid boldness of Creole, twisting and deforming English phonemic and grammatical laws, much as the midnight woman refuses subordination by her resistant spunk. Such a dialogic poem — neither wholly "Jamaican" nor wholly "British" — is a transnational discursive field in which the forces and counterforces of converging, jostling, competing nationalities meet.[28]

By the same token, McKay's later "American" poems in Standard English, written after he left Jamaica but was still a British subject, cannot be reduced to U.S. normativity without obscuring the extent to which they view America from the agonized stance of the migrant outsider: "the great western world holds me in fee."[29] "America," in a sonnet by that title, is allegorized as a source of nourishment and vitality, yet also "sinks into my throat her tiger's tooth, / Stealing my breath of life" — threatening a poetic afflatus that is therefore irreducible to American citizenship.[30] Moreover, the British "inputs" and "outputs" of a poem such as "If We Must Die" complicate its classification as "American"; "a counter-lynching poem," as Kamau Brathwaite calls it,[31] born of post–World War I anti-black rioting in U.S. cities, the sonnet is nevertheless cast in the heroic rhetoric of Shakespeare's *Henry V,* making it readily appropriable by Winston Churchill, who intoned it during World War II without attribution:

> If we must die, O let us nobly die,
> So that our precious blood may not be shed
> In vain; then even the monsters we defy
> Shall be constrained to honor us though dead!
> O kinsmen! we must meet the common foe!
> Though far outnumbered let us show us brave,
> And for their thousand blows deal one deathblow![32]

But neither is the sonnet merely "British" or "Jamaican." Various cultural conceptions and preconceptions dialogically contend even in its sonic texture, which contradicts Jekyll's claim that the "negro variant" of English "shortens, softens, rejects the harder sounds alike of consonants and vowels," instead drawing out assonances ("O let us nobly die") and rhyming on hard consonants (*spot/lot, pack/back*). And the poem belies the colonialist tags "languorous" and "feminine," instead asserting a defiant masculinity ("Like men we'll face the murderous, cowardly pack"). McKay's cross-national poetry, both early and late, cannot be declared "Jamaican" or "British," "American" or "European," "Afro-Caribbean" or "Euro-American," without limiting the array of cultural vectors that radiate from and converge within it.

Needless to say, the term "transnationalism" is not always associated with dialogic energies and interstitial identities of the sort I am ascribing to black and white modernisms. Often it is a synonym for neoliberal globalism or corporate jet-setting, and Aihwa Ong applies it not only to middle-class Asian entrepreneurs driven by capitalist interests but also to terrorist networks and diasporic peoples who transport narrowly conceived religious or ethnic solidarities.[33] The cultural politics of transnationalism, as of nationalism, is situational and cannot be predicted — both ethnic separatism and cross-cultural interchange, both global dialogue and imperial imposition are in some sense "transnational." What I would call the identitarian transnationalism that Ong spotlights merely distends traditional citizenship (*ethnos*): allegiances are owed to a single, unifying, "imagined community," albeit spread across the globe. As such, this transnationalist mode is readily adaptable to the disciplinary nationalisms of the humanities: whether Irish or Chinese, Indian or Arab, the diasporic group, though somewhat changed by migration or travel, reproduces and stabilizes itself in circulating across the globe. Literary transnationalism of the sort represented here by modernist poetry may suggest a different disciplinary model of "citizenship": instead of replicating the centripetal vortex of the nation-state or its dilated counterpart in unitary migrant communities, cross-cultural writing and reading can, if taken seriously in criticism and the classroom, evoke noncoercive and nonatavistic forms of transnational imaginative belonging. Some poetry is, of course, imperialist, appropriative, and flattening in its cross-cultural engagements. But when the intercultural tropes, allusions, and vocabularies of poetry outstrip single-state or single-identity affiliations, they can exemplify the potential for generative intercultural exploration.

2.

To discuss every example of a modern poet whose life and work deviate from the mononational would be impossible, since, as the examples of

Pound, Eliot, Stein, and McKay indicate, this would be to retell a great deal of twentieth-century literary history. And yet, as I have already suggested, only a review of that history — albeit in a telegraphic and preliminary manner — can highlight the distortions and inadequacies entailed in the organizing national categories. Though delimited by the somewhat artificial boundaries of language, period, and genre, the transnationalist paradigm carves out a disciplinary space shared by Euromodernists and Harlem Renaissance poets, by Beats and postcolonial Indian poets. It helps sketch a literary history in which transnational creolization, hybridization, and interculturation become almost as basic to our understanding of modernism as they are of the postcolonial. And it affords a cross-cultural comparatism grounded in the migrant and mingled tropes and forms and identities in the literature it studies.

While figures such as Eliot and McKay are typically isolated from one another by race, class, or nationality, even in criticism that spans white and black modernisms, a thoroughly cross-culturalist remapping of the field can reveal unexpected affinities between these accent- and nation-shifting poets who, displaced by modernity's ever-accelerating mobility, redefined their cultural identities in migration, worked in various Englishes, and, in poems such as "Outcast" and "East Coker," reimagined their ancestral homelands in England and in Africa. Yeats is another poet whose life and work exceed the bounds of a nationalist disciplinary framework. Although usually tagged unambiguously Irish, he shuttled between England and Ireland, identified with both Irish nationalism and the Anglo-Irish Protestant Ascendancy, pined after an Irishwoman and married an Englishwoman, and collaborated with such South Asians as Tagore and Shri Purohit Swami. His writing hybridizes English and Irish genres, meters, and orthographies, while also incorporating forms and motifs from East and South Asia.[34] Poetry is a means of geographic and temporal travel, he suggests in "Sailing to Byzantium," and in "Lapis Lazuli," he intercuts Renaissance England, modern Europe, ancient Greece, and China. Yeats and Mina Loy are generally thought of as having almost nothing in common — Yeats as a monolithically canonical Irishman, Loy as a recent entrant into a more experimental Anglo-American countercanon. But just as a transnational poetics can provide a unifying ground for poets as seemingly unlike as McKay and Eliot, Yeats's violent ambivalences toward his Irish and English inheritances, in a poem such as "Easter, 1916," can be compared with Loy's fractured identifications; his cross-national and cross-cultural interstitiality, with hers. Loy's "Anglo-Mongrel" verse reflects American, English, and Continental influences in its harsh, edgy surfaces and interlingual mixture. Doubly alienated, as indicated by her discomfiting manipulation of stereotypes of Englishness and Jewishness, this Anglo-Euro-Judeo-American poet had grown up with a Protestant English mother and a Jewish Hungarian immigrant father, wryly allegorized as "Alice the gentile / Exodus the Jew" in "Anglo-Mongrels and the Rose," before she left England for Italy, France, New York, Paris, again New York, and finally Aspen.[35] Helping to put in relief stylistic and cultural commonalities and differences, a cross-national paradigm enables us to recognize that both Loy and Yeats were bricoleur migrants entangled in, and tensely divided amid, the various cultural affiliations mediated in their poetry.

Similarly, D. H. Lawrence and Langston Hughes are thought of as belonging to entirely distinct literary universes. Yet a transnational approach helps illuminate — across enormous differences of geography, politics, and aesthetics — their mutual debt to, and distinct uses of, a shared progenitor. Though catalogued as singularly "English" or "British," Lawrence — who left England after World War I to rove across Europe, Australia, Mexico, the American Southwest, and elsewhere — hails Whitman as a model for the free-verse poet: "Whitman's is the best poetry of this kind," "the unrestful, ungraspable poetry of the sheer present," in contrast with British examples, such as the "treasured gem-like lyrics of Shelley and Keats."[36] Whitman is a no less foundational resource for Hughes, as the so-called poet laureate of Harlem acknowledges in "I, Too," though Hughes uses Whitman not to seize on the "sheer present" but to reclaim and honor a rich past denied to African Americans. Hughes's "The Negro Speaks of Rivers," an early paean to the wellsprings of African American identity, builds its transhistorical and transcultural "I," flowing freely across temporalities and metrical limits, on Whitman's example. The transatlantic circuit is completed when poets of a later generation in the United States — the Black Mountain poets Charles Olson, Robert Creeley, and Denise Levertov — take up Lawrence's poetry of the present as a model for a postwar poetics of "open," "projective," and "organic" form (despite the anxious Americanism of a document such as Olson's 1950 manifesto "Projective Verse").[37] And "black British" poets complete a parallel transatlantic loop by drawing on the example of the militant, vernacular poetics of the Black Arts movement, which in turn owed debts to the Beats and Black Mountain poets (as indicated, for example, by Amiri Baraka's mining of Olson's "Projective Verse") and to Harlem Renaissance poets such as Hughes.

A cross-cultural framework also makes more visible the intergeo-graphic mappings and postnational skepticisms of modernist poetry. The Pennsylvania-born H.D.—who spent most of her life in England and Europe, married the Englishman Richard Aldington, took as her life partner the novelist Bryher, daughter of perhaps England's wealthiest man, and wrote early verse modeled on Greek lyric fragments—palimp-sestically fuses ancient Egypt and Blitz-torn London in *The Walls Do Not Fall* (1944), the sequence's opening stanzas repeating and compressing "here, there," until the words' deictic force dissolves and the transcon-tinental locations become inseparable.[38] By the same token, to enlist the poems of Laura Riding—a New York Jew turned Southern Fugitive turned American expatriate, in England and Majorca—as citizens of a national literature would be, at the very least, to override their skepti-cism toward cartographic reduction: "The map of places passes," warns one of her poems, "The reality of paper tears."[39] The same could be said of the poetry of W. H. Auden, who reversed the direction of H.D.'s and Riding's transatlantic migrations. Written soon after his arrival in the States, his elegy for Yeats tropes the poet's death as a kind of denation-alization, comparable to Auden's own recent displacement: "Now he is scattered among a hundred cities / And wholly given over to unfamiliar affections"; "Let the Irish vessel lie / Emptied of its poetry."[40] Presumably Auden is at this moment but an English vessel for poetry that—mediat-ing between the formal and political proclivities of a leftist Englishman and a reactionary Irishman, ranging from "air-ports" to "evergreen for-ests," collating Rudyard Kipling and Paul Claudel, straddling "the floor of the Bourse," "mad Ireland," and "the dogs of Europe"—cannot be as-signed unitary citizenship without endorsing the national reduction-ism against which the poem pits its cosmopolitanism. As will be seen in chapter 4, the elegy's translocational grief stands against the virulent na-tionalism about to ravage much of the world: "the living nations wait, / Each sequestered in its hate." In "Prologue at Sixty" Auden asks, "Who am I now? / An American?" and answers, "No, a New Yorker," though the poem's intermappings of English, Austrian, German, Roman, Icelandic, Ischian, Slovakian, Swiss, French, and other landscapes as psychic sedi-mentation complicate even this humorously localized self-definition.[41] In short, these and many other instances of dislocation and hybridiza-tion, of creolized genres and idioms, of shared intercultural precursors and forms, of postnational skepticisms and sedimented geographies, re-veal the holes in nationalist disciplinary partitions.

Granted, neither the United States nor the United Kingdom lacked

literary regionalists or nationalists: A. E. Housman hymned the Shrop-
shire countryside, as did Carl Sandburg Chicago's cityscapes, while
E. A. Robinson told the stories of failed lives in Tilbury Town, Masters
in Spoon River, though these poets reanimated globally circulated traditions, such as Housman's Latin classicism and Masters's Greek epitaphs, to give expression to their local or regional experience. Perhaps
the most prominent among the American regionalists and nationalists,
William Carlos Williams, illustrates the difficulty of considering even
"nativist" poets outside an international context. With a father from
Birmingham, England, and a Spanish-speaking, Puerto Rican–born
mother of Basque-Dutch-Spanish-Jewish descent, this poet from a bi-
lingual household (who titled his first major book *Al Que Quiere!*) vocif-
erously promoted an American literary nationalism that was in part a reaction against the non-native classicism and symbolism he deplored ("IT
CONFORMS!"), particularly in Eliot and Pound — "Men content with the
connotations of their masters" and willing to rehash and repeat European prototypes.[42] Though Williams was not an expatriate, he lived, like
Wallace Stevens and Marianne Moore, in and around "mongrel Manhattan," as Ann Douglas calls it,[43] where all three poets came into contact
with avant-garde European art, engendering poems that have more in
common with the violent perspectivism of cubism than with American poetry of the previous generation. Comically disordering its num-
bered sections, wildly shifting from the vatic to the reportorial, disgorg-
ing large gobs of quotation, Williams's prologue to *Kora in Hell* bristles
with excitement over cubist dissections of space and dada experiments
in "ready-mades," such as Marcel Duchamp's porcelain urinal or *Foun-
tain*[44] — European examples of "found" art that would make possible
Williams's "quintessentially American" poetry. Responsive to local or
national conditions, modernist imaginings were nevertheless inseparable from modernity's intensified global flows.

3.

Because the transnationalism of modernist poetry conflicts with
nation-based curricula and literary histories, it is often absorbed and
deflected by several means, above all the strategy I term culture-of-birth
determinism. By this logic, poets born in Hailey, Idaho, St. Louis,
Missouri, Bethlehem and Allegheny, Pennsylvania, and raised in the
United States, cannot help but create American art, no matter where
they live, what styles and movements they respond to or foment, what

citizenship they claim. It is assumed that in the formation of a poet's sensibility, the essential ingredients are mother tongue and familial, religious, and educational background; and the frequent corollary is that no amount of geographic, cultural, or linguistic displacement can alter these fundamentals. While these views have some validity, they can easily be taken too far, neutralizing the often transformative, or at least defamiliarizing, effects of migration from an "original" to an "adopted" home or language or religious outlook, of being smitten by literary and artistic works across national boundaries. The culture-of-birth paradigm is most obviously problematic when applied to the children of immigrants: Sandburg first spoke Swedish; Louis Zukofsky, Yiddish; and Stein, French and German; and, indeed, Stein's early polylingualism helps explain her insistence on the material density of the linguistic medium, as does her engagement with the fractured planes of Picasso's cubist and Cézanne's proto-cubist painting.[45] In view of culture-of-birth determinism, Eliot's English accent, Anglo-Catholic conversion, and adoption of British citizenship and home are but evasions of his real Americanness. To keep him from falling outside the bounds of the Americanist narrative in *The New Princeton Encyclopedia of Poetry and Poetics*, the entry on "American Poetry" says, "his Am. roots, his growing up in St. Louis and New England, were the deepest sources of his personality and poetry."[46] Meanwhile, the author of the entry on "English Poetry" in the same encyclopedia has the reverse problem of qualifying Eliot for British literary citizenship: "The seminal figures, Pound and Eliot, were both Americans," grants the author, "though Eliot became very thoroughly Anglicized" and "can be seen as the man who brought Fr. symbolism (q.v.) to England."[47]

As this example indicates, culture-of-birth determinism gives way to other, sometimes contradictory, paradigms when the national narrative requires it. "American poetry" genealogies must switch horses to make sense of McKay or Loy, for example, turning from origination narrative to site-of-influence teleology—not "you belong where you came from" but "you belong where you had an influence." McKay's influence on the Harlem Renaissance qualifies him as "American," even though during it he was on the other side of the Atlantic; and, by the same logic, he might as well be deemed "Jamaican," given his influence on Creole poets such as Louise Bennett, or "postcolonial," due to his influence on African and African diaspora poets of negritude, such as Léopold Senghor. Because Loy caused a stir in New York after publishing "Songs for Joannes" (1915–17) in *Others*, her avant-gardism is likewise chronicled as American, de-

spite her English birth, Anglo-European formation, and close association with the leaders of Italian futurism, let alone her poetry's jarring
mixture of Pre-Raphaelite aestheticism, futurist typographic experi-
ment, and feminist satire. Among postwar writers, the "American poet"
Denise Levertov arrived in the United States at the age of twenty-five,
having already published her first book of poetry in England.[48] Whether
these poets were born and grew up in the United States or arrived in ma-
turity, their work is labeled "Made in the USA." Some poets are born to
Americanness, some achieve Americanness, some have Americanness
thrust upon them.

What is the cultural politics of this nationalization of transnational writing? What needs are met when ambiguously affiliated poets
are asked to serve nation-centered lineages? The expansiveness of the
American canon can be seen as a happy side effect of American multicultural openness or as an unfortunate consequence of American
cultural imperialism and its need for aggrandizing self-narration. In
Donald Pease's view, American literary studies "facilitated exchanges
between literary and political realms and effectively transformed the
field into an agency of neocolonialism. Americanist critics," he adds,
tried to "subsume other literatures and geopolitical spaces into a universal Americanism that reshaped the entire world in the images and
interests of the United States."[49] Although Pease is describing cold-war
Americanists and although American studies has begun to internation-
alize itself, the recently proliferating anthologies and literary histories
of modern and contemporary American poetry, even when this poetry
is conceived as subversive, frequently embody a cultural nationalism
that risks complicity in assertions of American political, economic, and
military power. Americanist multiculturalism, while usefully pluralizing
conceptions of American literature, likewise risks representing one nation's literature as a self-sufficient macrocosm that effectively internal-
izes and thus effaces all others.

Not that the American nationalist narrative stands alone. During
the waning of an older empire, poets and critics of the so-called Movement, such as Philip Larkin, told a parallel story about a "native" English line of poetry that goes back to A. E. Housman, Thomas Hardy,
and the English Georgians, abandoning an abstruse modernism imported from America and Ireland. But Larkin, whose poetry is steeped
in Eliot's early poetics of psychosexual alienation and Yeats's of irresolvable ambivalence, took the African American musical form of jazz
as his aesthetic paradigm — an art that he thought could, in its more

traditional forms, deliver sensual and emotional pleasure with great immediacy, as he wanted to in his poems.[50] Larkin's Anglo-nativism, like Williams's Americo-nativism, is inconceivable outside an international context — his reaction against the perceived foreignness of the modernism of Yeats, Eliot, and Pound, and his anxious and nostalgic response to the postwar collapse of the British Empire, in poems such as "Homage to a Government." Despite the standard assumption of a transatlantic gulf between postwar British and American poetry, other poets of the Movement who migrated to the United States — Donald Davie and Thom Gunn — adapted the influences of Pound and Yvor Winters in forging Atlantic-straddling formalisms, while Charles Tomlinson claimed Stevens, Moore, and the objectivists as models for his poetics of "otherness,"[51] and Geoffrey Hill based the harsh ethical self-scrutiny of his poetry on the model of Allen Tate's verse.[52] Various confessionalists, Beats, and New York poets had a still wider influence in Britain and Ireland from the 1960s onward.

Nor did these influences flow in one direction across the Atlantic. Living in the United States and presiding over the Yale Series of Younger Poets from 1947 to 1959, Auden helped shape the work of an array of form-hungry U.S. poets, from James Merrill, Elizabeth Bishop, and Robert Hayden to John Ashbery, Frank O'Hara, and Adrienne Rich.[53] Settling in England, Plath — usually anthologized as American, sometimes as British — assimilated the violence and grim sonorities of her English husband's verse, her irreducible cross-nationalism instanced by the semi-American, semi-English intonation of her poetry readings for the BBC. The collective unconscious presupposed by her poems — in which the global historical trauma of Auschwitz, Belsen, Hiroshima spills across national and psychic borders — exceeds the identitarian and Americo-centric paradigms typically clustered around the concept of "American confessionalism." A few years earlier, poets influenced by the Movement in England and the New Criticism in America, sharing a commitment to a rational syntax and a nonpolitical poetics, cohabited the landmark 1957 anthology *New Poets of England and America,* their transatlantic formalism representing a mutual suspicion of the rationalized irrationality that killed millions during World War II. At the same time, many of the antiformalists of Donald Allen's competing *New American Poetry* (1960), such as the Beats and the New York poets, looked to Continental surrealism and to East Asian thought and poetry for help in representing the unreal realities and delocalized locations of postwar experience. In the ensuing decades, the institutional circulation and networks of reputation, money, and poetry within booming graduate programs in the United States focused considerable attention inward, but the counterforce of transnational human and cultural flows continued as a strong stimulus to contemporary U.S. poetry, both inside and outside the university, as evidenced by extensive work in imported fixed forms (e.g., haiku, pantoum, ghazal), the surge in translation by poets (e.g., Robert Bly, W. S. Merwin, Robert Lowell, Agha Shahid Ali, Robert Hass, Lyn Hejinian), long residencies abroad (e.g., Bishop in Brazil, Gary Snyder in Japan, Ashbery and Marilyn Hacker in France), the arrival of expatriate and visiting poets (e.g., Czeslaw Milosz, Joseph Brodsky, Derek Walcott, Seamus Heaney, Agha Shahid Ali, Paul Muldoon, Eavan Boland, Geoffrey Hill, Kamau Brathwaite, Lorna Goodison, Wole Soyinka), and the emergence of poets born and reared elsewhere (e.g., Charles Simic in Yugoslavia; Jorie Graham in France and Italy; Li-Young Lee in Indonesia, Hong Kong, Macao, and Japan).

Because Irish poetry is often assumed to be even more "provincial" and "rooted" than other varieties of contemporary poetry, it deserves special attention in an exploration of what a transnational disciplinary paradigm can reveal and a national paradigm can make harder to see. Critical discussions of Irish poetry and culture often still bear vestigial traces of Irish Ireland — in Terence Brown's words, "an imaginative attachment to the local and a belief that history had allowed that local life a protracted protection from alien influences";[54] yet we should not forget that postwar Irish poetry frequently transnationalizes the local. Seamus Heaney has been both lauded and attacked as a nationalist, a poet (according to David Lloyd) of "reterritorialisation of language and culture."[55] But such provincialization of Heaney occludes his English models — Wordsworth's guilty explorations of emergent sexuality, Hopkins's sonically clustered and erotically charged religious verse, Ted Hughes's clenched and implosive poetry — not to mention subsequent American influences, such as Williams, Robert Creeley, Theodore Roethke, and Robert Lowell. Further, the imaginative topography of Heaney's poetry is an intercultural space, a layered geography. He renews *dinnseanchas*, the Irish place-name topos, by revealing the transnational sedimentation of the Irish ground. "Bogland," the first of his poems set in the bog, interprets Irish topography in relation to the American West, seeing Ireland's bog through a screen of negations — "unfenced country," "They'll never dig coal here," "We have no prairies / To slice a big sun at evening." Ireland's landscape is made visible only by juxtapositions with another geography—made readable only by the help of topographic diacriticals imported from across the Atlantic. In the semantic dissonance of "pioneers"—transatlantically punning on meanings both Old World (archaic for "diggers") and New ("American explorers")—the *here* becomes inseparable from the *not here*. Poetic archaeology ironically deterritorializes the ground, which is found to be ever "Melting and opening." Excavating bogland as he excavates words, the poet finds not the terra firma of the nativist but "Atlantic seepage. / The wet centre is bottomless," in a glance at the Irish diaspora and other transatlantic flows between Ireland and the Americas.[56] The bog poems' place-names "Tollund, Grauballe, Nebelgard" insist on an intercultural and interlingual collage of Norseman and Norman, Viking and Celt, Hibernia and Jutland, the latter extending across peninsular Denmark and northwest Germany.[57] Multidirectional vectors criss-cross in the Bog Queen's "dreams of Baltic amber," "peat floe," "phoenician stitchwork," and "nuzzle of fjords."[58] That poem's language, studded with Old Norse, Irish, Anglo-Saxon, also bears traces of the intimate transatlantic fusion of two poets: its anaphora of "I" and "my" and its prosopopoeia recall Ted Hughes's animal poems, while its concluding resurrection—"and I rose from the dark, / hacked bone, skull-ware"—evokes the ending of Plath's "Lady Lazarus." Though repeatedly enlisted, in Richard Kearney words, "as the poet of the patria, a home bird, an excavator of the national landscape,"[59] Heaney names an imaginative place that is local, yet irreducibly composite, in between, translocational: in his elegy for Francis Ledwidge, the "Criss-cross" of Irish and "true-blue" strains of an Irishman serving in the British Army; in "Station Island," the superposition of Dante's Purgatorio and Lough Derg; the multilingual dislocations of "Alphabets"; the intertroping of Irish and Old English words in *Beowulf;* the conflation of Horace's lightning-hurling Jupiter and the September 11 attacks under a "clear blue sky" in "Anything Can Happen"; and, in "Electric Light," the surprising intersections of a maternal grandmother's archaic speech and that of the Sybil of Cumae, of Chaucer's "straunge stronde" and the "Derry ground."[60]

Another poet from Northern Ireland who has spent much of his career in the United States, Paul Muldoon, pushes these cross-national proclivities still further in the geographically kaleidoscopic refractions of his poetry. "7, Middagh Street," for example, submits *dinnseanchas* to a violent scattering. Widening the cross-cultural bearings of Auden's poetry, as of the New York school, the section "Wystan" is a postnationalist *tour de force*, or perhaps *tour du globe*, intercutting Nineveh and Newfoundland, New York and Barcelona, the Spanish Civil War and the Sino-Japanese War, "Egypt, Gallipoli / and France," Germany, Ballylee, Oregon, New Hampshire, Bread Loaf, the English Midlands, and Venice.[61] In "The Grand Conversation," Muldoon antically dramatizes what Freud termed the "narcissism of minor differences."[62] He wryly recalls the place-names of *dinnseanchas:* Comber and Loughgall, but also Charlottesville, Korelitz (his wife's last name), and most humorously "the islets of Langerhans"—not a geographic place but the insulin-producing cells in the pancreas.[63] Seemingly anchors of identity, place-names instead become for Muldoon deceptive and fetishized signifiers of cultural distinctiveness, while the larger story of contemporary intercultural experience is "The Grand Conversation" across boundaries of place, tribe, ethnicity: in an ironic echo of the estranged Prufrock and his imaginary mermaids, the poem's Northern Irish husband and Jewish American wife cry out "each to each / from his or her own quicken-queach."

Nor are Heaney and Muldoon isolated examples: many other contemporary poets from Ireland, north and south, cannot be adequately understood within a narrowly national framework. To break the grip of Ireland's masculinist "Mimic Muse," Eavan Boland turned to the example of American feminist poets: she adopted Plath's performative language of personal extremity in a poem such as "Anorexic" ("I am skin and bone") and Adrienne Rich's use of emblematic, first-person female personae—in a poem such as "Mise Eire," collectivist figures such as the prostitute ("I am the woman— // . . . who practices / the quick frictions") and the emigrant ("I am the woman / in the gansy-coat / on board the *Mary Belle*").[64] Meanwhile, Medbh McGuckian's "dream-language" of "double-stranded words"[65]—syntactically unmoored, vividly imagistic, semantically oblique, steeped in unconscious materials—has less in common with Boland's declarative work than it does with neo-surrealist or Deep Image poetry. Having lived much of his life in New York and London, the Anglo-Irish, French symbolist-indebted Derek Mahon asks "what is meant by home,"[66] and it is a question that Irish poetry—like other modern and contemporary poetries—more often raises than answers. In sum, in the case of Ireland, as of Britain or the United States, let alone the more obviously transnational postcolonial world and "ethnic" U.K. and U.S., the paradigm of distinct national literatures, coherently transmitted, proves ill-suited to the powerfully intercultural dynamics of twentieth- and twenty-first-century poetry.

4.

If so, then perhaps more deconstructive pressure needs to be applied not only to mononational narratives but also to the distinction between indigenists and cosmopolitans (albeit without dissolving it altogether), for it risks obscuring the transnationality of the "indigenists" and artificially separating poetic "cosmopolitanism" from the main, nationally defined, strands of modern and contemporary poetry in English. The work of fellow Nigerian poets Wole Soyinka and Christopher Okigbo has often been contrasted with the "traditionalist," "authentic" poetry of other African writers, such as Okot p'Bitek[67]—except that Soyinka and Okigbo indigenize modernism through Igbo and Yoruba myth, syntax, and wordplay, and Okot's nativism is inseparable (as mentioned earlier) from his Western anthropological training. In the Caribbean, Walcott's internationalism is contrasted with the localism of such Creole poets as Louise Bennett, except that Walcott's calypso rhythms creolize Standard English ("'This is how, one sunrise, we cut down them canoes,'" begins *Omeros*),[68] while Bennett's Creole poetry is, like McKay's, framed by the British ballad stanza, as in her poem "Bans a Killin," which compares Jamaican English with the other dialects legitimized by "de Oxford Book / A English Verse":

> Dat dem start fi try tun language
> From de fourteen century—
> Five hundred years gawn an dem got
> More dialec dan we![69]

Bennett humorously deprovincializes Jamaican Creole, recontextualizing it globally as but one of the multitude of dialects spawned by a world-circulating language. Similarly, in the Harlem Renaissance, to turn from the transnational to the closely related question of the cross-ethnic, Countee Cullen's and Claude McKay's Euro-American technique is often contrasted with the more "indigenous" practices of Langston Hughes, or Jean Toomer's Anglo-Imagism with Sterling Brown's orally styled verse. But Whitman, Sandburg, and Robinson were also strong influences on the "indigenists," as evidenced by their use of collectivist personae and satiric character portraits. And the poetry of the "cosmopolitans," including the densely allusive and polyglot modernism of Melvin Tolson's *Harlem Gallery*, is inflected by African

American oral traditions, such as insistent rhyme, exaggerated irony, rhetorical indirection and extravagance:

> Convulsively, unexampledly,
> Snakehips' body and soul
> began to twist and untwist like a gyrating rawhide —
> began to coil, to writhe
> like a prismatic-hued python
> in the throes of copulation.[70]

Amiri Baraka's Black Arts nationalism, refusing assimilation to Euro-American poetic norms and celebrating instead blues and jazz models, might seem the polar opposite of the sonnet-embracing formalism of Rita Dove, Robert Hayden, and the early Gwendolyn Brooks. But Baraka's improvisatory aesthetic is based in the Beat and Black Mountain poetics of spontaneity, which in turn relied heavily on jazz and blues improvisation to resist New Critical norms of formal polish and closure (see, e.g., Robert Creeley's "I Know a Man" and Allen Ginsberg's "Kaddish").[71] Now that criticism has highlighted the homely and ethnically specific origins of even seemingly placeless or raceless modern and contemporary writing, it may be time to explore more vigorously the cross-cultural sources and reach of poetry such as Baraka's, Hughes's, Brown's, Bennett's, or Okot's, which seems securely rooted in indigenous tradition and local soil. Within the overarching context of the twentieth century's "traveling cultures" (in Clifford's phrase) and "dramatically delocalized world" (in Appadurai's), poetries that seem native or provincial or local often turn out to be vitally exogamous.

Even so, in a reframing of modern and contemporary poetic history, nationality and ethnicity still need to play important roles. An updated version of the universalist "Golden Treasury" model that erases national and ethnic experience must be avoided. Neither localist nor universalist, neither nationalist nor vacantly globalist, a *translocal poetics* highlights the dialogic intersections — sometimes tense and resistant, sometimes openly assimilative — of specific discourses, genres, techniques, and forms of diverse origins. Located in translocation, transnational and cross-ethnic literary history thus differs from "postnational" or "postethnic" history, in which writers are viewed, when these terms are used most broadly, as floating free in an ambient universe of denationalized, deracialized forms and discourses. Globalization has gone far, but to say that the nation-state is a tolerated anachronism understates the centripetal force of location and the undertow of national cultures. Nor should the "international modernist" paradigm articulated by an earlier, distinguished generation of critics, such as Hugh Kenner and Richard Ellmann, be recuperated without revision. Its internationalism was not always particularized, its Eurocentricism made scant room for the so-called developing world, and its supposed universalism tended to de-ethnicize writers—Jewish poets, for example, were seldom engaged or described as such. But Jewishness may help in understanding the objectivist George Oppen's almost sacred sense of the word in "Psalm"—

> The small nouns
> Crying faith
> In this in which the wild deer
> Startle, and stare out[72]

—or its inverse in the Language poet Charles Bernstein's satirically deflative iconoclasm about the verbal arts in what might be read as Jewish humor:

> Poetry services provide cost savings
>
> to readers, such
>
> as avoiding hospitalizations (you're less likely
>
> to get in an accident if you're home reading poems), minimizing
>
> wasted time (*condensare*), and reducing
>
> adverse idea interactions.[73]

Yet the ethnic or national descriptor, though helpful, is not sufficient in itself, as suggested by the differences between Muriel Rukeyser's revolutionary rhetoric and Oppen's distaste for hortatory political poetry, or between Adrienne Rich's confessionalism and Bernstein's anticonfessionalism (indebted to a Continental, poststructuralist suspicion toward subjectivity). A cross-cultural poetics depends on the identitarian paradigms it complicates—depends on them to trace the literary cultures that are being fused, ironized, and recast.

Identity tags such as "European" or "Anglo-American," attached to techniques and devices that were once taken to be culturally transcendent, can also be useful, since the ethnic legacy of the sonnet, for example, helps us to understand McKay's compacting of rage and ambivalence into a form that enables him to bespeak, even as it furthers, his cultural alienation: "I must walk the way of life a ghost / Among the sons of earth, a thing apart."[74] Unless we posit distinct locational reference points — a black migrant from Jamaica to the United States and Europe who adapts a prototypically European poetic form — we risk missing the sometimes tense relation among positionalities in such transcultural engagement. Jean Toomer's "Portrait in Georgia" starkly recasts the juxtapositional method of Anglo-American imagism (itself partly derived from East Asian sources) into a tool for encoding the violence of racial experience in America. Instead of evoking an inner state or impression, Toomer's poem superimposes a blazon-like description of a white woman's face onto the lynching of a black man:

Hair — braided chestnut, coiled like a lyncher's rope,
Eyes — fagots,
Lips — old scars, or the first red blisters,
Breath — the last sweet scent of cane,
And her slim body, white as the ash
　　　of black flesh after flame.[75]

The abruptness of imagist juxtapositions, such as Pound's of faces and flower petals ("In a Station of the Metro") or H.D.'s of pines and the sea ("Oread"), is powerfully redeployed and is given social and political content in light of the lived violence besetting African Americans. Toomer's dashes demarcate the color-lined chasm between races, yet also traverse it; they violate the erotically charged boundaries between white female and black male bodies, while highlighting the differences in their fate. The interracial crossings enacted within the poem figure, in part, an interethnic encounter between an African American poet and the white cultural inheritance he strenuously reconfigures — a fusion at the aesthetic level that confutes the historical prohibitions remembered within the text. Toomer's poem, like other African American and Jewish rewritings of European and white American inheritances, indicates how race, ethnicity, and nationality are necessary ingredients in a cross-culturalist account. The demarcation of difference can illuminate the interlingual, intercultural, and interethnic tensions and longings that vitalize much modern and contemporary poetry.

Yet overly nationalized and ethnicized narratives risk understating the energy of intercultural transfer and friction. Attuned to pieties or anxieties of influence, monocultural narratives of literary transmission mute the *ironies of influence*. Though Pound was a blatant anti-Semite living in Fascist Italy, his objectivist followers Reznikoff, Oppen, and Zukofsky were left-wing Jews based largely in New York. Zukofsky, referring to Pound as his "papa," put the anti-Semite's poetic methods to work in forging a second-generation modernist aesthetic that could include Yiddish song and humor: he jokes in "Poem Beginning 'The,'"

> . . . mother,
>
> Assimilation is not hard
> And once the Faith's askew
> I might as well look Shagetz just as much as Jew.[76]

Similarly, Reznikoff borrowed Pound's practice of using historical documents to piece together *Holocaust*, a long documentary poem based on the Nuremberg and Eichmann trials. Unless we transnationalize our syllabi and historical narratives of modern poetry, we may miss such abundant ironies of influence as that Pound could have been a primary influence on Jewish poets from Zukofsky to Ginsberg and Bernstein; that imagist juxtaposition could have been useful for Toomer's dramatization of the binaries of American racial violence; that the "English" poets of the Auden circle could have appropriated the right-wing apocalypticism of an "Irish" Yeats and an "American" Eliot for a left politics; that Gwendolyn Brooks could have remade a New Critical aesthetic of contrastive wit and understatement to explore social limits on African American expression; that the Hong Kong–born Marilyn Chin could redeploy the edgy, identity-centered poetics of Black Arts feminism to bespeak an Asian American cultural disinheritance; that the Cuban-born Dionisio D. Martínez could have turned to the surreal dislocations of the New York School to represent the literal dislocations of the Latino immigrant; that the Jamaica-born Linton Kwesi Johnson could have been spurred by African American poets to create his London-centered "dub" or "reggae" poems; that the "ethnic" U.S. poets Li-Young Lee, Joy Harjo, Lorna Dee Cervantes, and Alberto Ríos could have found in such privatistic modes as confessionalism and Deep Image poetry tools for memorializing collective cultural histories.

To highlight these transnational and cross-ethnic ironies is, ultimately, to reassert the very national and ethnic categories of identity that a cross-cultural poetics is meant to outstrip. Viewing poets as creolizing imagism or New Critical formalism, Euromodernism or Black Arts feminism, requires that we ethnicize and nationalize writers, each of whose aesthetics results from a complex history of earlier creolizations. Yet recently proposed alternatives risk still greater reductionism. To impose "modernism" as an umbrella category, for example, that encompasses postcolonialism as much as it does Euromodernism is to whitewash differences among peoples, continents, and histories, assimilating them in an undifferentiated mass of twentieth- and twenty-first-century "modernist" cultures. Or to see all literatures as uniformly "global" is, again, to risk evacuating the specificities of intercultural friction and assimilation. When using such contested terms as "transnationalism," "hybridization," and "creolization," we need to remind ourselves constantly that the cultures, locations, and identities connected or juxtaposed are themselves agglomerations of complex origin — though those earlier fusions have often been naturalized in ways that occlude the surprise or irony of their convergence. Indeed, the hybridities in recent postcolonial and cross-ethnic literatures can help in recovering the earlier hybridities in Euromodernism and in the Harlem Renaissance, which in turn can help reanimate those of still earlier cultural moments.

Celebrating "hybridity, impurity, intermingling, the transformation that comes of new and unexpected combinations," Salman Rushdie remarks that *"mélange,* hotchpotch, a bit of this and a bit of that is *how newness enters the world."*[77] When we track the twists and turns of transnational inheritance, we find stories with, in Eliot's words, "many cunning passages, contrived corridors / And issues."[78] To trace these complex intercultural relationships across boundaries of nation and ethnicity, without erasing those boundaries or the earlier hybridizations they contain, is to begin to explain how poetry helps newness enter the world.

5.

In their area- and nation-based pie-charting of the globe, humanistic disciplines have often helped reinforce — albeit in qualified ways — national and civilizational demarcations. "A tacit or explicit literary nationalism," writes Meredith McGill, "continues to organize departments of English despite the fact that continuities in language and demographics, as well as complexly intertwining histories of publication and of literary form, tug against the often unquestioned binary division of the field into British and American literatures."[79] Indeed, most English departments in the United States still apportion literary turf largely between American and British, making some space for "English Literature Other Than British and American," as the MLA division title revealingly names the most obviously transnational subarea. But as we move away from the mononational paradigm, as identitarian ways of structuring knowledge come under increasing scrutiny, as postcolonial and global studies make deeper inroads, English studies and other humanistic disciplines will be better able to project and delineate models of cross-national imaginative citizenship that are mobile, ambivalent, and multifaceted.

Although national labels impute singularity and coherence, poets make and remake their often interstitial citizenship, as we have seen, through formal and ideological rewritings, through mutations of sound and trope that can span multiple nationalities. More than norms of literary citizenship based on either political jurisdiction and place of birth (*dēmos*) or on their filiative counterpart (*ethnos*), a concept of poetic citizenship allows for poems formed by both unwilled imaginative inheritances and elective identifications across national borders. When living poets face the hard political boundaries of nation-states at airports and checkpoints, it may not count for much that they practice traveling poetries, that they are citizens of imaginative webs formed by cross-national reading and rewriting. Yet surely those of us working in English studies should do whatever we can to dissociate the disciplinary practices that define our subject from the immigration official's surveillance of territorial boundaries.

Transnationalism is not, as I've conceded, inherently emancipatory, any more than nationalism is always reactionary. In the wake of the decolonization of Kenya, Ngũgĩ wa Thiong'o famously led the movement in the late 1960s to abolish the English Department at the University of Nairobi and replace it with a Department of African Literature and Languages. In view of the imperial estrangement of African peoples from local languages and cultures, the argument for the nationalization of literary studies — akin to the nationalization of natural resources and industries throughout the decolonizing world — made sense, even if this institutional reform meant replicating in reverse British imperial assumptions about literature and nationality.[80] Arguably, literary studies today in the world's most powerful nations should be nudged in the opposite direction. I write from within the early twenty-first-century U.S. academy, when the most consequential nationalism in the world

is American, when assumptions about civilizational differences sometimes underwrite political discourse and even projections of U.S. military forces abroad. Under these circumstances and under the broader
conditions of post-cold-war U.S. hegemony, the usefulness of decon-
structing mononationalist paradigms and revealing the web of dialogic
interconnections that belie them, of pluralizing and creolizing our models of culture and citizenship, should not be underestimated. "The fact
is," as Edward Said puts it, "we are mixed in with one another in ways
that most national systems of education have not dreamed of. To match
knowledge in the arts and sciences with these integrative realities is, I
believe, the intellectual and cultural challenge of the moment."[81] A nuanced picture of cross-national and cross civilizational fusion and friction is badly needed today, and denationalized disciplines in the humanities may help provide it, however limited their extra-institutional
reach. As instanced by the intricate knotting together of seemingly antithetical influences and histories, the polyphonic layering of idioms and
ideologies, in a single poem by Yeats or Eliot, Loy or Toomer, Agha Shahid Ali or Lorna Goodison, poetic transnationalism can help us both to
understand a world in which cultural boundaries are permeable and to
read ourselves as imaginative citizens of worlds that ceaselessly overlap,
intersect, and converge.

CHAPTER 3

TRAVELING POETRY

Rapid, multidirectional, unexplained—such are the geographic displacements in the famous opening of Ezra Pound's Canto 81, written while the poet was incarcerated in the Disciplinary Training Center near Pisa:

> Zeus lies in Ceres' bosom
> Taishan is attended of loves
>   under Cythera, before sunrise
> and he said: "Hay aquí mucho catolicismo—(sounded catoli*th*ismo)
>   y muy poco reliHion"[1]

With the help of allusions repeated and elaborated elsewhere in *The Cantos*, we infer that the pre-dawn sun nestling behind mountains near Pisa is being refigured as a Greek sun god lying in the bosom of the fertility goddess Ceres. The cone-shaped mountain Pound could see from his detention cage is also troped as a sacred mountain in China, before the next line returns to Greece—an Ionian island sacred to Aphrodite—and the ensuing passage moves on to personal memories of Spain. Not all poetry travels at such velocity; but in the spirit of Edward Said's exploration of "traveling theory" and James Clifford's of "traveling cultures," I consider what enables *traveling poetry* by Pound and many other modern and contemporary poets to leap across national and cultural boundaries.[2] Recognizing the "inextinguishable taint" of the term "travel," its recreational, bourgeois, European, gendered associations, Clifford nevertheless reclaims the word, using it expansively to describe different "practices of crossing and interaction," "the ways people leave home and return, enacting differently centered worlds, interconnected cosmopolitanisms."³ How does poetry leave home and return? What makes possible poetry's differently centered cosmopolitanisms? And how does poetic travel differ from global transport by other means?

Poetry travels partly, of course, by means of traveling poets. Pound's incarceration in Italy reminds us that, as we saw in chapter 2, various expatriates, migrants, and émigrés transformed poetry in the first part of the twentieth century, and that modern and contemporary poets have been changing places and have been changed by places, from Euromodernists such as Yeats, Eliot, and Mina Loy and Harlem Renaissance poets such as Langston Hughes and Claude McKay, to postwar American poets Elizabeth Bishop, John Ashbery, and James Merrill (analyzed by Robert von Hallberg and Jeffrey Gray as tourists and travelers) and postcolonial and immigrant poets such as Okot p'Bitek and Lorna Goodison, Paul Muldoon and Charles Simic.⁴ Along with literal movement, as also indicated above, modern and contemporary poetry written in English is shaped as well by the circulation of images and ideas via radio, television, the Internet, and other fleet forms of global mediation.

Poetry also travels because poems travel. During his confinement, Pound is elated to find *The Pocket Book of Verse,* edited by Morris Edmund Speare, on a toilet seat — a surprising juxtaposition of the humble commode and poetic transport:

> That from the gates of death,
> that from the gates of death: Whitman or Lovelace
>   found on the jo-house seat at that
> in a cheap edition! [and thanks to Professor Speare]⁵

Modern printing and more recent technologies of dissemination help poems by Whitman, Lovelace, and Ezra Pound to travel via back pockets, iPods, and Web sites, particularly because of poetry's trademark compression. Having only Speare's poetry anthology, a Bible, and an edition of Confucius with him, Pound conjures other poems from memory. Indeed, another reason why poems travel is their mnemonic structure — the rhythmic, sonic, rhetorical, and syntactic patterning that led Auden to define poetry as "memorable speech."⁶

Poetry is especially well suited to traveling in yet another sense — that is, the imaginative enactment of geographic displacement, as in the rapid-fire transnational jumps in Pound's Pisan Canto, and it is this dimension of poetry's travel, briefly highlighted in chapters 1 and 2, that is the sustained focus of this chapter. Not that the Cantos' transnational displacements are unprecedented: Homer's epic similes sweep us from battle scene to snowstorm; Donne imaginatively wanders to a newfound land; Byron's Childe Harold peregrinates across Europe. But as the flows of people, technology, money, images, and ideas have accelerated across modern national boundaries in the twentieth and twenty-first centuries, poetry has made ever more use of the genre's motile resources.[7] Nor does poetic travel always outstrip travel by other genres and discourses. To the extent that poetry is what is lost in translation, travel writing, fiction, music, cinema, and the visual arts may travel more easily across cultural boundaries. Poetry is stitched and hitched to the peculiarities of the language in which it is written. Moreover, because of its reliance on the line and stanza as units of organization, poetry may be a less effective means of ethnographic transport than, say, a chapter of a realist novel or an act of a naturalist play. The detailed description of a wrestling match in chapter 6 of Achebe's *Things Fall Apart* — unlike fellow Igbo writer Christopher Okigbo's intensely self-reflexive lyric sequences — firmly situates the non-Igbo reader within the life world of a Nigerian village at the turn of the twentieth century. Because of its formal patterning and energetic verbal self-consciousness, poetry typically offers less transparent access to other cultural worlds. Similarly, whereas travel writing, the Odyssean tale, or, for that matter, the travel poem (as opposed to the traveling poem) involves "the *territorial* passage from one zone to another"[8]— that is, a macro-level transition, a mimetically plotted border crossing from home to foreign land — the travel in what I am calling traveling poetry often occurs at the micro-level: swift territorial shifts by line, trope, sound, or stanza that result in flickering movements and juxtapositions. A poem such Walcott's "The Fortunate Traveller" functions at both levels: as a travel poem, it traces the speaker's literal air flight from a shrinking England, seen from a cabin window, to Saint Lucia; but it is as a traveling poem, which can bound in a few lines from Canaries, Saint Lucia to Albert Schweitzer in Africa to Hitler's Germany, that we witness the distinctively compressed form of imaginative displacement that poetry affords.[9]

What poetry loses as a traveling medium that often eschews density of social detail, resists translation, interrupts mimesis, meditates on its linguistic surface, and fractures the spatiotemporal passage from one "zone" to another, it gains through structural efficiency and compression. Because the line is fundamental as a unit of meaning in poetry, each of the first four lines of the opening of Pound's Canto 81 can turn to a different geocultural space — Greek myth, Chinese mountain, Greek island, memories of Spain. Frank O'Hara's "The Day Lady Died" grounds itself in specificities of space and time — "It is 12:20 in New York a Friday / three days after Bastille day, yes / it is 1959") — yet, as first intimated by the seemingly throwaway "Bastille day," which superimposes Paris on New York, the jumps across national boundaries, from one line to the next, could hardly be more quick and nimble. From musings about "what the poets / in Ghana are doing these days" to Verlaine and Pierre Bonnard to Lattimore's translation of Hesiod, and so forth, the poem winds up with Billie Holiday at the 5 Spot — a headlong associative movement that, by its elegant flow (to adapt Appadurai's term), gives the prosaic details their "poetic" quality.[10] Such a poem is itself a kind of "contact zone," in Mary Louise Pratt's phrase, a site of migrating and mingling tropes, geographies, and cultural signifiers.[11] Such lyric poetry's intercultural "contact" tends to diverge, however, from that of tourist writing — a genre satirized by Ashbery in "The Instruction Manual" for exoticizing foreign places and fetishistically dwelling on their particulars, such as those of a dreamily wondrous Guadalajara, conjured up by a worker bored by having to write about the uses of a new metal. As indicated by O'Hara's and Ashbery's work, traveling poetry proceeds more quickly and abruptly, through translocational juxtapositions, which by their rapidity and lyric compression typically prevent us from believing that we are entering an alternative space and, instead, foreground the negotiations and fabrications of imaginative travel.

For other poets, the stanza is a mapping tool that helps efficiently establish location and translocation. The transnational dislocations in Yeats's "Lapis Lazuli" occur in the gaps between stanzas sited in the British Isles, then Greece, then China. In one stanza of "Vacillation," the Duke of Chou, author of the *I-Ching*, looks out on a Chinese field; and in the next, a conqueror in Babylon or Nineveh draws rein, both Chinese duke and Middle Easterner crying out, "'Let all things pass away.'"[12] By the logic of *stanza* as geographic room, the white space in between functions like a doorway between cultural worlds, also linked in this instance by a shared refrain, stanzaic pattern, and use of the *contemptus mundi* topos. Even when not strictly bounding regions by stanza, the stepwise *abab* structure of Archibald MacLeish's quatrains in "You, Andrew Marvell" helps track nightfall's westward sweep from Persia to Baghdad, and Arabia, to Palmyra, Lebanon, and Crete, to Sicily, Spain, and Africa. Also moving westward, from Brooklyn to California, Hart Crane's *The Bridge* enacts geopoetic migration through sectional divisions that, by shifting among free verse, blank verse, ballad, and other forms, poetically accentuate and propel dislocation. In these and other examples, the traveling reader never fully inhabits any of these spaces, but is brought up short by the formal framing and various rapid transitions. By sound, structure, and self-reflexivity, poems enunciate and play on the construction of, and movement through, multiple worlds.

Rhyme, rhythm, and poetry's many other forms of sonic patterning also enable imaginative travel. When Melvin Tolson sonically links the Christian god ("Great God A'mighty!"), the Greek god of fortune ("the whim / of Tyche"), and an American folk hero ("*The Birth of John Henry!*"), the connective force of rhyme helps his verse cross enormous distances.[13] "Rhyme," Walcott declares in *Omeros*, "is the language's / desire to enclose the loved world in its arms," and in this long poem, the rhymes of his zigzagging terza rima stitch sonic patterns that traverse much of the world's surface, from the Caribbean to the United States, Ireland, and Africa.[14] Like such lyricized epics, lyrics per se make use of a globe-traversing weave. The sound patterns echoing across one of the most humorously overloaded short poems of the twentieth century, Stevens's "Bantams in Pine-Woods," may not move across literal geographies, but its first lines, mocking the chief who turns out to be the solipsistically inflated "ten-foot poet," unmistakably evoke widely separated places: "Chieftain Iffucan of Azcan in caftan / Of tan with henna hackles, halt!"[15] With the help of a repeated phoneme, a pre-Columbian chief — perhaps Aztec, Mayan, or a conflation of the two — is dressed (from the Persian *khaftahn*) and dyed (from the Arabic *hinna*) like a Middle Easterner. At poem's end, the phoneme "*an*" of the pseudo-place-name "Azcan" helps stretch poetic topography all the way to the Appalachi*an* mountains. Riding the back of such caravans of sound, poetry traverses real and half-real landscapes — perhaps more nimbly than forms that are less sonically rich, more prosaically referential. Its self-signaling sonic textures foreground the linguistic and imaginative construction of poetic travel. Hardy's Drummer Hodge has voyaged from a North Atlantic home to a southern African grave, and the rhymes, assonances, syntactic parallels, and alternating four- and three-beat lines both connect and ironically disconnect these vastly discrepant spaces:

> Yet portion of that unknown plain
> > Will Hodge for ever be;
> His homely Northern breast and brain
> > Grow to some Southern tree,

And strange-eyed constellations reign
His stars eternally.[16]

Unlike Rupert Brooke's notorious World War I poem "The Soldier," which imperially extends national territory wherever the soldier dies ("there's some corner of a foreign field / That is forever England"), Hardy's poem, while acknowledging some cross-hemispheric fusion, emphasizes the unhomeliness of the deterritorialized English body thrown into a landscape that will remain forever "strange" and "unknown."[17]

Sometimes rhythm serves as a way of intertwining disparate cultural spaces, as when Gwendolyn Brooks merges the syncopations of African American speech with the norms of a Petrarchan sonnet, in a poem such as "The Rites for Cousin Vit": "Kicked back the casket-stand. But it can't hold her / That stuff and satin aiming to enfold her."[18] In "A Song in the Front Yard," Brooks entwines her iambs with vernacular triple rhythms and subtly inflected African American phrasing—"That George'll be taken to Jail soon or late / (On account of last winter he sold our back gate)."[19] Whether imposed or willingly adapted, meter, rhythm, stanza, and other prosodic elements have always traveled across cultural and territorial boundaries; consider, for example, the Japanese haiku, famously anglicized by the imagists, or the Arabic ghazal, adapted for over a thousand years into Persian (taking its canonical form in that language), Turkish, Urdu, German, and English—most recently by Agha Shahid Ali. Despite William Carlos Williams's nativist fulminations against European prosodic strictures, he can write a poem that employs a rolling, waltz-like triple rhythm to evoke the dancing of the Dutch peasants in Brueghel's painting *The Kermess*:

the dancers go round, they go round and
around, the squeal and the blare and the
tweedle of bagpipes, a bugle and fiddles
tipping their bellies. . . .[20]

Sometimes the allure of a rhythm, a formal structure, or a "foreign" aesthetic is stronger than ideological fortifications against cross-cultural contamination.

A figuratively rich discourse, poetry enables travel in part by its characteristically high proportion of figures of thought, as well as figures of speech. Since *metaphor* derives from the Greek "transfer" or "carry across," it should come as little surprise that poetry's figurative language enacts geographic and other kinds of movement. "Moving on or going back to where you came from, / bad news is what you mainly travel with," begins Amy Clampitt's elegy for her mother, "A Procession at Candlemas."[21] The mourning daughter figuratively associates the vehicles she sees moving westward on the highway with examples of "transhumance," or seasonal migration, in the Pyrenees, the Andes ("red-tasseled pack llamas"), and the Kurdish mountains; her tropes for travel travel across three continents in three lines. As Bonnie Costello writes, "Clampitt reveals how poetry might become a guide in developing this nomadic imagination: searching out and crossing boundaries, scavenging, finding value in what has been ignored, setting up formal patterns which she then works to defeat."[22] Clampitt's nomadic embroideries might seem to have little in common with Sylvia Plath's emotionally eruptive work. But the rapid rush of figurative substitutions in Plath's "Cut" enacts intercontinental, among other forms of displacement. Having seen her thumb as a pilgrim scalped by an American Indian, the speaker addresses it as a

> Saboteur,
> Kamikaze man —
>
> The stain on your
> Gauze Ku Klux Klan
> Babushka
> Darkens and tarnishes. . . .[23]

In these few words, the poem's pain-exhilarated metaphorical substitutions arc across vast cultural distances, from the Allied saboteur (French) to the Axis kamikaze (Japanese), from the Klansman's hood to a Russian head kerchief. Plath's figurative leaps, especially from herself to Jews in Nazi concentration camps and Japanese victims of nuclear bombs, have been criticized as too free and indiscriminate; even the sympathetic Seamus Heaney worries about her "rampaging so permissively in the history of other people's sorrows."[24] Yet Heaney's poetry, as seen in chapter 2, shuttles back and forth across discrepant spaces — especially, in his early work, across the North Sea to connect the present-day victims of Northern Ireland's atrocities with the sacrificial victims deposited in Jutland's bogs.

Indeed, geopoetic oscillation, as we might term such imaginative movement back and forth between discrepant topographies, is prominent in, though not exclusive to, much modern and contemporary verse. In Ted Hughes's "Out," the lived reality of the Yorkshire farmland is continually sucked under by his father's searing memories of the carnage in Gallipoli — "jawbones and blown-off boots, tree-stumps, shellcases and craters."[25] In "The Glass Essay," Anne Carson shuttles between a wintry Canadian landscape and the English moors of Emily Brontë's *Wuthering Heights*; in "The Great Palaces of Versailles," Rita Dove's Beulah reimagines the white women who come to Charlotte's Dress Shoppe as variants of the French court ladies of Versailles; and in "Memphis Blues," Sterling Brown's bluesman sees little difference between the flood-ravaged Memphis along the Mississippi and "de other Memphis in / History."[26] Lyric highlights the ways in which lines of thought, analogy, and cross-cultural reading — whether strong ligaments or tenuous filaments — connect disparate human experiences. If sometimes the oscillating poem merges landscapes, at other times it plays ironically on the differences between the terrains it shoves together. Walcott's poem "The Sea Is History," for example, wryly juxtaposes biblical and Caribbean historical geographies, and Sherman Alexie's "Crow Testament" sardonically superimposes bible-scapes on American Indian history and myth:

> Cain lifts Crow, that heavy black bird
> and strikes down Abel.
>
> Damn, says Crow, I guess
> this is just the beginning.[27]

Instead of situating themselves imaginatively in the interstices between two geographies, poems by Pound, Tolson, Kamau Brathwaite, Paul Muldoon, Susan Howe, and other poets skip around a multitude of locations. Howe's "Rückenfigur," for example, seems to plant its first line unambiguously in Cornwall: "Iseult stands at Tintagel."[28] But within a few stanzas, the name Tristan is morphing across cultural landscapes,

> Tristran Tristan Tristrant
> Tristram Trystan Trystram
> Tristrem Tristanz Drust
> Drystan . . . ,

while Iseult becomes "Iseut Isolde Ysolt Essyllt / bride of March Marc Mark."[29] The seeming stability of a proper name fractures into the improprieties of its variants in a multitude of texts from different times and places, sometimes by means of the shift of a single letter — "Marc Mark." Orthographic differences are shown to signify and miniaturize geocultural migrations of names and legends. In poetry, travel — not merely the plot-driven excursus into a foreign land — may occur at the level of a substituted letter, a varied rhythm, a pivoting line.

This ease of movement by lines and stanzas, sounds and tropes, juxtapositions and morphologies may not always seem a winning aspect of poetry. Such cross-cultural forays may appear to ride roughshod over significant differences. Alexie's humorous juxtapositions, for example, may risk the very insensitivity to differences between biblical and American Indian narratives that have been catastrophic for native peoples in the Americas — except that he highlights the jarring discrepancies as much as the similarities. Plath may seem irresponsible for linking the Allied saboteur to the Axis kamikaze, the Ku Klux Klan hood to the Russian babushka, and for eliding their political and historical differences — except that her metaphorical connections also underscore the cross-regional and global violence registered and compressed in the poetic unconscious at mid-century. Does Stevens's sonic yoking of the pre-Columbian with the Middle Eastern and in turn the Appalachian repress the regions' historical and geocultural dissimilarities? Perhaps, although part of the burden of his poem is the bantam's rebuke to the grandiose poet for his reductive and idealist insensitivity to specifics, such as those riotously played on by Stevens. Does Clampitt's association of her mournful journey with seasonal migrations in the Pyrenees, the Andes, and the Kurdish mountains trip too easily across inequalities and erase cultural specificities? Maybe, but surely we would not wish to crimp the cross-geographic reach of the twentieth- and twenty-first-century globalized imagination, forcing a poet like Clampitt to ignore connections among migrant mountain populations and limit the range of her associations to the United States. Does Pound's syncretic verse too easily appropriate Chinese, Greek, and Spanish locales and myths and place-names for his self-elegiac purposes? Surely the risk, as in these other poetic examples, is there — a risk that arises in each instance partly from the velocity of the traveling poem, partly from the relative freedom of the aesthetic. But such criticisms may assume a too rigid model of identity.

To wag one's finger at these poems' metaphorical, sonic, and structural "stretch" (Giddens's term for modernity's translocalism) is to presuppose the discreteness and stability of each cultural unit, when each culture is always already thoroughly enmeshed in a multitude of others.[30] It is to impose an ethical and quasi-legal notion of cultural ownership that is inimical to poetry's radial connections, imaginative leaps, and boundary-crossing ventures. And it is to box creative expression within identitarian preconceptions resisted by poetry's hybridizing, associative force. Surely, some poetic maneuvers may be harder to defend, such as William Stafford's foray into Wounded Knee in "Report to Crazy Horse," Robert Duncan's into the primitive and primal Africa of "An African Elegy," and June Jordan's to the same continent in "Poem about My Rights"—poems that may less self-consciously and dialogically traverse uneven cultural terrain. But these risks are inextricably bound up with the characteristic strengths of poetry, as seen in traveling poems by Hardy, Stevens, Pound, Plath, Heaney, Okigbo, Walcott, Howe, and others. Cross-cultural contamination and leakage are congenial to poetry. Traveling poetry helps foreground how, through imaginative as well as literal mingling and merging, new coinages, new intergeographic spaces, even new compound identities come into being.[31]

* * *

Although examples could be spun out ad infinitum, closer travelogical analysis of poems by an early twentieth-century African American poet, a mid-century Euro-American expatriate, and a late-century Latino poet may shed light on how, why, and to what effect poetry travels and what the implications are for a poetics of transnational identity. Langston Hughes recounts being inspired to compose "The Negro Speaks of Rivers" while he crossed the Mississippi, a recent high-school graduate en route to see his father in Mexico.[32] In a mere four lines, his poem crosses four rivers, one in Southwest Asia, two in Africa, one in North America:

I bathed in the Euphrates when dawns were young.
I built my hut near the Congo and it lulled me to sleep.
I looked upon the Nile and raised the pyramids above it.
I heard the singing of the Mississippi when Abe Lincoln went down to New
    Orleans, and I've seen its muddy bosom turn all golden in the
    sunset.[33]

What makes it possible for the poem to cross such distances? By the logic of poetic lineation, each of these end-stopped lines locates itself in a different place, and the gap between one line and the next marks a distance that can be thousands of miles. The disjunctive logic of poetic lineation instructs us not to expect geographic continuity. Each line is a different scene, a different chapter, a different cultural world. Still, the poem's countervailing connections — the "centripetal" quality we saw Bakhtin identify with poetry — moderate the effect of these dislocations.[34] The gelatinous Whitmanian "I" binds together globally disparate experiences. A figure of speech, anaphora also functions as a figure of thought, a trope for the replications of diverse human experiences in different times and places. All the different rivers are seen as resembling one another, and all figuratively fuse with the poet's blood flow and all-knowing soul.

Although Hughes's poem is often read as an example of what Walter Benn Michaels calls "a commitment to a poetry of identity,"[35] specifically an African American or an African diaspora identity, its affirmation of a new "Negro" identity is paradoxically enmeshed in, and dependent on, a declaration of transracial, planetary identity — "the flow of human blood in human veins." The poem's naming of rivers in particular is often described as evidencing the speaker's racial identity; yet two of the four rivers, the Euphrates and the Mississippi, are hardly African, and only one of the other two is mainly in sub-Saharan Africa. The poem "maps a truly global geography of rivers," as Jeff Westover notes, in keeping with Brent Hayes Edwards's "black internationalist" reading of Hughes's poetry.[36] Hughes wrote "The Negro Speaks of Rivers" in 1920 and published it in 1921, when another writer with whom he is seldom linked was composing a poem that juxtaposes rivers on separate continents — the Thames, the Rhine, the Ganges, and perhaps subliminally the Mississippi. Both Eliot's and Hughes's poems assert knowledge of rivers represented as distant sites of human origin: the ancient Ganges for Eliot and the civilization-cradling Euphrates for Hughes. The epistemological claims in these poems — to have "known rivers" far and wide, even at the dawn of civilization — brashly overstep the bounds of each writer's lived experience. But Eliot's poem seems overburdened with the knowledge garnered by global imaginative travel, while Hughes's speaker exuberantly claims the authority to know. Instead of representing himself as being at the end of an enervated civilization, looking elsewhere for moral and spiritual guidance, Hughes, at the birth of the Harlem Renaissance, looks backward to look forward, to summon a boldly affirmed power to speak as a "Negro"—a new "Negro" whose knowledge is both racial (the Congo and the Nile) and extraracial (the Euphrates), both African and transcivilizational.[37] Like the trope of the river, the blood in the poem functions paradoxically as a signifier of the speaker's racial specificity and his shared humanity. The lyric instantiates its dual emphasis on racial and transracial identity in its hybridization of African American and Euro-American cultural forms. Written in a free-versifying and multitude-encompassing Whitmanian voice, the poem also summons the rhetoric and imagery of spirituals, in which to go "down by the riverside" is to seek a site where conflict can be reconciled—"Ain't gonna study war no more."

Although racial identity is often conceived in terms of roots, this poem takes multiple routes leading in different directions. Its allusions to slavery—the building of the pyramids in Egypt and Lincoln's trip to New Orleans—suggest that the poem energetically displaces one kind of travel, the horror of slaves bought and sold down rivers against their will, with the New Negro's imaginative and literal travel across continents at will. Its rapid, voluntary, nonsequential movements are thus the reverse of the terrifying constraints of enslavement. Although the poem tracks the sun's diurnal course, the lyric's global river travel cannot be mapped as a linear trajectory across historical time: it turns from what was then considered the original site of human civilization, the Euphrates, to the Congo, where the Kongo kingdom was in place from the fourteenth through the sixteenth century; to the ancient civilizations of the Nile; to the nineteenth- and twentieth-century Mississippi. Nor is a linear spatial mapping possible from east to west, because of the middle lines about the Congo and then the Nile. This zigzag movement across time and space emphasizes that the verse turns where the speaker wants to turn it (*vertere*), asserting the authority of an unfettered and globe-traversing poetic "I." From a narrowly identitarian perspective, Hughes may seem to travel too freely and quickly, eliding important geocultural differences among ancient Babylonians, Egyptians, Africans of the Kongo kingdom, and nineteenth-century Americans. Yet his free-wheeling poetic travel looks different when seen in the contexts that inform it: the haunting transgenerational memory of forced travel down the river; the claiming of a common humanity historically denied to African Americans; and an understanding of poetry as a discursive space that—by means of place-leaping lineation, cross-cultural symbols, and aesthetic hybridization — affords a remarkable freedom of movement and affiliative connection.

Fifty years later, another American poet explores questions of travel, once again staging poetic self-discovery within a global context. Like Hughes's lyric "I," the "I" in Elizabeth Bishop's "In the Waiting Room" (1971) defines itself in relation to other cultures in distant parts of the world. But whereas Hughes's poem traverses continents to embrace continuities between distant civilizations and the poem's "Negro" speaker, whose soul contains cross-cultural multitudes in a display of new-found traveling freedom and a newly affirmed (cross-)cultural identity, Bishop's almost seven-year-old "Elizabeth" shrinks from the shocking difference-in-sameness she sees in the indigenous peoples pictured in the *National Geographic*. Instead of stabilizing, authorizing, and enlarging the lyric "I," as in Hughes's poem, imaginative travel puts the subject in Bishop's poem at risk — risk that, paradoxically, affords the articulation of lyric self-consciousness. Recounting, in a phrase Mutlu Konuk Blasing borrows from Wordsworth, the "growth of a poet's mind,"[38] the poem explores how the media's global circulation of images impinges on an individual's emerging subjectivity. The young "Elizabeth," Lee Edelman observes in an astute reading, discovers that gender is hardly natural but artificially fashioned and constrained.[39] But the girl's revelation about her common condition as a female human being — akin to both the naked women in the pictures and the heavily clad women in the dentist's office, including her aunt — is no less a revelation about cultural difference:

> A dead man slung on a pole
> — "Long Pig," the caption said.
> Babies with pointed heads
> wound round and round with string;
> black, naked women with necks
> wound round and round with wire
> like the necks of light bulbs.
> Their breasts were horrifying.[40]

In Worcester, Massachusetts, in February 1918, the young girl suddenly finds herself traveling imaginatively to a place visited and photographed by the explorers Osa and Martin Johnson. The mass media present to the imagination, as Appadurai writes, "a rich, ever-changing store of possible lives."[41] Elizabeth's encounter with alien bodies and "disembedded" cultural practices (in Giddens's term for the dislocations of modernity) shocks her into the recognition not only of sameness but also of difference, destabilizing the naturalness of her own cultural world, which suddenly shrinks into one among an indefinite array of contingent possibilities.[42] Her vertiginous

> sensation of falling off
> the round, turning world
> into cold, blue-black space

is in part due to her initiation into becoming a global subject, once anchored to part of the world by the illusion of its completeness, but now unmoored and floating free among cultural and racial differences.

Falling into the knowledge of her apartness and isolation, the girl confronts a terrifying continuity with the alien other, figured especially as "those awful hanging breasts," which would normally signify primal connection but here also signify a dialectically constitutive difference. Written in the shadow of worldwide movements for decolonization in the 1960s, Bishop's poem projects backward in time the rupturing of the First World subject by the forceful emergence of indigenous peoples onto the global stage. As Gayatri Spivak observes of the protagonist of *Jane Eyre*, the "'subject-constitution' of the female individualist" takes place through the contrast with the "'native female.'"[43] First World subjectivity—the child's sense of apartness and her emergence into self-recognition—is "stretched": it depends here on the Third World, on both a recognition of continuity with these women and an exoticizing, primitivizing warding off of the cultural other as different from her own discrete, insular self-identity. The metropolitan female subject is shocked into a differential self-understanding as non-native, as other than the horrifying Other in the magazine. Emphatically defined as a reader—"(I could read)"—Elizabeth is represented in terms of what Spivak calls a "self-marginalized uniqueness" (246), as a reader of images and texts ("Long Pig," "the date"), in contrast to the sheer visuality of the Third World bodies she sees. As Elizabeth "articulates herself in shifting relationship to what is at stake, the 'native female' as such (*within* discourse, *as* a signifier) is excluded from any share in this emerging norm" (244–45). As for the mature poet, she, like the *National Geographic* and like the Johnsons, reproduces and circulates images of Third World bodies and practices for First World consumption. The extent to which these images represent undifferentiated otherness is indicated by Bishop's later confusion over their origin, which she referred to as "African" in an interview, claiming that they derived from what has proved a nonexistent issue of the *National Geographic*.[44] But Bishop most likely echoes the phrase "Long Pig" and the description of infants' heads wound with coconut string, as Edelman notes, from Osa Johnson's 1940 book *I Married Adventure*, and the Johnsons encountered these cultural phenomena not in Africa but during what Osa Johnson describes as an early adventure, in the Melanesian islands of Malekula and Vao in what was then the New Hebrides and is now Vanuatu, among a chain of Pacific islands west of Fiji and east of Australia.[45] The encircled heads and necks are cast in a symmetrical relation to each other, an imagistic repetition given sonic emphasis ("wound round and round"), but Bishop's echoic imagery and language traverse large distances, since the Johnsons photographed women with multiple brass and horsehair necklaces in British East Africa, as seen in *Four Years in Paradise* (1941), while the bare-breasted women pictured in *I Married Adventure* are Pacific Islanders and so-called Pygmies of the Belgian Congo.[46] Bishop's simile for ornamented necks—"wound round and round with wire / like the necks of light bulbs"—jarringly yokes together the primitive and the modern, and indeed the First World girl's lightbulb moment of self-recognition depends on the African/Pacific Islander primitivity against which she defines herself. Bishop's language of shock and estrangement, "horrifying," "awful," recalls the similar affective vocabulary—"horrible looking" (117), "frightful" (120), "terror" (121, 122, 132), "terrifying" (123), "horrible" (131), "horror" (145, 156), "awful" (153)—in Osa Johnson's descriptions in *I Married Adventure* of her encounters with Malekulans.

One way to reconsider the poem's cross-civilizational shock is to juxtapose the young American girl's horror of the "awful hanging breasts" with the reverse ethnography of an indigenous village woman in a poem published just five years earlier, Okot p'Bitek's *Song of Lawino* (1966). For Lawino, it is the breasts of white women and their non-European mimics that are horrifying. She cries out about her would-be white rival, Tina:

> Her breasts are completely shrivelled up,
> They are all folded dry skins,
> They have made nests of cotton wool
> And she folds the bits of cow-hide
> In the nests
> And call[s] them breasts![47]

The poetry of this passage's hyperbole ("completely shrivelled up") and circumlocution ("nests of cotton wool") mirrors the speaker's estrangement from a cultural practice — wearing bras — that has traveled from the "developed" to the "developing world." Just as Bishop's Elizabeth cannot fathom the binding of heads or necks, as formally signaled by the perplexed repetitions and the troping of ornamented necks as the necks of lightbulbs, so too the Ugandan villager is dumbfounded by the strange cultural practices of white women:

> They mould the tips of the cotton nests
> So that they are sharp
> And with these they prick
> The chests of their men! (39)

Whereas the nakedness of the hanging black breasts frightens the young Elizabeth, Lawino proclaims the virtue of the Acoli dancing without hiding anything:

> Small breasts that have just emerged,
> And large ones full of boiling milk,
> Are clearly seen in the arena. . . . (43)

For Lawino, the object of revulsion is the customary behavior of white women, who cover up their bodies and hold their mates in stultifying proximity, pricking "the chests of their men." Bishop's Elizabeth associates native women with violence to the body — cannibalism, head elongation, neck binding — whereas Lawino's language links such violence with white women ("sharp," "prick") and the bizarre ways they treat their bodies and the bodies of men. For all their differences, both Okot's poem and Bishop's treat the breast — seemingly the primal locus of mammalian connection — as the bodily site around which the traveling female subject establishes her distinctiveness vis-à-vis the cultural other. For these writers of widely divergent backgrounds, poetry enables the exploration of modernity's intensified circulation of images and practices, in part because poetic figures can richly evoke alienating encounters with cultural others (whether clothed women with "cotton nests / On their chests" or naked women with necks "like the necks of light bulbs"), and in part because the articulation of personal and communal subjectivities has been a hallmark of poetic forms.

In Bishop's poem, Elizabeth's First World "othering" of native women is unmistakable, so if Hughes's traveling poem can easily be attacked for eliding geocultural differences, Bishop's can be accused of exaggerating them. Yet what distinguishes the encounter with otherness in "In the Waiting Room" from the Johnsons' exoticist language and unselfconsciously triumphalist photographs is the poet's foregrounding the precarious act of self-fashioning in a differential relation to the cultural other (as Okot does in *Song of Lawino*). In Spivak's account, the subject's civilizational self-construction entails the unconscious suppression of the Third World other; but in Bishop's poem, the poetics of self-definition, including the girl's fragile dependence on the other to become herself, is front and center. The speaker's grown-up consciousness frames and drolly ironizes the young Elizabeth's self-discovery: "I scarcely dared to look / to see what it was I was." In the crisis moment in which the girl feels on the brink of oblivion, in danger of falling "into cold, blue-black space," the heightened self-consciousness that has long been a staple of lyric comes to the fore, particularly in Elizabeth's self-address and self-nomination:

> . . . you are an *I*,
> you are an *Elizabeth*,
> you are one of *them*.

In Rimbaud's famous declaration, "JE est un autre," the subject is split, represented as both self and other, as indicated by Elizabeth's doubling of pronouns.[48] In Bishop's quintessentially "lyric" moment of emerging self-consciousness, the vulnerable subject turns to address itself. It individuates itself by seizing on the first-person pronoun and bestowing on that self its proper name, yet it also deindividuates the self, employing indefinite articles that plunge the objectified self-as-other into a pool of resemblances ("an *I*," "an *Elizabeth*"), as in Paul de Man's apostrophic whirligig.[49] The girl thinks to herself, "how 'unlikely'" it is to be "like them," and the poem's play on likeness and unlikeness underscores the figurative comparisons between self and other on which self-understanding depends — the "similarities" that "held us all together / or made us all just one." By virtue of lyric's heightening of figuration, its self-reflexive framing, and its sharp attention to how trope and image fashion selves, cultures, and worlds, the traveling poem illuminates the differential structure through which the globalized subject enunciates and understands itself.

An adequate defense of time-and-space travel by lyric poetry needs to take account of both its connective (Hughes) and differential (Bishop) tendencies in relation to cultural others, since lyrics of cross-cultural sameness and those of cross-cultural difference are equally vulnerable to critique. Should a poem, like Hughes's, travel along vectors of poetic commonality, it may be suspected of eliding differences, colonizing and cannibalizing cultural others, appropriating alterity for self-interested projects cast in universalist guise. Should a poem, like Bishop's, emphasize difference (cultural otherness) within sameness (gender), it is exposed to the reverse criticism of exoticizing and stereotyping others, of overemphasizing and even manufacturing differences for the sake of propping up First World civilizational identities. Yet the parallels between these critiques — damned if you claim sameness, damned if you claim difference — indicate the dangers of a too stringent cross-cultural policing of literary identities. The metaphorical and lineal stretch of poetry — readily affording cross-cultural engagement, contact, and contamination — puts into question the adequacy of such limiting models, which are identitarian even when presented as postcolonial, postmodern, or planetary, at least insofar as their logic appears to favor the foot-bound over the fleet-footed poem. Lyric's nuanced attention to self-enunciation and self-construction in dialogic relation to the other should also give one pause before assimilating the genre to more blindly manipulative forms of global mediation.

While traveling poetry clearly has much in common with other globe-skipping forms, commodities, and discourses, some such poems, though glancing at their complicities with global market circulation, are at pains also to highlight the distinctiveness of poetry. Like Bishop's and Hughes's lyrics, a later traveling poem explores points of intersection among widely scattered images, further revealing what enables poetry to travel, particularly as physical and mental travel have accelerated in the contemporary world. What do Carl Sandburg's face, a plastic surgeon on TV, an American newspaper, signs forbidding laughter in Tiananmen Square, and the poem that records them all have in common? — so asks "Hysteria," by the Cuban-born, Florida-based poet Dionisio D. Martínez.[50] Riding the rails of "line," this poem moves rapidly and unexpectedly among these disparate sites: the lines on Sandburg's face, the wrinkles that the plastic surgeon claims are caused by all facial expressions, the folds of an American newspaper, the signs in Tiananmen Square, and implicitly the lines crossed and recrossed in writing and "reading the lines" of verse. Yet despite all these similarities, the poem implicitly contrasts its idiosyncratic and nonviolent global shuttlings with a more coercive form of epistemological globalism, troped as the way each section of an American newspaper "is folded independently and believes it owns / the world." A humorous enjambment that fractures the politically loaded word "inter- // national" figures the poem's travel across topographic, stanzaic, and lineal gaps:

> There's this brief item in the inter-
>
> national pages: the Chinese government has posted
> signs in Tiananmen Square, forbidding laughter.
> I'm sure the plastic surgeon would approve, he'd say
>
> the Chinese will look young much longer, their faces
> unnaturally smooth, but what I see (although
> no photograph accompanies the story) is laughter
>
> bursting inside them.

Newspapers, governments, and doctors try to hold and even reinforce lines, whereas the poet uses lines to cross, rupture, and question what political and other kinds of normative lines would hold back ("laughter // bursting inside them"). The lyric "I" enables the poet to weave chiastically together both Sandburg's windy Chicago and the prohibitions in Tiananmen Square, both China and North America:

> I think of wind in Tiananmen Square, how a country
> deprived of laughter ages invisibly; I think
>
> of the Great Walls of North America. . . .

We are back to Hughes's Whitmanian all-encompassing, cross-civilizational, lyric "I," the poet's first-person meditative utterance as omnium gatherum — translocal, binding disparities, forging new and surprising connections in its travel across the globe. We are also back to the tropological exploration of sameness-in-difference in Bishop's poem, the poem as site of cross-cultural global comparison, contrast, and self-definition. Of course Bishop's and Hughes's poems were already, in their own ways, mediating between home and elsewhere, between Bakhtin's centripetal and centrifugal propensities, between what distinguishes our locational identities and what holds us "all together" or makes us "all just one." Not that these poetic globalisms are identical: Hughes accesses the transnational as New Negro subject claiming a common humanity, Bishop as First World female subject divided against itself by women of the decolonizing global South, and Martínez through the linguistic and cultural displacements of the Latino migrant. Yet in all these poems—as in Pound's Canto 81 and Stevens's "Bantams in Pine-Woods," Okot's *Song of Lawino* and Howe's "Rückenfigur"—the nimble leaps of cross-cultural figuration and rhythm, the nation-straddling juxtapositions of image and sound, compress, vivify, and illuminate the globe- and identity-traversing force of the traveling imagination.

CHAPTER 4

NATIONALISM, TRANSNATIONALISM, AND THE POETRY OF MOURNING

As we have seen, genres travel. Although tragedy was born in Greece, the ghazal in Arabia, the sonnet in Italy, the Bildungsroman in Germany, and haiku in Japan, these and other genres, far from staying put, took flight across seas or continents, assuming new languages and local colors. As a transhistorical and transcultural template for literary analysis, genre can help track how the Persianization of the ghazal, the Americanization of the sestina, and the Caribbeanization of the Bildungsroman effected profound changes in these and other forms. If you study a work generically, as an instance of ode or pantoum or epic, you transnationalize it. Even with the benefit of a "historical poetics," you cannot dispense altogether with interculturality or cross-historicity in approaching genre.[1] When you circumscribe nationally and historically your generic object of study — say, the American sonnet in the 1920s — extranational (other than American) and extrahistorical (other than the 1920s) vectors cling to the generic descriptor (sonnet). Indeed, if you analyze a text without reference to its cross-border generic cousins, as well as antecedents and successors, you preclude, ironically, an understanding of its specificity.

Take the elegy — the focus of this chapter and a particular instance of the transnationalism traced in earlier chapters through different kinds of poetry. When you interpret a work as an elegy, I would suggest, you understand it differentially in relation to other elegies of other times and places. All elegies have time- and place-specific bearings. Anne Bradstreet's anguished poems for dead relatives reflect and resist seventeenth-century Puritan American assumptions; Tennyson's *In Memoriam* is a quintessentially Victorian English monument of grief; Seamus Heaney's poems for the victims of the Troubles instance the response of a poet from the Northern Irish Catholic community. Yet when you read these poems as elegies — as works that take up and recast specific literary conventions of mourning for the dead — you necessarily place them within a cross-nationally comparative framework, even when you insist on the seventeenth-century Americanness, nineteenth-century Englishness, or twentieth-century Irishness of their elegiac modulations.

The transnational bearings of elegy can also be seen in the genre's affective content: wherever there are bonds of family and friendship, death produces grief, mourning, and melancholia. Psychological responses to death are also, of course, culturally and historically conditioned. The elaborate Victorian display of bereavement in *In Memoriam* diverges sharply from the spare, minimalist modern mourning in an elegy such as William Carlos Williams's "Death." Yet whether magnifying or compacting grief, elegy's affectivity is recognizable by family resemblances across cultural and historical boundaries, from Bion and Moschus and Milton to Whitman and Anne Sexton. Hence, even as the psychological profile of the elegy changes, we can usually find precedents for later developments in earlier elegies. The modern elegy's melancholic resistance to the resolution of mourning, as seen in Wilfred Owen's "elegies . . . in no sense consolatory,"[2] is already evident in an elegy such as Ben Jonson's "On My First Son." If we compare Jonson's poem with African American poet Michael S. Harper's elegies for his dead infant children, such as "Nightmare Begins Responsibility," or if we compare the Kashmiri American poet Agha Shahid Ali's elegy for his mother, "Lenox Hill," with American poet Amy Clampitt's elegy for hers, "A Procession at Candlemas," or Igbo poet Christopher Okigbo's elegy for Yeats, "Lament of the Masks," with West Indian poet Derek Walcott's "Eulogy to W. H. Auden," we recognize elegy's ever-mutating affective universe across boundaries of place and culture: grief, love, and anger; the search for, and thwarting of, consolation; commemorative and anticommemorative impulses.

Later in this chapter, I distinguish among varieties of, and develop a taxonomy for, elegiac transnationalism, as an example of the various transnationalisms we've been exploring more generally in twentieth- and twenty-first-century poetry. But first I examine dialectically the nationalist and antinationalist strands of elegy, considering how poetry of mourning can be made to serve both nation-specific and cosmopolitan ends. Having argued in the first three chapters for a transnational approach, I now shift the course of the argument, acknowledging that nationalism also animates much modern and contemporary poetry, as exemplified by the elegiac genre. Elegies provide an opportunity to investigate poetic nationalism under conditions of globality. But elegies, as I also try to show, reveal how the very fabric of poetry, by virtue of the long intertextual strands that thread through it, contravenes the nationalism to which it sometimes gives powerful utterance.

1.

Mourning, memorialization, nationalism — the political uses of mourning in the service of the nation-state are everywhere to be seen. In *Imagined Communities,* Benedict Anderson memorably describes the significance for the modern nation of cenotaphs or tombs for unknown soldiers: "void as these tombs are of identifiable mortal remains or immortal souls, they are nonetheless saturated with ghostly *national* imaginings."[3] Such abstractive monuments mirror the fictive nature of the national community they yoke together. Since the temporary and then permanent construction in London of Edwin Lutyens's Cenotaph in 1919, it has been a major site of collective mourning for the British war dead and thus for symbolically expressing national identity. In addition to such empty tombs, the modern nation makes prolific use of communal mourning for public figures. As a child growing up in the United States, I was herded into my elementary school auditorium to watch the funerals of statesmen on TV, though the elaborate mourning of my Persian relatives reminded me that I lived in a society where public support for private mourning of loved ones was often lacking or was even discouraged.[4]

Despite their many transnational features, elegies can also serve nationalist identification with dead political leaders and heroes. Because the communal sense of loss or victimization is often instrumental in founding and fostering the nation-state, public elegies for national paragons sometimes play an ideological role comparable to that of the war memorial or political obituary. As recalled in chapter 3, when Rupert Brooke elegizes himself in "The Soldier," he imagines his dead body as marking a real estate claim on behalf of the nation:

> If I should die, think only this of me;
>   That there's some corner of a foreign field
> That is for ever England. There shall be
>   In that rich earth a richer dust concealed;
> A dust whom England bore, shaped, made aware. . . .[5]

The memorial logic of "dust to dust" is nationalized as "English dust to English dust," in a poem that, in its final phrase, even annexes the realm of the transcendent — an "English heaven." While such elegiac poems sustain state-sanctioned nationalisms, others support dissident or alternative nationalisms. Amiri Baraka's elegy for Malcolm X, "A Poem for Black Hearts," mourns a militant African American leader as a "black god of our time," the leader's and poet's black nationalism contesting official U.S. nationalism.[6]

The twinning of elegy and nationalism is hardly new. Lawrence Lipking uncovers the nationalist implications of Milton's "Lycidas," speculating more generally:

> Most guardian spirits, in short, serve national ends, and grievances are often the mark of the nation. Too many theories of nationhood prefer to forget this disturbing historical fact. The imagined community united by bonds of sympathy and interest makes a more satisfying picture than people bound together by bitter memories and common hatreds. . . . If recent history teaches any lesson about the rise and fall of nations — in the Balkans, for instance — it seems to be the amazing power of old resentments to endure and be revived, even after the ideals have died. Nor is it only losers who feel aggrieved: the Serbs and the Afrikaners are martyrs in their stories. Poets help to keep these memories alive, with elegies as well as epics that identify great wrongs and beautiful victims. Even as Milton was mourning a friend, he also was forging a nation.[7]

Perhaps the most horrifying recent example of poetry put in the service of nationalist extremism is the work of Radovan Karadzic, which glorifies the slaughter of Balkan Muslims to right old wrongs to the Serbian nation.[8] The psychoanalyst Vamik Volkan has theorized the role of narratives of victimization to national identity as a people's "chosen trauma" — a historical wound made to serve as a source of group identity, such as the fourteenth-century Ottoman defeat of Serbia at the Battle of Kosovo, or the U.S. defeat of the Dakota Indians at Wounded Knee. Volkan writes:

> As injured self- and internalized object-images pass from generation to generation, the chosen trauma they carry assumes new functions, new tasks. The historical truth about the event is no longer of psychological moment for the large group; what is important is the sense of being

linked together by the shared chosen trauma, which usually becomes highly mythologized. In other words, the chosen trauma is woven into the fabric of the canvas of the large-group tent, and becomes an integral part of the large-group identity. . . . [T]ransgenerational transmission of chosen traumas provoke[s] complicated tasks of mourning and/or reversing humiliation; since all are carriers of unconscious psychological processes of past generations, chosen traumas bind group members together more powerfully [than chosen glories].[9]

The ritualized, collective commemoration and group mourning of traumatic loss has often played a role in ethnic or national identity, to vastly different effects at different times, whether for Irish Catholics or Irish Protestants, Jews or Palestinians, Arabs or Iranians, Kurds or Turks, Germans or African Americans.

Nations imbue citizens with love and devotion, and poetry in general and the elegy in particular have often reinforced such feelings. As Anderson writes: "The cultural products of nationalism — poetry, prose fiction, music, plastic arts — show this love very clearly in thousands of different forms and styles."[10] Anderson famously describes the novel and the newspaper as providing the technical means for representing the nation, since they create the illusion of homogeneous empty time in which events can be played out simultaneously across a horizontal space. But evocatively he singles out poetry and song as sites for imagining the nation:

[T]here is a special kind of contemporaneous community which language alone suggests — above all in the form of poetry and songs. Take national anthems, for example, sung on national holidays. No matter how banal the words and mediocre the tunes, there is in this singing an experience of simultaneity. At precisely such moments, people wholly unknown to each other utter the same verses to the same melody. The image: unisonance. Singing the Marseillaise, Waltzing Matilda, and Indonesia Raya provide occasions for unisonality, for the echoed physical realization of the imagined community. (So does listening to [and maybe silently chiming in with] the recitation of ceremonial poetry, such as sections of *The Book of Common Prayer.*) How selfless this unisonance feels! If we are aware that others are singing these songs precisely when and as we are, we have no idea who they may be, or even where, out of earshot, they are singing. Nothing connects us all but imagined sound.[11]

The repetitive, rhythmic elements that contribute to what Roman Jakobson terms the "poetic function of language"[12] are key to this feeling of an "echoed physical realization"—sonic dimensions of poetry that bind together the imagined community. Anderson also cites funeral elegies, such as "The Burial of Sir John Moore" by Charles Wolfe, as exemplifying his theory.[13] Language is crucial in connecting fellow citizens affectively with the dead, in Anderson's account, especially the intensified and heightened form of language that is poetry.[14]

We can thus identify two distinct elements that fuse in the imaginary of national elegies, each playing a separate role: first, the collective mourning that is often fundamental in the formation of group identity, and second, the recursive or echoic quality of poetic language that can foster the sense of simultaneous community. When poetic uses of language are made to serve public mourning, we have the imagined-community-in-mourning of the public elegy. A resonant example of the elegy in a nationalist key, Tennyson's "Ode on the Death of the Duke of Wellington," defines the duke's heroism through his self-sacrificial fending off of foreign dangers, from Lisbon to Waterloo, which have threatened a personified England. The elegy for the Anglo-Irish British hero begins with an exhortation:

I
Bury the Great Duke
   With an empire's lamentation,
Let us bury the Great Duke
   To the noise of the mourning of a mighty nation;
Mourning when their leaders fall,
Warriors carry the warrior's pall,
And sorrow darkens hamlet and hall.

II
Where shall we lay the man whom we deplore?
Here, in streaming London's central roar.
Let the sound of those he wrought for,
And the feet of those he fought for,
Echo round his bones for evermore.[15]

Establishing itself immediately as the vehicle of massively collective feeling across empire and nation and as an utterance intoned not by one person but by the multitude, the poem is a sonic echo chamber:

end rhyme, consonance, assonance, alliteration, anaphora, and other re-
sounding figures of speech become figures of thought for the imagined
national community of mourners, as if to incarnate their multitudinous
harmony in poetic sound. When the poem summons "the sound of those
he wrought for, / And the feet of those he fought for," the sound and feet
of poem and mourners are made to echo each other, as if to "Echo round
his bones for evermore." Imagining an enormous horizontal comrade-
ship of mourners, the poem also projects this community into the future: "Peace, his triumph will be sung / By some yet unmoulded tongue /
Far on in summers that we shall not see."[16] Chanting these very words,
readers-to-be will extend the community of mourners and thus of the
nation into an endless but definite perpetuity.

"Mourn," exhorts Tennyson's elegy, "for to us he seems the last, /
Remembering all his greatness in the past."[17] The same command re-
sounds three times in the young Yeats's elegy for Parnell, which calls out
"Mourn" to all the countrymen of "our sad nation."[18] This poem of collective mourning is no more shy about its nationalism than Tennyson's,
though as an elegy mourning the shattered hopes of an as-yet-stateless
nation, "Mourn — and Then Onward!" bespeaks a bitter woe that diverges from the "civic revel and pomp" of Tennyson's lament for an empire's "great commander."[19] Yeats's elegy entwines grief and grievance:

> Mourn ye on grass-green plains of Eri fated,
>   For closed in darkness now
> Is he who laboured on, derided, hated,
>   And made the tyrant bow.

This youthful poem's moment of linguistic exuberance — "derided,
hated" — arises when it passionately identifies with Parnell's heroic victimization. Quickly redirecting this anger, the poem urges a movement
"onward," redeeming Parnell as a Mosaic figure, "a tall pillar, burning /
Before us in the gloom!"

Yeats provides a rich and complex example of the intersections
between nationalism, antinationalism, and transnationalism in the
English-language elegy, as revealed by analysis of a few of his poems,
which I juxtapose in turn with those of the twentieth century's other
preeminent civic elegist, W. H. Auden. Unlike the early monotone elegy
for Parnell, Yeats's most famous public elegy, "Easter, 1916," is a poem
of multiple shifts and sudden turns.[20] It commemorates the revolutionary nationalist leaders executed for their part in the failed Easter Rising

against the British government, an event that helped galvanize the creation of the Irish Free State in 1921–22. Does this poem, like the Wellington elegy and the Parnell elegy, exemplify elegiac nationalism?

The most obvious evidence for such a reading is the poem's installation of a national symbol at its climax. Having thought he "lived where motley is worn" (the jester's multicolored clothes suggesting a people's comic inability to cohere around national purpose), the speaker now anticipates the memory of the Easter rebels enduring "Wherever green is worn," though the indefiniteness of "Wherever" subtly departs from territorial nationalism. Paralleling this imagistic transformation of motley into green is the change in the poem's social fabric. Recalling his dissociation from the rebel leaders, as an "I" often encountering a remote "them," Yeats refers twice to their exchanges of "Polite meaningless words"—language that, empty and mechanical, has been holding them as much apart as together. By poem's end, Yeats foregrounds his use of language for secular blessing, language seemingly at its most flush with presence and least fissured by the gap between signifier and signified, incarnating the rebels in their eternized names and his eternally recurring performative act:

> I write it out in a verse —
> MacDonagh and MacBride
> And Connolly and Pearse. . . .

Every time we read the poem, we reenact this inscription of heroic names, proper names of the dead veiled until this climax. Anderson describes nationalism as secularizing religious impulses in taking up the task of "transforming fatality into continuity,"[21] and Yeats's elegy seeks to effect the transformation of the dead rebels into the continuing life of nation and poem. Closing the gap between the rebels and himself, the poet assimilates their nationalist "dream," their "love" for the nation, to his long-suffering and frequently proclaimed romantic love for the ardent nationalist Maud Gonne: "And what if excess of love / Bewildered them till they died?" Having seen the rebels through the cold lens of indifference, the poet is suddenly awakened to his, and by inference his larger society's, relational proximity to them.

"Dramatizing" his "detachment," as Judith Butler writes in theorizing the social dimension of mourning in *Precarious Life*, Yeats had been "trying to minimize" his "relationality": "What grief displays, in contrast, is the thrall in which our relations with others hold us, in ways that we cannot always recount or explain, in ways that often interrupt the self-conscious account of ourselves we might try to provide, in ways that challenge the very notion of ourselves as autonomous and in control."[22] The first stanza's narrative of detachment is suddenly interrupted by the refrain: "All changed, changed utterly: / A terrible beauty is born." The shift from the loosely paced syntax of remote description to the poetically loaded refrain (ellipsis; lexical repetition; caesura; near chiasmus; alliteration; half-rhyme of "they and I" with "utterly") enacts the break in the poet's consciousness. The refrain's use of the passive voice suggests, in Butler's terms, how death and loss challenge the speaker's sense of autonomy, showing him and his society to be held in "thrall" to the rebels. The larger national project subsumes their differences.

But even with these forcefully nationalist strands, the elegy cannot be reduced to a monochromatic nationalism, "a martyrological lament," as it has recently been called.[23] To do so is to impose on the poem the single-mindedness it criticizes: "Too long a sacrifice / Can make a stone of the heart." Threaded through the fabric of this antinationalist national elegy are also equivocations, hesitations, and questions, the poem giving voice to republicanism and constitutional nationalism, but also to suspicions about the distortions of nationalism. In this regard, it would be hard to imagine the poem recited or sung like one of Anderson's national anthems, chanted in a "unisonance" that is "the echoed physical realization of the imagined community." Hence Gonne's complaint that the poem was not "a living thing which our race would treasure & repeat, such as a poet like you might have given to your nation."[24]

The dissonant notes struck by the nonheroic portraits of the rebels are the clearest indication of the elegy's ambivalence. Someone singing the poem as an anthem to the birth of the new nation might well falter over the line "A drunken, vainglorious lout." Although the epithet applies to Major John MacBride as Yeats perceived him before his metamorphosis, its bitterness isn't smoothly assimilable to hero-historiography, any more than is the putative shrill-voicedness of Constance Markievicz.[25] In the final stanza, the poem finds rhetorical correlatives for its conflicted views of the rebellion in the form of questions. Roiling with doubts and uncertainties about blood martyrdom, these lines even dare to ask, since "England may keep faith" and implement Home Rule after World War I, was the rebellion "needless death after all?" This stanza's language of self-correction ("No, no, not night . . .") and self-redirection ("That is heaven's part . . .") rhetorically echoes the natural flux in the preceding stanza ("Minute by minute they change"). The poem acknowledges that the stone's resistance to flux initiates a nationalist revolution, but it is far from certain that such rigid resistance is ultimately necessary. The oxymoronic phrase "terrible beauty" encapsulates these ambivalences. As an imaginative product of the rebels' action, the incipient nation is beautiful; but it is also "terrible," a word that evokes the bloody excesses of the French Revolution's Terror and violent political methods that strike hearts with terror.

In varying degrees and at varying times, Yeats's elegies exemplify the compatibility of elegy with nationalism but also with dissent from nationalism. This dissent in some of his public elegies is informed, paradoxically, by Yeats's nationalism. A reader of Yeats's elegies for Robert Gregory may initially be surprised that the dead man finds no redemption in the continued life of the nation for which he fought in World War I. But part of the reason for this short-circuiting of the logic of national salvation is that Gregory died as a member of the British Royal Flying Corps, and the Fenian Yeats could hardly look to the continued life of the British Empire as a source for the dead airman's redemption. Although "In Memory of Major Robert Gregory," like Tennyson's elegy for the Duke of Wellington, celebrates the dead man as soldier, Yeats's poem offers no indication of the official cause for which this soldier fought. "An Irish Airman Foresees His Death" states the impossible inbetweenness of Gregory's situation: "Those that I fight I do not hate, / Those that I guard I do not love."[26] As such, the dead man is seen as fighting not out of duty to king and country but out of a purely existential thrill in encountering death: "A lonely impulse of delight / Drove to this tumult in the clouds." Elegy here is made to transcend politics, ironically, for a political reason — the logjam in which Irish nationalism found itself during World War I.

Elegiac antinationalism is still more strongly evident in one of Yeats's later poems, "In Memory of Eva Gore-Booth and Con Markievicz."[27] This elegy sharply contrasts the prenationalist beauty of the Gore-Booth sisters and their "withered old and skeleton-gaunt" desiccation as political instruments. In his final apostrophe to the sisters, who have in death reverted to their prepolitical state, the speaker imagines them as joining him in burning down the framework of nationalist and other ideological movements:

Arise and bid me strike a match
And strike another till time catch;

> Should the conflagration climb,
> Run till all the sages know.

The elegy purifies the sisters on the funeral pyre that consumes tempo-rality. Death is seen not as national but as postpolitical and postnational. That this poem adapts the envelope rhyme (*abba, cddc*, etc.) monumen-talized in Tennyson's *In Memoriam* may offer a subtle indication of the elegy's departure, at the level of form as well as theme, from a nationalist poetics — a poem of transnational form and antinationalist content.

Elegy, as Yeats's poetry indicates, can be put in the service of nation-alism, equivocal nationalism, antinationalism, transnationalism, and many combinations of these positions. That Yeats's preeminent public elegy, "Easter, 1916," should at one and the same time vaunt and question nationalism accords with the polyvalent richness, the internalized dia-logism, the ability to express multiple, contending viewpoints that have frequently been prized in poetry, if not in national anthems. Still, even in national anthems, poetic and musical form often betrays mono-nationalist ideologies. For example, when Americans perform the "con-temporaneous community" of the nation by intoning "My Country 'Tis of Thee," their sense of self-contained communal identity is neverthe-less infiltrated by a melody that has been used for British, Danish, and Prussian national anthems, as well as Beethoven's commemoration of the Duke of Wellington. So too Tennyson's imperial elegy for Welling-ton is based in part on Roman models, and Yeats's "Easter, 1916" echoes the "Mutability Cantos" ("all shall changed bee") of would-be Irish-exterminating Edmund Spenser — a poet whose sometimes nationalist poetry was in turn redolent of Italian and other non-English models.[28] Because poetry and song are long-memoried forms, they are traversed, even when doggedly nationalist, by twisted cross-cultural skeins. Yeats's elegies, however Irish in subject matter, are saturated with classical and English conventions, tropes, and forms, drawn from an array of poets, from Virgil to Spenser, Jonson, and Donne, Shelley, Tennyson, and Swin-burne.

Admittedly, such weak transnationalism, as it might be termed, can be attributed to a wide variety of English-language but non-English po-etries that draw on forms and symbols originating in Euro-American nations sometime in the past, as distinct from the strong transnational-ism that aggressively splices together discrepant cultural materials from global North and South, East and West. But particularly in a poem or an-them that asserts the identity or self-sufficiency of the nation, the irony that these assertions depend on extranational tropes and forms should not be lost. Nor should a distinction between West-West and East-West transnationalisms occlude the ways in which, particularly in the first half of the twentieth century, Englishness, Irishness, and other European formations, despite their manifold interconnections, were hardly seen as culturally continuous.

Yet for all their occasional antinationalism and perhaps even transnationalism, most of Yeats's elegies center on the Irish dead, from Parnell and the Easter rebels to Robert Gregory and the Gore-Booth sisters, whereas the dead mourned in Auden's more forcefully transnational elegies may seem like occupants of a United Nations cemetery: an Irish poet, an Austrian psychoanalyst, a German expressionist, an Anglo-American novelist, an American president, an Anglo-Irish poet, and so forth. Preceding the elegies he wrote for Sigmund Freud, Ernst Toller, Henry James, Louis MacNeice, and John F. Kennedy, Auden's "In Memory of W. B. Yeats" may be the twentieth century's first great transnational elegy.[29] If elegiac nationalism makes use of the powerful links between mourning and nationalism, elegiac transnationalism in its genetic, intrageneric diversity redirects poetic mourning across national borders, building affective microcommunities that instance the possibilities of a public sphere not contained and subsumed by the nation-state. An Englishman in America poetically mourns an Irishman, the poem straddling a variety of political and geocultural divides. Writing on the brink of the world's most deadly war, when right-wing nationalist ideologies were about to tear apart nations, Auden names but overlooks Yeats's nationalism, putting the Irishman's poetry in the service of cosmopolitanism. Although grief is often conceived as "privatizing" and "depoliticizing," Butler writes,

> it furnishes a sense of political community of a complex order, and it does this first of all by bringing to the fore the relational ties that have implications for theorizing fundamental dependency and ethical responsibility. If my fate is not originally or finally separable from yours, then the "we" is traversed by a relationality that we cannot easily argue against; or, rather, we can argue against it, but we would be denying something fundamental about the social conditions of our very formation.[30]

The social conditions of Auden's very formation include his being influenced by poems such as Yeats's ambivalent public elegies. Yeats's example, I argue elsewhere, helps make it possible for Auden to name Yeats's perceived flaws — his parochial aristocratic pretensions and nationalist obsessions ("The parish of rich women" and "mad Ireland"); Yeats's "Under Ben Bulben" furnishes the stanza pattern for the last section of Auden's elegy for him; word clusters from "In Memory of Eva Gore-Booth and Con Markievicz" reappear in the Englishman's elegy; and Yeats's Nietzschean philosophy of tragic joy is transmuted into Auden's humanistic exhortation to "rejoice":[31]

> With the farming of a verse
> Make a vineyard of the curse,
> Sing of human unsuccess
> In a rapture of distress. . . .

The tissue of connections and echoes makes of the poem's language, technique, and philosophy an Auden-Yeats hybrid. As such, the elegy explores the relationality that mourning foregrounds, in Butler's view — "a relationality that is composed neither exclusively of myself nor you, but is to be conceived as *the tie* by which those terms are differentiated and related."[32] Words, tropes, forms, techniques, outlook — these are among the fibers of the transnational "tie" that Auden emphasizes in his twain-converging elegy.

Instead of being "privatizing" or "depoliticizing," mourning in this poem is, as a transnationalist act, intensely communal and even political, despite frequent misreadings of Auden's statement that "poetry makes nothing happen." Poetic mourning's cross-national microcommunity of English-leftist-Auden and Irish-rightist-Yeats is shown to be a model of affiliative connection, in contrast with the bitter divisions separating European nations on the brink of war:

> In the nightmare of the dark
> All the dogs of Europe bark,
> And the living nations wait,
> Each sequestered in its hate;
>
> Intellectual disgrace
> Stares from every human face,
> And the seas of pity lie
> Locked and frozen in each eye.

National hatreds sequester and freeze, divide and separate. Because of nationalist extremism, "the seas of pity" have been "Locked and frozen." "Pity," Wilfred Owen's word for compassion and tenderness, is seen as a potentially oceanic force that can overwhelm national and other political divisions.[33] Poetry is associated with the flow of a river across dividing lines ("it survives / In the valley of its saying"; "it flows south"), whereas phrases such as "the Irish vessel," "sequestered in its hate," and "Locked and frozen" link nations with containment and division. The flow of Yeats's poetry into this very poem is the elegy's most immediate evidence for its transnationalist claims.

Not that the poem's theory of literary inheritance, of community forged in mourning, is blindly utopian. According to this elegy's embedded theory of its own genesis, the transnational flow of Yeats's language and ideas into the community of his survivors, the transformation of the poet into his "admirers," the preservation of the poet's work by "mourning tongues" that include this very poem, is difficult:

> Now he is scattered among a hundred cities
> And wholly given over to unfamiliar affections;
> To find his happiness in another kind of wood
> And be punished under a foreign code of conscience.
> The words of a dead man
> Are modified in the guts of the living.

The transition from living poet into his afterlives involves estrangement, deracination, even punishment. While literally signaling Yeats's literary reception in countries other than his own, Auden also figuratively depicts the transmission from poet to reader, intention to reception, as exilic: Yeats's self-estrangement in death involves submitting to the "foreign." Since the poem is in some respects Auden's own initiation in his exilic American life, this theory of poetic transmission as exile parallels Auden's transatlantic migration with Yeats's postmortem literary journey. Ultimately, the poet's survival requires submission to being a sacrificial meal for others, like the totem animal that unites the band of brothers who devour it in Freud's *Totem and Taboo*. Although cosmopolitanism is often thought of as abstract, here it is vividly embodied, requiring both disembodiment at death and reembodiment in the "tongues" and "guts" of the poet's mourning survivors.

Auden's "In Memory of Sigmund Freud" similarly both theorizes and enacts a cross-national transmission, its Freudian mourning for Freud instancing further "the tie" Butler attributes to mourning. Freud, too, undergoes deterritorialization: a Jew living amid enemies in Austria, then in England, and beyond that "a whole climate of opinion"; indeed, his transnational reach is such that it extends to "even / The remotest most miserable duchy."[34] In dissolving boundaries between mourner and mourned and establishing microcommunities between them, Auden's elegies bear witness to the transformative potentiality of cross-national mourning. "[O]ne mourns," Butler writes, "when one accepts that by the loss one undergoes one will be changed, possibly for ever. Perhaps mourning has to do with agreeing to undergo a transformation (perhaps one should say *submitting* to a transformation) the full result of which one cannot know in advance."[35] Merging with those he mourns across national and cultural lines, Auden embraces the unpredictably transformative effects of grief. Whether nationalist or transnationalist, Yeats's and Auden's elegies show mourning to be destabilizing and transfigurative ("All changed, changed utterly"), exemplary of the power of grief to make and unmake the world.

2.

So capacious and amorphous is the term "transnational," like such related world-wrapping abstractions as "international," "global," and "planetary," that it warrants being broken down into distinct varieties that intersect and overlap in the elegy, as in other poetic genres. Elegiac transnationalism can be tracked intrinsically and extrinsically. An obvious extrinsic source is influence across national lines—Baudelaire on Swinburne; Swinburne on Yeats; Yeats on Auden and Okigbo; Auden on Plath, Heaney, and Walcott; Okigbo on Linton Kwesi Johnson; and so forth. Insofar as elegies embed within themselves the histories of their own literary genesis, self-consciously recycling tropes, motifs, and words from different places, they announce their non-isolation within national boundaries. Constructing transnational cultural spaces of mourning, spilling grief across boundaries of race, ethnicity, and nation, they build structures of feeling that represent alternatives to modern nationalist efforts to bind mourning within an imagined community of compatriots.

The elective affinities knitting elegists with the dead in border-spanning microcommunities of poetic mourning are not limited to poetic influence. In wartime elegies, many poets extend the reach of poetic mourning across the national lines that divide soldiers. Wilfred Owen's

"Strange Meeting" metaphorizes as subterranean escape the transnational traversal of no man's land:

> It seemed that out of battle I escaped
> Down some profound dull tunnel, long since scooped
> Through granites which titanic wars had groined.
>
> Yet also there encumbered sleepers groaned,
> Too fast in thought or death to be bestirred.[36]

At the same time that the speaker tunnels beneath the battle line, Owen's pararhymed sonic couplings — *escaped/since scooped*; *groined/groaned* — tunnel poetically through the phonemic differences of language. In the duplicative but differential fashion of Owen's discordant rhymes, the dead man who springs up—"a German conscript" in an early draft of the poem, identified by his abundant literary allusions as a poet—doubles and diverges from the speaker: "I am the enemy you killed, my friend," he declares. The dead man would have told the world, as the living man is doing in the writing of his elegy, about "The pity of war, the pity war distilled." If, as Owen wrote in his draft manifesto, "The Poetry is in the pity,"[37] then pity, instantiated in rhyme, metaphor, and doppelgänger, is the elegiac tissue knitting together the living with the dead across "enemy" lines.

Fifty years later, when Geoffrey Hill's "September Song" mourns a child deported and gassed in the Holocaust, elegy again functions as a nation-crossing "tie," to recall Butler's term.[38] The Holocaust victim's birth date nearly coincides with the poet's, though the child's being born one day apart from him, let alone having suffered a horrible death probably by Zyklon, suggests again the slant-rhyming of elegiac transnational solidarities, by which the otherness of the dead person's fate is respected, yet also brought into a difficult relation of resemblance with the poet. "(I have made / an elegy for myself it / is true)," concedes the poet parenthetically, wishing to elegize across their vastly discrepant experiences, while recognizing the impossibility of ever closing the gap and the intractable self-referentiality of poetic mourning.

A third extrinsic factor transnationalizing the elegy, in addition to influence and solidarity, is the movement of poets to foreign lands, by migration or diaspora. Having immigrated to the United States from Britain and married the Dada poet-boxer Arthur Cravan, Mina Loy elegizes his disappearance in a poem that redeploys the African American jazz of Loy's adopted home as "An uninterpretable wail."[39] Elegies by another English immigrant to the United States, Denise Levertov's "Olga Poems," use place-names to place grief with precision in the English landscape she shared with her sister: the River Roding, Wanstead Park, New Forest. Levertov's central metaphor toward the climactic end of the sequence — "Your eyes were the brown gold of pebbles under water"—allows her both to situate her sister in a pastoral England and to write into the poem her geographic displacement elsewhere.[40] She says she could not cross the River Roding

> without remembering your eyes. Even when we were estranged
> and my own eyes smarted in pain and anger at the thought of you.
> And by other streams in other countries; anywhere where the light
> reaches down through shallows to gold gravel. Olga's
> brown eyes.[41]

The river figures the sister's veiling in death and marks her separation; yet in the Roding's replication by "other streams in other countries," Olga's eyes always seen in the riverbed, the trope of the river also enables the speaker to span distances and reach toward her sister even in death. "I cross / so many brooks in the world," she continues, hinting also at the resemblance between the sister's final migration, as if across the River Styx, and her own geocultural displacement to the United States.[42]

Although Kamau Brathwaite has written many poems mourning victims of enslavement, colonialism, and neocolonialism, particularly in the West Indies but also elsewhere in the global South, he composed — after moving like Levertov, Loy, and Auden to the United States — a long and perhaps unexpected elegy for the Trade Center victims of September 11, including an imaginary relative:

> my Filenes Bargain Basement uncle
> nvr going shopping there or anywhere so wonderful again. his cell-
> ular titanium lip no more complain. ing from the 92nd Floor
>
> we nvr find his body . we nvr find the phone
> some somewhere in this wide gaping river of the city's
> wound.[43]

Mourning, like Milton and other earlier elegists, the dead person's unplaceable loss, the West Indian New Yorker contrapuntally interweaves his voice of mourning with that of Beth Petrone, who recalled at a first anniversary memorial service the moment when one of the towers collapsed and she knew that her husband, a captain in the New York fire department, was "incinerated" (written out in large, bold type): "I just felt a complete disconnection in my heart," she said; "It was just like everything was just ripped-out-of-my-chest." Brathwaite assimilates Beth Petrone's grief to that of "all the women of this poem's world in New York Rwanda Kingston Iraq Afghanistan. . . ."[44] Invoking Coleman Hawkins's jazz saxophone, heard in London in the 1960s, as an upwelling of wordless grief, Brathwaite draws no lines between his grief and Beth Petrone's, between black and white mourning, between First and Third World loss, catastrophe, and desolation.

Among the three intrinsic sources of elegiac transnationalism that can also be delineated is, first, the translocal geography we have already glimpsed in some elegies. Elegies have long emphasized the placement of grief in a specific location as part of the apparatus of consolation. "If only I knew where to mourn you, / I would surely mourn," bitterly laments James Wright; "But I don't know."[45] The most obviously placed form of elegy is the epitaph, literally the inscription upon (*epi*) the tomb (*taphos*). An epitaph of *The Greek Anthology* such as that of the Spartan dead at Thermopylae employs deixis to point to the specific *here* of the dead: "Go tell the Spartans, stranger passing by, / that here obedient to their words we lie."[46] But when war, no longer isolated within a narrow Grecian pass, spreads globally, the epitaph undergoes a congruent metamorphosis. Rudyard Kipling's "Epitaphs of the War" deterritorializes the epitaph — or, more precisely, multiterritorializes it.[47] The World War I epitaphs in this sequence move from France, Egypt, and Sudan to Canada, London, Italy, and Greece, as indicated by the wide-ranging geographic scope of Kipling's titles: "Hindu Sepoy in France," "A Grave Near Cairo," "Pelicans in the Wilderness (A Grave Near Halfa)," "Two Canadian Memorials," "Bombed in London," "A Drifter off Tarentum," and "Salonikan Grave." The atlas of the epitaph, like that of the novel in Franco Moretti's analysis,[48] dramatically widens, remapping the relations among distant sites and spatial matrices. Playing on the long-lived conventions of the epitaph, such as epigram and prosopopoeia, Kipling follows the model of *The Greek Anthology* in placing the dead in specific sites; yet the world-traversing geography of the poem situates these dead translocally, showing modern warfare to intertwine the fate of the dead in North America, Europe, the Middle East, and North

who is normatively human: what counts as a livable life and a grievable death?"[63] Although elegies often function within national ideologies of grievability, emphasizing deaths within the orbit of the nation, they also sometimes extend across these boundaries. "I am the enemy you killed, my friend," writes Owen, profoundly undoing what Butler calls "the differential allocation of grief" to serve "the derealizing aims of military violence."[64] While nations erect hierarchies of grievability, transnational elegy's cross-cultural influences, solidarities, and migrations, its border-crossing influences, forms, and ontologies, suggest other ways of mourning death than within physical barriers and conceptual lines patrolled by militaries and enforced by violence.

CHAPTER 5

MODERNIST BRICOLAGE, POSTCOLONIAL HYBRIDITY

> I arise and go with William Butler Yeats
> to country Sligoville
> in the shamrock green hills of St. Catherine.

So begins an homage by the Jamaican poet Lorna Goodison.[1]

> We walk and palaver by the Rio Cobre
> till we hear tributaries
> join and sing, water songs of nixies.
>
> Dark tales of Maroon warriors,
> fierce women and men
> bush comrades of Cuchulain.
>
> We swap duppy stories, dark night doings.
> I show him the link of a rolling calf's chain
> And an old hige's salt skin carcass.

This African Caribbean poem for a Euromodernist traverses cultural, racial, and gender boundaries via intersections of place-names (Sligo, Sligoville), mythical heroes (Ireland's Cuchulain, Jamaica's ex-slave rebels), and premodern magic (Yeats's mysticism, Jamaica's skin-shedding witches and neck-chained, calf-like ghosts). Goodison Irishes Jamaica, making its hills "shamrock green," and Jamaicanizes Ireland—Cuchulain now has African Caribbean "bush comrades." Apostrophizing a dead poet who often discoursed with the dead, Goodison writes:

William Butler, I swear my dead mother
embraced me. I then washed off my heart
with the amniotic water of a green coconut.

Conjoining myths and magic, topography and words across hemispheres, Goodison figures her intercultural relationship with Yeats as
reciprocal exchange ("We swap duppy stories"): his work has changed
hers, and, notwithstanding chronology, her postcolonial reception of his
transforms it metaleptically. Poetry, she suggests, is for crossing boundaries between the living and the dead, between times, places, cultures.
The space of a poem is neither local — a securely anchored signifier of Jamaican authenticity — nor global — a placeless, free-floating noumenon.
It is a translocation, verbally enabling and enacting — between specific
times and places — cross-cultural, transhistorical exchange.

This intercultural conception of poetry is central to both Euromodernism and to what Martinican theorist and writer Édouard Glissant
has called the cross-cultural poetics ("poétique de la Relation") of the
Caribbean.[2] Yet postcolonial criticism has sometimes represented the
relation between postcolonialism and Western modernism as adversar-
ial. Now that the postmodern is no longer seen as an outright rejection
of the modern, we also need to reconsider whether and to what extent
postcolonial literatures repudiate — "write back to" — an imperial modernism. In his pathbreaking analysis of African Caribbean fiction, Simon Gikandi offers a nuanced statement of the agonistic position: "Caribbean modernism is opposed to, though not necessarily independent
of, European notions of modernism." Gikandi thus proposes a "Third
World modernism distinct from the prototypical European form, which
in Houston Baker's words, 'is exclusively Western, preeminently bourgeois, and optically white.'"[3] The authors of *Toward the Decolonization of
African Literature* assert a sharper divide: "African literature *is* an autonomous entity separate and apart from all other literatures. It has its own
traditions, models and norms." The influence of Euromodernist "pri-
vatism" can only obscure authentic African expression under "dunghill
piles of esoterica and obscure allusions."[4] Other critics assume, in Fredric Jameson's words, that the "traces of imperialism can . . . be detected
in Western modernism, and are indeed constitutive of it."[5] Bill Ashcroft
and John Salter represent modernism's influence beyond the metropole
as unambiguously imperialist: "The high-cultural discourse of modernism, with its imposition of a set of largely uncontested parameters upon
a non-European cultural reality, may be seen to be metonymic of the op-

eration of imperial domination. Modernity and modernism are rooted in empire."[6]

But far from being an obstruction that had to be dislodged from the postcolonial windpipe, Western modernism — in one of the great ironies of twentieth-century literary history — crucially enabled a range of non-Western poets after World War II to explore their hybrid cultures and postcolonial experience. For these poets, the detour through modernism was often, paradoxically, the surest route home. In his *History of the Voice*, Kamau Brathwaite offers one of the most vivid testaments to the importance of modernism for the postcolonization of postcolonial literatures. T. S. Eliot, he asserts, was the primary influence on Caribbean poets' "moving from standard English" to creolized English, or "nation language": "What T. S. Eliot did for Caribbean poetry and Caribbean literature was to introduce the notion of the speaking voice, the conversational tone. That is what really attracted us to Eliot." Emphasizing the oral/aural medium of transmission and thus assimilating Eliot to West Indian orature, Brathwaite further explains in a footnote:

> For those who really made the breakthrough, it was Eliot's actual voice — or rather his recorded voice, property of the British Council (Barbados) — reading "Preludes," "The love song of J. Alfred Prufrock," *The Waste Land* and later the *Four Quartets* — not the texts — which turned us on. In that dry deadpan delivery, the "riddims" of St Louis (though we did not know the source then) were stark and clear for those of us who at the same time were listening to the dislocations of Bird, Dizzy and Klook. And it is interesting that, on the whole, the establishment could not stand Eliot's voice — and far less jazz!

Uncovering an intercultural heterogeneity even in the heart of the empire, Brathwaite cites the parallel influence of a BBC cricket commentator's "natural, 'riddimic' and image-laden tropes in his revolutionary Hampshire burr": "he subverted the establishment with the way he spoke and where: like Eliot, like jazz . . . ."[7]

Brathwaite hails Eliot for his conversational orality and jazz dislocations, his nonstandard diction and improvisatory rhythms. That a revolutionary Afrocentrist could hear the flat British monotone of an Anglo-Catholic royalist as subversive, could embrace Eliot as an antiestablishment poet for the 1950s and '60s, might well seem bizarre, especially since for many North American poets of the time, Eliot *was* the establishment. When Robert Creeley, Allen Ginsberg, and Amiri

Baraka turned to jazz as a model for improvisatory rhythms and phrasing, they were repudiating Eliot's academic embodiment in New Critical, formalist norms of coherence, polish, and impersonal wit. In a 1950
manifesto for the new American poetries, "Projective Verse," Charles
Olson implicitly mocks "O. M. Eliot" (that is, Order of Merit) for his
imperial affinities.[8] Meanwhile, in Britain, Philip Larkin and other poets of the Movement were also renouncing Eliot and Pound, put off
by their polyglossia, syntactic dislocations, and arcane mythologies.
But while the Beats, the Black Mountain poets, poets of the Black
Arts movement, as well as poets of the Movement in Britain, saw a
stiff-necked modernism — aestheticist, elitist, writerly — as the dominant mode needing demolition, many leading poets of the "developing
world," including the Barbadian Brathwaite, Saint Lucian Walcott, Indian A. K. Ramanujan, Ugandan Okot p'Bitek, and the Nigerians Christopher Okigbo and Wole Soyinka, seized on modernism as a tool of liberation. These postcolonial poets, all born in the five-year span 1929–34
and thus initially educated under British colonial rule, came of age during the formal breakup of much of the British Empire from the late
1940s through the 1960s. They leveraged modernism against British
Romantic, Victorian, and other imperial norms calcified in their local
educational and cultural establishments — norms that resulted in the
stilted neo-Romantic poems enshrined by organizations such as the Jamaican Poetry League.[9]

For the young Brathwaite, Eliot's impersonality and unpredictabil-
ity seemed an emancipatory alternative to the closed, emotive, monologic voice of the canonical English lyric purveyed in the schools. For
Ramanujan, modernist astringency served as an antidote to the mawk-
ishness and monologism of much postwar Indian poetry in English.
Okot p'Bitek employed brisk, image-rich, modernist free verse to satirize the hypocrisy and pomposity of African missionaries and politicians. Against the restrictive "platform poetry" of negritude, Okigbo
and Soyinka unleashed an intercultural polyphony they derived in part
from modernism. The opening lyric of Walcott's *Collected Poems* redeploys the agonized self-divisions of "Prufrock," with auxiliary echoes
of *The Waste Land*:

I go, of course, through all the isolated acts,
Make a holiday of situations,
Straighten my tie and fix important jaws. . . .

The modernist topos of self-alienation, far from being "metonymic of the operation of imperial domination," serves to contest the imperialist image of West Indians found

> In tourist booklets, behind ardent binoculars;
> Found in the blue reflection of eyes
> That have known cities and think us here happy.[10]

The choice for Walcott, Brathwaite, Ramanujan, Okot, Okigbo, and Soyinka was not between an imported modernism and a pristine native culture, since the forms of cultural dominance against which they struggled were often local instantiations of the *imperium*—Victorian sentiment and monologue, missionary prudishness and hypocrisy, colonial education and racism, a tourist industry complicit in the production of imprisoning stereotypes, and nationalisms and nativisms that mirrored European norms in reverse. To insist, in the name of anti-Eurocentrism, that Euromodernism be seen as an imperial antagonist is to condescend to imaginative writers who have wielded modernism in cultural decolonization; and it is also, ironically, to impose as universal a Eurocentric standard: the antimodernism of postwar American and British poetry.

The intercultural poetic forms of modernism, in particular, have been especially attractive to so-called Third World poets in their quest to break through monologic lyricism, to express their cross-cultural experience, despite vast differences in ethnicity and geography, politics and history, from the Western modernists. Modernist bricolage—the synthetic use in early twentieth-century poetry of diverse cultural materials ready to hand—has helped postcolonial poets aesthetically encode intersections among multiple cultural vectors. Writing in the metropole at a time of imperial and ethnographic adventure, massive immigration, world war, interlingual mixture, speedier communication and travel, the modernists—many of them exiles and émigrés themselves—were the first English-language poets to create a formal vocabulary for the intercultural collisions and juxtapositions, the epistemic instabilities and decenterings, of globalization.[11] By contrast with the disjunctiveness and perspectivism of the modernist poem, the premodern English lyric was, Brathwaite suggests, a model that risked suppressing the cultural complexity of postcolonial experience: it could not adequately articulate such intercultural discordance as being schooled to write poems about unseen snowfall while living in the hurricane-swept tropics.[12] In

short, for many postcolonial poets, even though on the receiving end
of imperial dominance, what was more important than the modernists'
complicity in empire and in orientalist fantasy, or their imbrication in
European literary tradition, was their creation of answering forms and
vocabularies for the transcultural, interreligious, and polyglot minglings
and juxtapositions of cross-hemispheric experience.

But while postcolonial poets emergent in the 1950s and '60s weren't
antimodernists, neither were they Euromodernist wannabes. If postcolonial criticism has often been too eager to depict postcolonial writers as revolutionary Calibans struggling heroically against hegemonic,
Euromodernist Prosperos, modernist criticism has at times been perhaps too eager to assimilate postcolonialism to Euromodernism as "part
of the same movement."[13] Yet the contrasts should not be bleached out,
since Western modernists, even if marginal to the British cultural and
political center by virtue of nationality (e.g., Irish or American), class,
sexual orientation, or aesthetics ("épater les bourgeois" avant-gardism),
were finally less marginal than poets growing up in Castries, Bridgetown,
Mysore, Srinagar, Ojoto, Ibadan, or Gulu. Postcolonial hybridity and
modernist bricolage are thus, in James Clifford's phrase, "*discrepant cosmopolitanisms.*"[14] The conditions of possibility for postcolonial hybridity
are violent occupation and cultural imposition at home, across immense
differences of power, topography, culture, and economics. Its non-West
is primary and profoundly experiential, not the object of extraterritorial questing via tourism and museums, books and ethnography, friend-
ships and translations. By contrast, the modernists make use, as Lévi-
Strauss says of the bricoleur, of a limited heterogeneity,[15] their materials
often made available by imperial and ethnographic forays. Even the
most boldly cross-hemispheric modernist poets occasionally import a
subaltern text or artifact or genre and embed it within a Western literary universe. Since the postcolonial writer inhabits the multiple cultural worlds forcibly conjoined by empire, hybridity — the knotting together of countless already knotted together indigenous and imposed
languages, images, genres — is not an aspect but the basic fabric of the
postcolonial poem. In redeploying modernism across these differences,
postcolonial poets have had to refashion it for resisting local and imperial monisms, for articulating a cross-culturalism still more plural and
polyphonic than Western modernism. They have reshaped it through
indigenous genres and vocabularies, have recentered it in non-Western
landscapes and mythologies, and have often inverted its racial and cultural politics.

1.

Among the hybridizing literary strategies of postcolonial poetry that can be traced in part to modernist bricolage are translocalism, mythical syncretism, heteroglossia, and apocalypticism. Translocalism is key to A. K. Ramanujan's "Chicago Zen":

> Watch your step. Sight may strike you
> blind in unexpected places.
>
> The traffic light turns orange
> on 57th and Dorchester, and you stumble,
>
> you fall into a vision of forest fires,
> enter a frothing Himalayan river,
>
> rapid, silent.
>
>   On the 14th floor,
> Lake Michigan crawls and crawls
>
> in the window.[16]

In this morphing of Lake Michigan into a South Asian river, of the traffic light in a Chicago neighborhood into Indian forest fires, Ramanujan adapts the modernist technique of translocal "super-position," as Pound called it — Eliot's layering of the Thames and the Ganges, Pound's of a mountain near the Disciplinary Training Center in Pisa and Mount Taishan. He renews both modernist technique and its indigenous counterpart, fusing superposition to what he termed the "montage" and "dissolve" effects of Dravidian poetry, as well as the startling paradoxes of Zen.[17] As in Goodison's melding of Ireland's Sligo and Jamaica's Sligoville, Walcott's of the Greek islands and the Antilles, distances between North and South collapse: "you drown," Ramanujan writes in an echo of "Prufrock," "eyes open, // towards the Indies, the antipodes." Not that postcolonial and modernist translocalisms are identical. The modernist superpositional poem imports into an experiential Western place (the Thames, Pisa) an "other," exoticized, Eastern place (the Ganges, Mount Taishan), whereas in "Chicago Zen," the speaker "falls" from one floor of his migrant experience, Chicago, to another, India — two worlds that he has lived and that now live in him. And whereas the Western modernist poem often derealizes the local (Eliot's London, Pound's Pisa) by silhouetting it against an Eastern alterity, Ramanujan's poem revises this modernist strategy by oscillating between fully real but discrepant locations. Ramanujan assimilates modernist translocalism to what Salman Rushdie calls the "migrant's-eye view of the world"—born of a more fully interstitial migrancy than that of the modernists, because of its layering upon a prior postcolonial dislocation, and thus a more thoroughgoing "experience of uprooting, disjuncture and metamorphosis (slow or rapid, painful or pleasurable)."[18]

African, Caribbean, and Asian poets have also adapted mythical syncretism from the modernists as a key device for their intercultural poetics: like Cuchulain, so Goodison's maroon warrior; like Shango — Yoruba god of lightning—so electricity in Soyinka's "Idanre." The modernists helped make the high art poem a space for the cross-religious syncretism that was basic to life in the colonies and postcolonies, so that, once again, an imported modernism paradoxically serves as a means for transmuting into literary discourse "postcolocal" experience—a portmanteau word I coin that, combining "postcolonial" with "local," also highlights the translocalism ("colocal") of the postcolonial. Having in modernist fashion developed his "own personal religion," out of Christian, classical, and Igbo sources, Okigbo said in an interview, "The way that I worship my gods is in fact through poetry."[19] Yeats also thought of poetry as a syncretic rite, and Okigbo delivers an appropriately ritualistic homage to Yeats as "the arch-priest of the sanctuary" in his "Lament of the Masks," published by the University of Ibadan in a book celebrating Yeats's centenary in 1965.[20] In this late poem, which has been described as marking Okigbo's shift to a more African aesthetic,[21] Okigbo paradoxically Africanizes his poetry in the act of praising a Euromodernist. Indigenization and aesthetic modernization, for Okigbo as for Ramanujan, are not polar opposites but closely linked. Direct references within the poem to classical panegyric and to praise song indicate Okigbo's remaking of European genres within an African framework (the contributor's note also states that the poem "is based on a traditional Yoruba praise-song").[22] Drawing on the traditional praise song's ritualistic imagery of the hunt, animals, and heroic action, Okigbo arrays an African elephant, a jungle, a plantain leaf, and a giant iroko tree alongside symbols adapted from the temple of Yeats's poetry—iron-throated singers in bird-masks—and from classical myth—"Waggoner of the great Dawn." He reterritorializes Yeats, Africanizing him as an elephant hunter, his masks as ritual objects, while deterritorializing the praise song, centering it on a European subject. It is hard not to hear a wry pun on "canon" in Okigbo's modest self-representation:

> Warped voices —
> For we answer the cannon
> From afar off —
>
> And from throats of iron —
>
> In bird-masks —
> Unlike accusing tones that issue forth javelins —
> Bring, O Poet,
>
> Panegyrics for the arch-priest of the sanctuary . . .

Having spent much time in an "ethereal ivory tower," Yeats comes across as an idealistic — if tireless and heroic — chaser of "the white elephant." But Okigbo was also a passionate idealist as a poet, and on balance, the relation of his poem to Yeats's verse is more affiliative than corrosive; like Goodison, Okigbo credits Yeats with having helped to translate lived, "postcolocal," transreligious feeling into poetry. Elsewhere, Okigbo's poetry of polymythic syncretism draws extensively on the intercultural amalgamations of Pound's poetry — from *The Cantos* he even adapts archaisms, shifting cadences, and the refrain "& the mortar is not yet dry" — especially resonant in the newly formed but internally fractious Nigeria of the 1960s, where "mortar" could suggest not only building material but also a firing device.[23] Okigbo remarked that he "never felt" a "conflict" between his European and his African cultural inheritances,[24] and his praise song for Yeats synthesizes mythologies of diverse origins: Euro-classical ("rumour awakens"), Christian ("Water of baptism"), and precolonial African ("Thunder above the earth").

Although Walcott sometimes highlights the tensions among the various points on his religious and cultural compass (e.g., the early "A Far Cry from Africa"), he, too, is often an organic syncretist, to draw on Bakhtin's distinction between "organic" and "intentional" modes of hybridity.[25] In an especially high-spirited scene of *Omeros* that humorously pumps up modernist comparativism, Walcott imagines a cyclone pounding Saint Lucia as a raucous party to which he invites

European, African, and Caribbean gods. They play Yoruba and African Caribbean "Shango drums" that "made Neptune rock in the caves," while the Haitian love goddess Erzulie rattles "her ra-ra," the African Caribbean snake god Damballa winds, and the Yoruba and African Caribbean blacksmith Ogun fires drinks with "his partner Zeus."[26] Unlike Okigbo or Soyinka, Walcott aestheticizes the transreligious, displaying his intercultural groupings as artifacts. Still, his compression of deities from diverse pantheons into one polyphonous space energizes both party and poem. Like Okigbo's, the later Walcott's syncretism tends to be more exuberant than elegiac — a celebration of transregional inheritance in the Caribbean — unlike Eliot's "mythical method," where the parallels often encode a narrative of degeneration, a Eurocentric lament over decline and dissipation.[27]

More nearly affiliated with Eliot's elegiac syncretism, if still distinct, is the work of a poet of the next generation. In "Ghazal" ("Where are you now? Who lies beneath your spell tonight"), the different faiths of Agha Shahid Ali's Kashmiri youth jostle alongside one another, in references to biblical stories, a Hindu temple, a Shi'a god.[28] Repulsed by violence in the name of religion — executions, smashed statues and idols — "A refugee from Belief seeks a cell tonight," perhaps in the discontinuous two-line cells of the ghazal itself:

> Executioners near the woman at the window.
> Damn you, Elijah, I'll bless Jezebel tonight.
>
> *Lord,* cried out the idols, *Don't let us be broken;*
> *Only we can convert the infidel tonight.*
>
> Has God's vintage loneliness turned to vinegar?
> He's poured rust into the Sacred Well tonight.
>
> In the heart's veined temple all statues have been smashed.
> No priest in saffron's left to toll its knell tonight.
>
> He's freed some fire from ice, in pity for Heaven;
> he's left open — for God — the doors of Hell tonight.
>
> And I, Shahid, only am escaped to tell thee —
> God sobs in my arms. Call me Ishmael tonight.

In the echo chamber of this final stanza, Ali commingles Job ("only am escaped [alone] to tell thee"), *Moby-Dick* ("Call me Ishmael" and the Job quotation), and Islamic tradition (Ishmael as ur-ancestor). In this further example of what I term the dialectics of indigenization, Ali reinvigorates both the "native" and the foreign, both the Urdu-Persian form of the ghazal and the Western modernist mode of mythical syncretism, bracing them together through their homologous conjunctures and fissures. When ghazalified, modernist syncretism, hardly a disabling imperial influence, functions for Ali as a counterweight to tyrannies closer to "home"—the religious and nationalist absolutisms that have ravaged Kashmir. As required by the ghazal, the poet names himself (the *takhallos*), but he then gives himself another name, Ishmael—an intercultural node in which Judaism, Christianity, and Islam intersect, as they have in the poem's formal junctures and syncretic layerings. This *takhallos* may also recall the strange fusion of self-reference and scattershot quotation in a famous retrospective coda—"These fragments I have shored against my ruins"—particularly in view of Ali's discussion of the "sense of loss and desolation" in *The Waste Land*, in his dissertation-turned-monograph, *T. S. Eliot as Editor*.[29] Lamenting exile, linguistic displacement, and political violence in his poems, Ali is drawn to Eliot's work by its resemblance to the melancholy of Urdu poetry, to the disjunctive collage and impersonal personality of the ghazal. Yet whereas Eliot grieves in the gaps between one version of a myth and its successors, in the ruptures of cultural multiplicity, Ali moves freely among intimately felt inheritances from English, American, and Urdu literatures and from Buddhism, Hinduism, Islam, Judaism, and Christianity, mobilizing these against both public and private losses and against monistic structures of recuperation from such losses. The differential appropriations of Eliot by a poet of Shi'a Muslim and African Caribbean origin—that is, the differences between Ali's Eliot and Brathwaite's satiric, jazzy, creolized Eliot—again instance the diverse ways postcolonial modernism is indigenized. For Ali, as for Brathwaite, Goodison, Okigbo, and Ramanujan, modernism represents not an "imposition of a set of largely uncontested parameters upon a non-European cultural reality," but a multifaceted and mutable resource, amenable to different localizing strategies and syntheses.

Modernist heteroglossia—rapid turns from high to low, standard to dialect, English to Sanskrit or Chinese, preeminently in Eliot and Pound—is another form of literary bricolage submitted to the dialectics of indigenization by postcolonial poets, especially in the Caribbean. Whereas Eliot and Pound, as Michael North has shown, made ambivalent use of African American vernacular as vital yet debased,[30] Brathwaite, Walcott, and Goodison have adopted heteroglossia as a poetic structure to figure the code switching of Barbados, Jamaica, and Saint Lucia—an everyday oral practice that was largely absent from earlier West Indian poems, which were usually written in Creole, Standard English, or a comic medley of the two. Although Brathwaite hears a hint of nation language in a voice recording of Claude McKay's Standard English poetry,[31] he suggests that the English lyric had rendered largely inaudible the poet's Afro-Euro-American creolization. In Brathwaite's "Calypso," a signature poem of his *Rights of Passage* (the first part of *The Arrivants*), his echo of *The Waste Land* makes clear the literary template for his criss-crossing voices: Black Sam "carries bucketfuls of water / 'cause his Ma's just had another daughter" (the moonlight shines on Eliot's "Mrs. Porter / And on her daughter / They wash their feet in soda water").[32] Like Eliot, whose irregularly placed rhymes and shifting rhythms he redeploys, Brathwaite plays various Englishes and cadences against one another—in "Calypso," a prophetic voice intoning a creation myth of the Caribbean ("curved stone hissed into reef / wave teeth fanged into clay"); a satiric ode on white plantation life, built on Eliot's "so elegant / So intelligent" Shakespeherian rag ("O it was a wonderful time / an elegant benevolent redolent time—"); calypso itself ("Steel drum steel drum / hit the hot calypso dancing"); the limbo dance ("For we glance the banjo / dance the limbo"); and West Indian Creole ("please to take 'im back"). Brathwaite's early heteroglossia, like Eliot's, exemplifies Bakhtin's "intentional hybridity," a poetry of satiric tensions and incongruities among voices, languages, sociolects. By the time Walcott was publishing "The Schooner *Flight*" in 1977–79 and Lorna Goodison her first volumes of poetry in the 1980s, they, Brathwaite, and other West Indian poets were more nimbly and pervasively switching between standard and dialectal codes, even as they had altered, abandoned, or inverted the linguistic hierarchies of modernism.

Modernist apocalypses have also served poets from different parts of the postcolonial world, and the apocalyptic is intimately tied to the intercultural in *The Waste Land* and other modernist poems, the crossing from West to East affording an extrinsic vantage point that reveals or uncovers (*apokalyptein*) the crisis of modernity. Indeed, the apocalyptic mode evinces the intense ambivalence toward modernity both in modernist and in postcolonial writing. At the end of "The Fire Sermon," in-

veighing against the West's unhinging of sex from religion, Eliot fuses
the Buddha and Augustine — "Burning burning burning burning" — in
what his note names "this collocation of these two representatives of
eastern and western asceticism."[33] In "Irae," Brathwaite reroutes Eliot's moral apocalypse into a postcolonial confrontation with the West,
intoning "burning burning from tomorrow" in an early version of the
poem.[34] In this instance of the dialectics of indigenization, of the transformative twinning of the Euromodernist with the postcolocal, Brathwaite fuses Eliotic and Rastafarian apocalypses, as he earlier had in the
vision of Babylon burned in "Wings of a Dove." Aggressively dislocat-
ing "Dies Irae" to address contemporary circumstance — a dislocation
that also recalls Eliot's violent decontextualization of traditional material to simulate crisis — Brathwaite pounds out a prophecy of doom
in the insistent rhymes and rhythms of the thirteenth-century hymn:
"dies irae dreadful day / when the world shall pass away." In two of the
tercets' middle lines, he chillingly compacts the names of massacres and
weapons — "mi lai sharpville wounded knee"; "poniard poison rocket
bomb" — that occasion the poem's rage. The poet sees divine retribution
in the violent resistance of Jamaica's Maroon leaders — "nanny cuffee
cudjoe." Brathwaite thus remakes Eliot's fiery apocalypse to condemn
an imperial West that — technologically superior but ethically insane —
is responsible for unspeakable injustices and atrocities and thus deserves its imminent implosion:

> day of fire dreadful day
> day for which all sufferers pray
> grant me patience with thy plenty
> grant me vengeance with thy sword[35]

The political implications of Brathwaite's poem could hardly be more
different from those we usually associate with Eliot's work. Even so, in
translating Eliot's apocalypse across the North/South divide and melding it, via a medieval hymn, with Rastafarian chant, Brathwaite renews
the apocalyptic mode: like the Western modernists, he uses religious
language for a compressed, visionary evocation of modernity as cata-
clysmic violence, a modern history trembling on the verge of dramatic
and perhaps ultimate transformation.

Another poem of cosmic symbolism, including the thunder and
lightning mythologized in West Africa, Okigbo's "Come Thunder" also
adapts modernist apocalypticism to bespeak a liminal moment in Third

World history, the first of numerous civil wars that have ravaged post-colonial Africa. Okigbo presents as a second coming, complete with birds that seem almost Byzantine, the events leading up to the Nigerian civil war, in which he was to fight and die:

Magic birds with the miracle of lightning flash on their feathers . . .

The arrows of God tremble at the gates of light,
The drums of curfew pander to a dance of death;

And the secret thing in its heaving
Threatens with iron mask
The last lighted torch of the century . . .[36]

As in Yeats's prophecies, the violence of modernity inspires a troubled joy — "laughter, broken in two, hangs tremulous between the teeth" — and a joyous terror, the threat of an unknowable, iron-masked future. Okigbo, again like Yeats, lexically achieves the apocalyptic by combining the concrete ("The smell of blood," "myriad eyes of deserted corn cobs") with the indefinite ("immeasurable," "unnamed," "unprintable"). He Africanizes the affective and formal structures of the modernist apocalypse — his title evoking also "What the Thunder Said" — for a postcolonial vision of a rough beast about to be born. Since modernist apocalypses are thought to represent a Eurocentric response to the decline of a Western *imperium*, such adaptability may well seem surprising, but British poets of the 1930s, as Stephen Spender indicates, already believed that "[c]onsidered as an apocalyptic vision, the Communist view coincides with that of T. S. Eliot in *The Waste Land* or Yeats in *The Second Coming*."[37] African, Caribbean, and Asian poets have been no less ready to remake Western modernist apocalypses for their ambivalent visions of modernity's historical rupture.

2.

Having explored how "Third World" poets postcolonize Euromodernism and Euromodernize the postcolonial, I reverse the lens, reconsidering the cross-cultural bricolage of a few of the most canonical modernist poems. As I've already suggested, the North-South syncretism and trans-hemispheric interstitiality in modernist poems differ from the more thoroughly hybridized language, mythology, genres, and geography of many postcolonial texts. The primary transhemispheric currents in Western modernist poems include the importation of East and South Asian materials. These poems invoke Asian religious texts, such as the Upanishads and the Fire Sermon, as well as literary genres or visual artifacts, such as haiku or a lapis lazuli carving, as potential solutions to Eurocentric crises of faith, war, literature, and tradition. They often exotically construct the East as spiritual Other, as site of ancient wisdom, frozen in an archaic state, voided of a contemporary history with real human beings. In keeping with other familiar patterns of circulation and long-lived orientalist assumptions, the literary West, as site of artistic and epistemic production, arrogates to itself raw materials mined in Asia and makes of them new elite forms of literary capital.

How then could Eliot, Yeats, and Pound furnish enabling examples for postcolonial poets? Aren't the modernists, as Neil Lazarus writes of such Western musicians as Paul Simon, guilty of a "profound insensitivity to the politico-ethical implications of cultural appropriation across the international division of labor," of a "distressing unilateralism of influence," a "complete lack of cultural dialogism"?[38] In an essay on *The Waste Land* and empire, Paul Douglass has argued that Pound and Eliot's "aesthetics of the jagged and the juxtaposed," of the "fragmentary and syncretic," is inherently "reactionary," part of a larger project in "defense of . . . empire": such literary wreckage demands the imperial, reconstructive labor of a learned elite.[39] More generally, these modernist texts are increasingly thought to belong seamlessly to the orientalist project of fabricating, managing, and disciplining the East. But the postcolonial poetic response compels us to ask whether such views are fully adequate to the cross-cultural dimensions of modernist poetry, whether the manner of this poetry's assimilation of non-Western texts and artifacts — often inorganic, incomplete, self-conscious — might enable these to interact dialogically with the predominantly Western texts into which they are imported.

In my view, because of *The Waste Land*'s and *The Cantos*' polyglot representation of the East, partly in its languages, these indigenous texts — the Upanishads, Confucian writings — retain at least some capacity to question both their Western host texts and the ways in which the non-West is represented. In an essay on the uses of India in *The Waste Land*, Harish Trivedi argues that "for Eliot, there aren't in this poem, there never were and never would be, any solutions outside Christianity. Here, near the climax of his poem ['What the Thunder Said'], he takes up, in order to interrogate, the traditional claim of Eastern spiritual efficacy,

and finds it wanting."[40] But in Eliot's collage of his own poetry with
the text of the Brihadaranyaka Upanishad, the discordance between
the ethical injunctions *Datta, Dayadhvam, Damyata* and the English responses shows up not the East's but the West's spiritual inefficacy, its
helplessness to redress its crisis. The Sanskrit texts — though perhaps
framed like objects in the British Museum — nevertheless write back to
an empire that in the early 1920s continued to assert its superiority and
mastery over these texts' site of origin. By way of an imperfect analogy,
imagine if during the U.S.-led occupation of Iraq, John Ashbery or Jorie
Graham embedded Koranic verses in their poetry as signifiers of spiritual wisdom. "Shantih   shantih   shantih," normally the closing bene-
diction of an Upanishad, suggestively reframes *The Waste Land*, as if to
say, this poem aspires to the peacefulness of an ancient, sacred, meditative text from still-colonized India, but, as perhaps indicated by Eliot's
omission of the standard prefix "Om," again shows the West to fall short.
Ultimately, even the poem's critique of the West, though offered in the
voice of the other, can be seen as problematically appropriative, since
Eliot is using Eastern materials to Western ends — Eastern supplements
that are, finally, appendages to a fundamentally Western project. But we
should be wary of the naïve presupposition that a poetic text could, as
if released from all ethnocentric moorings, engage a text from another
hemisphere without assimilative pressure, without using it for its own
cultural ends. Moreover, the poem's shadowing of a non-Western religion with a Christian intertext — Trivedi cites the translation of the poem's last line as the biblical "Peace which passeth understanding" — is
common to some of the most celebrated postcolonial works (Achebe
reshapes Igbo stories to fit Christian paradigms in *Things Fall Apart,* and
Okigbo, as we've seen, returns in *Heavensgate* to Igbo myth and culture
through the story of the prodigal son).[41] While Christian yearning plays
a part in *The Waste Land*, to read back into the poem the logic of the salvific Christianity Eliot later embraced is to allow this telos to evacu-
ate the melancholic specificity, the painful splaying across hemispheres,
of this literary moment. We do violence to its intercultural dialogism
and disjuncture, its textual "fragments" and personal "ruins," if we overemphasize the recuperative clause wedged between these two substan-
tives — "I have shored against." *The Waste Land*, while not escaping the
orientalism of modern Western representations of the East, also sets
Eastern and Western texts in dialogic relation with one another, and in
this double-voicedness, in the seams between the pieces of the transhemispheric collage, in the cross-cultural slippage between text and

embedded text, the Eastern quotations retain at least some capacity to make themselves heard.

Yeats's "Lapis Lazuli" also both participates in and questions orientalist assimilation, exoticism, and supplementarity. Like *The Waste Land*, the poem enacts a psycho-geographical movement from a Western panorama of destruction to an Eastern alterity. Here again, the onset of large-scale terror and destruction occasions the poet's cross-cultural excursion to the Orient, where Yeats stages the last in a series of rejoinders to the view that artistic gaiety is frivolous in wartime — fiddling while the metropole burns. Edmund Dulac had written Yeats that he feared London would be bombed, and in 1936, Hitler, Mussolini, and Spanish generals were indeed mobilizing for war. The eighteenth-century Chinese carving, arrived at in the poem after a typically modernist leap across hemispheres, seems at first to offer an exotic refuge:

> Two Chinamen, behind them a third,
> Are carved in Lapis Lazuli,
> Over them flies a long-legged bird
> A symbol of longevity;
> The third, doubtless a serving man,
> Carries a musical instrument.[42]

After the scenes of death and ruin in the earlier stanzas, the calm enumeration of hierarchical social roles, twinned with signifiers of hermeneutic certainty (the bird "A symbol of longevity"), suggests a timeless, oriental world of order, harmony, and stability. But in the ensuing lines, East-West binaries begin to collapse, as time and ruin invade the scene:

> Every discolouration of the stone,
> Every accidental crack or dent. . . .

If the poet has tried to displace Western war and chaos with an atemporal, Eastern security, the surface of the carving fissures this orientalist presumption. Although Yeats's poem isn't, like Eliot's, polyglot, his modernist close reading of the artifact enables its surface to assert a reality that contravenes the orientalist abstractions with which he began: the poem self-correctively pivots, undoing its reified image of the Chinese stone. Here, as in Eliot's poem, this slippage, though limited, allows a counterview to emerge: the East is not the timeless haven the poet hoped for.

But no sooner has Yeats established the stone's fractured surface as primary than he begins to project onto it his poetic fantasies, troping each mark as

> . . . a water-course or an avalanche,
> Or lofty slope where it still snows
> Though doubtless plum or cherry-branch
> Sweetens the little half-way house
> Those Chinamen climb towards, and I
> Delight to imagine them seated there. . . .

His poetic self-consciousness foregrounded by the second use of "doubt-less" and the enjambment that suspends the lyric "I" at the end of a line, the poet shows us a Western mind at the moment of its interplay with an Eastern artifact, of inspiration by and transformation of Chinese art into something other than itself. Although these lines belong to the discourse, in Edward Said's words, "by which European culture was able to manage — and even produce — the Orient," they also open a reflective space within that discourse, because they thematize the literary work of producing the Orient.[43] Instancing the imaginative joy of building again out of things that fall, the poet indulges orientalist fantasy, writing over the stone's surface with stock plum or cherry branches and an imagined trek halfway up the mountain. Yet set off by the stone's corrective, his construction of a self-affirming Western lyric moment out of the fissures and interstices of an Eastern artwork is shown to supplement and twist. While the poem assimilates the Chinese other to Nietzschean tragic joy, and while the poet is returned to himself through the wrinkle-eyed gaze of the other, this assimilation also impedes itself; after all, the poet needs the other to remain at least somewhat other, if only so that he can use the Orient as an alternative space from which to look back critically at the anguish and terror gripping the contemporary Occident. That he imagines the men climbing not to a transcendental site atop the mountain but to a half-way house figures their in-betweenness. In a letter about the carving, Yeats similarly interrupts himself, unable to decide whether to write about the East as other or as assimilable to Western tragedy: "The heroic cry in the midst of despair. But no, I am wrong, the east has its solutions always and therefore knows nothing of tragedy."[44] Self-interrupting, self-thematizing, the poem emphasizes what we might call the orientalist wobble, caught as it is between assimilation and acknowledgment, between exoticism and historicity.

Another key poem in the modernist canon, Pound's "In a Station of the Metro," also crosses from West to East, but dramatically miniaturizes the journey:

The apparition of these faces in the crowd;
Petals on a wet, black bough.[45]

The poem's imaginative leap — often celebrated for its modernist compression and ellipsis — is again transhemispheric, from an urban Western scene, specifically located by the title in a Parisian Metro station, to an unmistakably East Asian, painterly image of flower petals against a branch. In his well-known account of composing the poem, Pound writes of "trying to record the precise instant when a thing outward and objective transforms itself, or darts into a thing inward and subjective."[46] His implicit association of the East with the "inward and subjective," as contrasted with the historicized, materialized objectivity of the urban crowd scene, accords with the orientalist abstraction of the East as spiritual and immaterial that we also saw in *The Waste Land* and in "Lapis Lazuli." Also like Eliot and Yeats, Pound turns to Asia in a moment of crisis or, in his own word, "impasse," seizing on Japanese haiku as a literary model that enables his breakthrough — a mirror image of the later postcolonial importation of Western modernism to shatter the impasse of a colonial poetics. Pound famously recounts how he reduced the poem from thirty lines to two under the influence of the compression and "super-position" of haiku, suggesting that an Asian literary structure helped engender the starkly juxtapositional poetics of modernism and, insofar as this is an intercultural formation, again complicating the view that such jaggedness is inherently imperialist.[47] With its title seen as integral, the poem is still more closely linked to the three-line structure of haiku (short to long to short line).[48] Pound's prototypically imagist poem thus encrypts and enacts within its split, transhemispheric textual body a miniaturized psycho-biographical narrative of its genesis out of a cross-cultural imaginative passage from West to East. By at once internalizing and displaying the logic of its East-West dislocation, by refusing connectives that would discursively paper over the gap between the Western urban scene and Eastern ideality, by formally alluding to the three-line haiku without flattening its differences from this generic paradigm, the poem represents an orientalism that is also antiorientalist, that is cross-cutting and counterdiscursive. Pound's later free translations of *Cathay* will — through the use of Japanese for Chinese names of places and poets — also foreground a densely mediated reception history that similarly impedes, even as other features of the texts advance, orientalist transparency and penetration.

In sum, these three poems exemplify orientalist appropriation, exoticism, and misreading, but the intercultural crossings they enact are also self-divided, self-impeding, and self-critical. While incorporating a non-Western text, artifact, image, or genre, they also reveal the friction between figure and frame, the wobble of assimilation or alterity. Monologic imperialism is thus inadequate as a description of their intercultural work — their jagged cross-cultural juxtapositions, their dialogic counterpointing of here and there, their leveraging of the East in their critique of the West, ultimately their openness, if only partial, to the potentially transformative impact of the voice of the other.

A later generation of poets on the margins of empire can thus help us reconsider what we think we know about modernist poetry. Not that the modernists in their own time are identical with their subsequent reception. The postcolonial uncovering of generative potentiality in modernism does not literally change the historical reality of the poets' words or actions. By the same token, Pound's profound influence on the second-generation Jewish modernists — the objectivists Reznikoff, Zukofsky, and Oppen — does not make some of his poetry any less virulently anti-Semitic. Nevertheless, that later poets have been able to read the poetry of Eliot, Yeats, and Pound against the grain of its limitations should indeed shape our understanding of Western modernist aesthetics. Eliot's uses of Donne's forced, cerebral conjunctions, Yeats's transmutation of Shelley's and Blake's visionary poetics, Langston Hughes's and Sterling Brown's adaptations of Whitman's omnivorous personae release and revitalize aspects of a precursor's work. "The words of a dead man," in Auden's aphorism, "Are modified in the guts of the living."[49] The Language poets, as Marjorie Perloff has argued, take up and expand certain features of modernist poetry—constructivism, antiabsorptive artifice, the poetics of adjacency and surface fragmentation—that make us see it anew.[50] This modernism is by and large the reverse of the witty, paradoxical, ironic modernism that the mid-century American formalists — the early Robert Lowell and Richard Wilbur — made the foundation of their poetry. In what we might term the postcolonial metaleptic, modernism's relation to postcolonial poetry illuminates yet other features — translocalism, polymythic syncretism, heteroglossia, ambivalent modernity, apocalypticism, interstitial migrancy, cultural self-alienation and self-critique and dialogism — that otherwise might be obscured.

As the critical debate over whether and to what extent modernism was imperialist and racist continues, not only the pieties or anxieties but also the ironies of influence need to play a role: Goodison's swapping duppy stories with Yeats, Brathwaite's hearing his own Creole rhythms in Eliot's poetry, Okigbo's Africanizing of Yeats's masks and of Pound's cross-religious syncretism, Ali's use of modernist disjunctiveness and melancholy to translate the ghazal. Modernism is often praised or blamed for its cross-cultural appropriations with scant awareness of its postcolonial afterlives. But these afterlives are vital in reconceptualizing the cross-cultural forms and languages of modernism, while dialectically yielding new insight into the still more vividly cross-cultural poetries beyond the Euro-American metropole. "Despite the celebrated internationalism of the modern," as Andreas Huyssen observes, "the very structures of academic disciplines, their compartmentalization in university departments of national literatures, and their inherent unequal power relations still prevent us from acknowledging what one might call modernism at large, that is, the cross-national cultural forms that emerge from the negotiation of the modern with the indigenous, the colonial and the postcolonial in the 'non-Western' world."[51]

In an important essay, Ramanujan cites Eliot's famous description of European texts as forming "'a simultaneous order,' where every new text within a series confirms yet alters the whole order ever so slightly, and not always so slightly."[52] Indigenizing and pluralizing Eliot's theory of literary tradition, he argues that Indian texts reflect and refract, invert and subvert one another, that in India "a whole tradition may invert, negate, rework, and revalue another." The same holds for the relation of his own and other postcolonial poets' work to modernism: postcolonial hybridity "confirms yet alters," reworks yet revalues modernist bricolage. It thus re-begets a poetic mode that helped beget it. Only by breaking out of exclusionary models of tradition as either Eliot's "mind of Europe" or its postcolonial obverse ("an autonomous entity separate and apart from all other literatures") can we begin to grasp the continuous remaking of "traditions" by one another across the twentieth century and beyond, the mutually transformative relations between the poetries of metropole and margin.

CHAPTER 6

CALIBAN'S MODERNITIES, POSTCOLONIAL POETRIES

If we grant the shared cross-culturalism and transhemispheric influences explored in chapter 5, the question remains, to what extent do Louise Bennett, Wole Soyinka, Agha Shahid Ali, and other postcolonial poets belong among the modernists? Would calling these poets of the global South *modernists* be what philosophers term "a category mistake"—a misattribution of properties, a confusion of classifications? Or is it possible that as Monsieur Jourdain in Molière's *Le Bourgeois Gentilhomme* didn't realize he had been speaking *prose* all his life, these poets of Africa, Asia, and the Caribbean have been modernists all along without anyone's noticing?

Geography helps explain this apparent category mistake. Anglophone modernism—conceived as a literary response to the anonymity, stress, and speed of modern life—is usually attributed to First World cities from London and Dublin to New York and Chicago. Way off the canonical map of English-speaking modernism are the colonial outposts of European empires, except as sites from which adventurous poets and artists are seen as importing primitive or exotic materials to shore up their ruins.

A second reason for the seeming oddity of critically conjoining modernism and postcolonialism is chronology. Most period-based conceptions of literary modernism locate it in the first half of the twentieth century; and postcolonial poetry, so called because of its emergence in the aftermath of European colonialism, flourished for the most part in the second half, after World War II. Like novelists Chinua Achebe and V. S. Naipaul, poets such as Derek Walcott, Wole Soyinka, and A. K. Ramanujan cut their literary teeth in the 1950s and '60s, after the death rattle of high modernism. As we saw in chapter 5, their contemporaries were not T. S. Eliot and Ezra Pound but the supposedly "anti-" or "post-modern" generation of the confessionals, the New York poets, the Beats, and the Black Arts poets.

A third and final reason for this apparent incongruity is stylistic. Modernism is often understood, by analogy with other "-isms" such as communism and feminism, as espousing form-shattering newness and radical experimentation in the arts, exemplified by works such as Gertrude Stein's *Tender Buttons,* Mina Loy's "Anglo-Mongrels and the Rose," and Pound's *Cantos.* Under this definition, early twentieth-century writers who composed formally patterned verse, such as W. B. Yeats, Robert Frost, Wilfred Owen, Langston Hughes, and Hugh MacDiarmid, might qualify as "modern" but not "modernist." This view of modernist style would likewise leave aside the work of most postcolonial poets, whether metrical or unmetered, monoglot or heteroglot, realist or surrealist.

These and other objections to calling postcolonial poetry *modernist* are sufficiently forceful that a critic might be tempted to pack up his paragraphs and quit. Instead, as you will have guessed from the previous chapter, I propose another option: neither to elide the differences between modernism and postcolonialism nor to quarantine these poetries in disciplinary isolation from one another, but, by identifying a cross-hemispheric and transhistorical common terrain, to explore significant points of intersection between them. After all, as we've seen, many renowned postcolonial poets, including the Caribbeans Derek Walcott and Lorna Goodison, the South Asians A. K. Ramanujan and Agha Shahid Ali, and the Africans Wole Soyinka and Christopher Okigbo, have testified to the role modernism played in the formation of their aesthetics. Yet influence may seem an insufficient reason for this conjunction, since, after all, many decidedly antimodernist postwar poets of the "developed world" were also influenced by the modernists. The further question that needs to be asked is whether a primary historical paradigm for modernism can also be used to shed light on the distinct but related historicity of postcolonial poetry.

Let us return, then, to the three principal objections to claiming postcolonial poetry as modernist, reconsidering them in reverse order: can we acknowledge their force, avoiding a collapse of the postcolonial and the modernist into a "postcomodernist" soup, while still bringing these poetries into overlapping, if not identical, critical frameworks? To narrow the criterion of genuinely "modern" or "modernist" to the formal experimentation of "open-form" or "avant-garde" poetries risks obscuring the various shapes that innovation can take. "Here the question of criteria is obviously key," writes Andreas Huyssen; "rather than privilege the radically new in Western avant-gardist fashion, we may want to focus on the complexity of repetition and rewriting, *bricolage* and translation, thus expanding our understanding of innovation."[1] A more porous yet still period-based conception recognizes the breakthroughs of modern Irish and Scottish poets in reimagining both national and transnational identities (e.g., Yeats and MacDiarmid); the ingenuity of Harlem Renaissance poets in infusing literary verse with the blues and jazz, among various oral and musical forms (e.g., Langston Hughes and Sterling Brown); and other examples of the hybridization of distinct aesthetics and discourses, the poetic re-creation of cultural and cross-cultural paradigms. This broader conceptualization may help make recognizable the analogous "experimentation" of postcolonial poets.

As for period boundaries, while we need to grant the center of modernist and postcolonial gravity in different halves of the twentieth century, this line should not be drawn too neatly, lest it obscure shared terrain. Just as modernist mastodons — Ezra Pound, Marianne Moore, Wallace Stevens, Langston Hughes, W. H. Auden — still trod the earth in the second half of the century, so too a few influential poets of the colonized world, such as the Bengali Rabindranath Tagore and, especially important for the present discussion of anglophone poetry, the Jamaicans Claude McKay and Louise Bennett, were publishing significant work before the 1950s. McKay's publications are contemporary with those of the first-generation modernists, such as Eliot and Marianne Moore. Thus the poetry of a writer working in the shadow of British colonialism can be considered, like that of Yeats and other Irish poets, both "modern" and "postcolonial."

As for the assumption that literary modernism represents a response to the pressures of technological and social modernity, particularly in Western cities, rich evidence of a complex encounter with modernization — accelerating after World War II in the "developing world" — can also be found in postcolonial poetry. Since modernity is the most widely recognized historical feature of modernism, the first part of this chapter is devoted to the question of its possible relevance to postcolonial poetry. This approach may seem peculiar, for critics have more often explored the affinities between postcoloniality and postmodernity.[2] But to characterize the historical experience of the postcolonial world as postmodern may be premature, when in these countries traditional agricultural forms of work still exist alongside industrialization; millions of subsistence farmers and day laborers alongside a tiny elite of knowledge workers; donkeys, camels, and horse-driven carts alongside cars and airplanes. The shock of new technologies and new transportation systems, of newly intrusive bureaucracies and newly murderous instruments of warfare, has been a catalyst for writers of the postwar "developing" world, as it was for writers in the early twentieth-century West, before this modernity could, in postmodern fashion, be taken for granted as an always-already banality. For these reasons, and because the ongoing reaction against modernization has emerged as one of the most volatile and dangerous features of the contemporary world, it behooves us to ask, as we do of modernist poetry, how does postcolonial poetry give aesthetic expression to the experience of trying to square "tradition" with the transforming effects of modernity? And how does this response to modernity compare with that of modernist poetry?

Another historical dimension of modernist experience that may be compared with that of postcolonial poetry is its social imaginary. Western modernist poetry is typically understood as being deeply formed by the alienating social effects of modernity. So in the second part of this chapter, I juxtapose poetry from the global South with early twentieth-century poetries by poets of European and minority backgrounds in the global North, asking, what is the implied audience for postcolonial poetry? How do poets of the global South conceive their relation to their emerging national communities? Do they represent themselves as citizen-spokespersons, fully immersed in and writing from their communities of origin, or as marginal outsiders, writing in estrangement from them?

To borrow critical templates associated with Western modernism is to raise the specter of academically recolonizing the ex-colonials, subjugating an emergent alterity under Eurocentric dominion. Yet a greater risk to postcolonial poetry as an academic subfield is posed by critical isolation and neglect. The institutionalization of the study of Caribbean, Asian, African, and other English-language poetries of the global South remains uncertain: this body of work is regularly passed over in postcolonial studies in favor of fiction and theory, and in modern and contemporary poetry studies in favor of American, British, and Irish poetries. Moreover, through its syncretic layering of mythologies, religions, and cultural frames of reference, postcolonial poetry acknowledges that "the foreign" can be approached only through inevitably distortive yet potentially illuminating parallels with the familiar. A transhemispheric (North/South) and cross-period (modern/contemporary) approach might help not only to bring postcolonial poetry into more classrooms, anthologies, and critical books, but also to globalize modern and contemporary literary studies.

1. Janus-Faced Modernities

I have been referring to the early twentieth-century literary response to modernity — urbanization, industrialization, technological and scientific advance, and so forth — as if it were unified. It wasn't. F. T. Marinetti's fire-breathing Futurist Manifesto (1909) famously glorifies the racing and roaring automobile and other aspects of the modern technological revolution. The vorticist manifesto of Wyndham Lewis's London-based journal *Blast* (1914), while defensively mocking futurist "automobilism," is likewise intoxicated with machinery and mobility.[3] Yet, despite these initial cheers for early twentieth-century modernization, many of the leading English-speaking modernists were less enthusiastic than the futurists and vorticists about smashing tradition and embracing new technologies. Indeed, Western poetry in English of the first half of the twentieth century is rife with anxious and conflicted responses to modernization, producing the notoriously paradoxical antimodernity of the anglophone modernists. Disgusted by the spectacle of modernity, Yeats decries "that discordant architecture, all those electric signs," on O'Connell Bridge in Dublin.[4] Ezra Pound blasts the "tawdry cheapness" of mass-produced goods; even beauty, he complains, has been reduced to a commodity in "the market place."[5] In the middle of Eliot's *Waste Land*, a tryst is made to seem all the more mechanical and degraded because the typist precoitally "lays out food in tins" (or cans) and post-coitally "smoothes her hair with automatic hand, / And puts a record on the gramophone."[6] This vehement resistance to modernization as mechanistic, cheapening, and alienating softens among second-generation modernists. Near the end of his life, Auden looks back nostalgically to the industrial machinery of his youth, including parts of old steam engines and other "beautiful old contraptions, soon to be banished from earth."[7] Yet even Auden is hardly sanguine about the effects of mass-scale bureaucratization on modern life ("The Unknown Citizen") and of anonymous, mass warfare on modern death ("Chinese Soldier"). Tortuously ambivalent, Hart Crane hails the Wright Brothers' first flight as the technological counterpart of imaginative flight into "unvanquished space," even as his descriptions also hint at the constraints on merely physical ascent ("axle-bound, confined / In coiled precision").[8] These poets give compressed and vivid expression to what Marshall Berman calls the "thrill and dread" of modernity.[9]

Bringing into our comparisons between Euromodernism and post-colonialism a third term, and thus triangulating this cross-cultural framework, we should remember that, also in the 1910s and 1920s, Harlem Renaissance poets rejoiced in, yet recoiled from, modernization, as exemplified by Jean Toomer. On the positive side, in "Her Lips Are Copper Wire," Toomer uses the electrification of cities—lamplights and billboards and a powerhouse—to metaphorize the connective energy of sexual love: a kiss removes the insulation from "wires" and turns lovers' lips and poetic language "incandescent."[10] A similar exuberance, mixed with wry humor, marks the ironic conjunction in "Gum" of large electric signs advertising Jesus Christ and chewing gum. Modernity thus avails a poet like Toomer of figurative leaps and ironic juxtapositions. Yet the lyric "Reapers" evokes the horror of the machine's displacement of traditional agriculture.[11] That poem begins with the sibilant-smoothed "sound of steel on stones" and "silent swinging" of black reapers' scythes, but ends—its syntax and rhythms and sonorities cut up—after a squealing field rat has been sliced by the indifferent force of a horse-driven mechanical mower proceeding relentlessly on its brutally uncaring course: "I see the blade, / Blood-stained, continue cutting weeds and shade." Not that the ambivalence toward modernity in Toomer's poetry and that of other Harlem Renaissance poets is identical with that of the white modernists. As Toomer indicates in "Song of the Son," the early twentieth-century African American poet mourns the passing of a rural black culture in harmony with nature and with the song forms born of slavery, incorporating the spiritual form into his poem; yet the demise of a slave- and sharecropper-based economy and culture is not entirely to be regretted. Even as the speaker plaintively grieves that "the sun is setting on / A song-lit race of slaves," he metaphorically recalls the atrocities that have beset African Americans in lines that recall the spectacle of lynching: "O Negro slaves, dark purple ripened plums, / Squeezed, and bursting in the pine-wood air."[12]

Are technology and other forms of modernization avenues to new promise, mobility, and freedom, or are they new tools for containing and oppressing African Americans? Langston Hughes's early blues poems, especially in *Fine Clothes to the Jew* (1927), honor by their brevity and *aab* stanzaic form the early blues recordings of the 1920s. Yet if technology can be used to embody and transmit African American voices, it can also be used to stifle them. In Sterling Brown's uproariously funny "Slim in Atlanta," the geography-traversing promise of the telephone morphs into its opposite—a tool of spatial confinement. According to Georgia law, claims the speaker, blacks are forbidden to laugh outdoors and must "do deir laughin / In a telefoam booth."[13] When the trickster Slim Greer learns of this absurd Jim Crow law, he bursts into a phone booth, making hundreds of other African Americans wait as he laughs over and over at the spectacle of their effort to contain their laughter, his interminable antiracist laughter — and the poem's — overbrimming such limits.

Against this backdrop of early twentieth-century Western poetry, black and white, greeting, while grimacing at, the complex forces of modernity, how do we understand the similar yet distinctive response of poets from the global South? Claude McKay, as a Jamaican-born immigrant to the United States and Europe, bridges the gulf between Western and postcolonial poetic responses to modernization, offering a first glimpse into the conflicted poems on modernity by Third World writers born under British colonial rule. When the speaker of his Standard English poems looks upon the modern urban world, he is filled with a vitalizing hatred. Racially marginalized in what he calls "The White City," he watches "The strident trains that speed the goaded mass, / The poles and spires and towers vapor-kissed."[14] The speed of modern mass transport and the vertical sublimity that cheap steel has made possible are alluring, "sweet like wanton loves," yet, shutting out the black immigrant, poison him with "hate." Alienated from "the great western world," the speaker of "The Tropics in New York" and "Outcast" pines for the tropical fruits and pastoral landscape of his youth, the "forgotten jungle songs" of his ancestors.[15] These poems aesthetically embody the ambivalences to which they give utterance by twinning traditional poetic form — sonnet, pastoral plaint, blazon — with the embittering torsions and distortions of a racially divisive and uneven modernity.

If the pace and effects of modernization often struck white and black Western poets as dehumanizing and estranging, many post–World War II poets of the global South — with McKay straddling periods and geographies — describe even more rapid upheavals along these lines, even more startling juxtapositions of traditional custom and onrushing industrial development. While the many faces of modernity — technological change, bureaucratic impersonality, capitalist entrepreneurship, disenchanting rationality, and so forth — often looked menacing to early twentieth-century writers, they have had a special significance for poets whose societies of origin are still grappling with the aftereffects of the violence and exploitation of colonial rule. And while the benefits of a Janus-faced modernity that enriches and impoverishes, empowers and enchains, have long been evident in the West,[16] they have less often materialized, amid urban squalor, poverty, and massive inequality, in much of the developing world.

The colonization of Africa brought native peoples into often alarmingly disjunctive contact with Western development, beginning with the late nineteenth- and early twentieth-century "scramble for Africa" and continuing through the second half of the twentieth century. Kofi Awoonor of Ghana laments the upending of traditional economies and societies. The speaker of one of his poems feels dispossessed, like an unhoused wanderer amid the thorns or "sharps of the forest"—an estrangement reproduced in the deliberate awkwardness of such literal translations of Ewe idiom ("sharps" for "thorns"), discordantly joined to traditional songs.[17] Fracturing temporality, modernity and colonialism are seen as rupturing the ties between generations. In the same poem, a parent attached to the traditions of his ancestors feels abandoned by his descendants, having no sons to mourn or daughters "to wail when I close my mouth." African and other postcolonial poets often represent the ongoing processes of modernization as iterations of colonialism's fraying of the seams of traditional life. Lenrie Peters of Gambia allegorizes this sense of sudden, jolting historical change: "The violent arrival / Puts out the joint," he says of "Parachute men," "Jumping across worlds / In condensed time."[18] The lacerating disorientations of modernity and colonialism, Peters's metaphor of parachuting suggests, dislocate peoples from one world into another, compress and conjoin discontinuous epochs.

Although the centuries-long history of European subjugation and settlement was less abrupt in South Asia and the Caribbean than in Africa, the poetry of these regions also figures modernity as entwined with the violence of colonialism, especially in tearing the fabric of custom and community. Fabric is indeed a locus of colonial violence in "The Dacca Gauzes," a poem by Agha Shahid Ali.[19] The soft, seamless muslins once woven in Dacca but now completely lost are remembered through his grandmother as "woven air, running / water, evening dew," the sequence of images and enjambments verbally evoking the flowing texture of the gauzes. But modernity, with its insatiable appetite for new spaces and new markets, dismembers: because Indian muslins threatened the sale of British fabrics in India, "the hands / of weavers were amputated," preventing Indian weavers from competing with the British or passing on their skills to their children. Modernity severs thumbs from hands, parents from children, soft fabric from coarse. Recalling gauze so fine in texture it was like "dew-starched" morning air, the verbal fabric of the poem — stitching together generations cut off from one another — attempts to redress these catastrophic losses; yet in remembering Bengali muslin-weaving as "a dead art now, dead over / a hundred years," Ali's poem also acknowledges the impossibility of compensating for the atrocities it memorializes.

To reveal fully the violence of Western modernity, postcolonial poets must, as Ali's poem suggests, rewrite dominant narratives of history, in which it is the non-West that is often figured as violent, cruel, barbaric. In "The Fortunate Traveller," Derek Walcott disputes the "imperial fiction" of Joseph Conrad's *Heart of Darkness,* declaring, "The heart of darkness is not Africa," as Kurtz imagines it. Instead, "The heart of darkness is the core of fire / in the white center of the holocaust."[20] Strenuously reversing the ethical associations of dark and white, Walcott sees "darkness" in Europe's systematically planned, bureaucratically managed, and technologically enacted mass killing: "The heart of darkness is the rubber claw / selecting a scalpel in antiseptic light" and "the hills of children's shoes" that are left behind after Jews and others have been clinically slaughtered.

Dislocation and dispossession, systematic violence and colonization, intergenerational and memorial rupture — modernity, it would seem, could scarcely be imagined more grimly. In some of the most chilling postcolonial representations of modernity, its victims become in turn strident victimizers. Satirizing monomaniacal African modernizers, Okot p'Bitek bestows on his character Ocol a voice that eerily echoes the demolition plans of the futurist and vorticist manifestos:

> To hell
> With the husks
> Of old traditions
> And meaningless customs,
>
> We will smash
> The taboos
> One by one,
> Explode the basis
> Of every superstition,
> We will uproot
> Every sacred tree
> And demolish every ancestral shrine.[21]

Across the "developing world," many supposedly forward-looking dictators, internalizing colonial views as does Ocol, have called for the obliteration of tribal affiliations and backward-facing traditions, often with disastrous results. The Euromodernist thrill in blasting the past becomes, in the African context, sadistic destruction and masochistic self-negation: "Smash all the mirrors" of the "blackness of the past," shouts the European wannabe Ocol.[22] Whereas Euromodernists such as F. T. Marinetti, Wyndham Lewis, and Gertrude Stein, secure as inheritors of an officially sanctioned high culture, could gleefully disavow traditions and libraries and museums, Western colonialism threatened the indigenous cultural inheritances of Third World writers, as Frantz Fanon observes, with defacement, defilement, and destruction.[23] Postcolonial poets such as Okot — deeply aware of their cultural riches and resources, both premodern and modern — satirize and lament the effects of such blindly modernizing aggression, whether internally or externally afflicted. Like Harlem Renaissance poets such as Hughes and Brown, and like Irish and Scottish Renaissance poets such as Yeats and MacDiarmid, they champion subjugated cultural inheritances and identities that have been at risk of destruction. At the same time, unlike fundamentalist revivalists or reactionary terrorists, these postcolonial poets avoid fetishizing an idealized precolonial past. While resisting the obliteration of their cultural inheritances, they nevertheless concede the inevitability of modernization, working in hybrid forms, idioms, and genres, acknowledging in their double-visioned sensibilities and language modernity's irreversible permeation of their world.

Both rooted and modernizing, recuperative and hybrid, located and mobile, the poetry of the global South does not, in short, represent modernity unequivocally as a negative force. Take modern technologies of transportation. Flight, travel, transport — these are the subject of an initial sequence of poems in Wole Soyinka's first book of poetry, *"Idanre" and Other Poems* (1967), where they evoke both the exciting speed and the unnerving collisions of development. The jet passengers in "Around Us, Dawning" feel, like the flyers in Crane's *The Bridge*, helpless, "bound to a will of rotors // Yielding" their will to an "alien" mechanism. Yet, also as in Crane, they are availed of power, possibility, ecstatic movement — the sunlit speeding plane, hurtling into the dawn, is an "incandescent / Onrush," the poem's surge of syntactically propelled and lightly punctuated exhilaration replicating the forward momentum of modern technology.[24] In "Death in the Dawn," another poem in the series, a driver en route to Lagos, Nigeria, encounters a car in which a man has been killed: "Brother, / Silenced in the startled hug of / Your invention."[25] In his apostrophe to the dead man crushed by his automobile ("Your invention"), Soyinka metaphorizes the automobile as "this mocked grimace / This closed contortion." For him, technology both entraps and advances, both kills and empowers; in this regard, it almost seems a latter-day manifestation of the doubleness of Ogun, the Yoruba god of creation and destruction, as well as metallurgy, artisanship, and the road. Here, the car speeds the speaker toward his destination, yet it becomes a death-dealing adjunct to the Yoruba mythologization of the road as "famished." The poem ends with the question of whether this image of a man crushed within something of his own making is "I," which would make the culturally and formally hybrid contraption of the poem itself a mechanism at once destructive and propulsive.

Indeed, for poets, the most immediate technologies are those of writing and performance, and in this respect, too, modernization is imagined as a curse and also a potential blessing. On the verge of developing a highly visual style of poetry reliant on computer-generated fonts and spacing, Kamau Brathwaite acknowledges the Western technology of the computer as a kind of "muse," even as he worries about the word processor's origins in the scientific, capitalist, imperial culture denounced in his work. Addressing a poem to his mother, he confesses that he writes "pun a computer o/kay? / like I jine de mercantilists! // well not quite!"[26] His pun on "upon" verbally intimates the transformative reworking he hopes to enact with Western technology, wringing from it unexpected possibilities, as a poet does with words. Invoking the Caliban/Prospero duality, Brathwaite affiliates himself with Caliban, since the Barbadian is also "learnin prospero linguage," yet distinguishes Caliban's curses, seen as ultimately serving Prospero, from his own (84). Naming Chauncery Lane — as his note says, "not the London walkway, but downtown Kingston (Jamaica) reggae-making and recording centre" — Brathwaite places his transvaluation of technology within the context of a larger postcolonial transvaluation of the tools of modernity, akin to the postcolonial remaking of colonially named sites (127). The resulting paradoxes for postcolonial poetry run deep. The "dub" or performance style of poetry developed by Linton Kwesi Johnson, who acknowledges Brathwaite as a precursor, is intimately bound up with technologies of electronic recording, staging, and distribution. As with Brathwaite's visuality, the mechanisms of modernization ironically enable the recovery and reinvigoration of a poetic orality that seemed endangered by the spread of print culture. For these writers, as for the

Western modernists, modernity and tradition become strange partners in fashioning a new aesthetic.

Sometimes seen as rupture and dismemberment, sometimes as both repressive and enabling, modernity is cast by some writers as postcolonial irony. In her Jamaican Creole verse, Louise Bennett turns the distress and disorientation of modernity into a subject of considerable comedy. In a humorous variation on the motif of the country boy come to the city, "Country Bwoy" is a dramatic monologue spoken by a young Jamaican riding a store elevator in Kingston. Mistaking one technology for another, an elevator for an airplane, he pompously announces on arrival at the top floor, "Dis is Cuba, I presume"—a wry turn, as editor Mervyn Morris notes, on "Dr. Livingstone, I presume" (the remark attributed to Henry Morton Stanley, a late nineteenth-century white explorer of Africa).[27] While mocking the ignorant country boy's bafflement, this allusion also redounds on explorers in Africa, who are made to seem no less ridiculously disoriented and displaced. In other poems, Bennett's speakers are terrified by speeding trams ("Rough-Ridin Tram") or baffled by ballots that need to be marked ("Sarah Chice").

Although locals confused by the technology and the rationalizing processes of modernity are often the butt of her humor, Bennett's irony cuts both ways: she is no less scathing in her ridicule of the supposedly advanced purveyors of modernity. The bureaucrat who maps and rationally administers modern society — for Max Weber, that society's mainstay — runs into considerable resistance in Bennett's verse. The speaker of one poem wards off the intrusive questioning of a census taker, who pries into "fimiliar tings," the intimate details of her family, property, marital status, even age: "Me stare right eena census face / An tell him bans a lie!" (23–24). The modernity-thwarting speaker in "Census" is, as often in Bennett's poetry, a female trickster whose resistant guile affords refuge. In the contest between the sly figure of Anancy and a flat-footed, bureaucratic modernity, Bennett gives the advantage to Anancy's linguistic subterfuge, even as her using it hybridizes the mythical paradigm with a modern predicament. Bringing a robust Jamaican English into poetry and disseminating her verse through such media as newspapers, radio, and TV, she refuses to be bound by either an infatuation with, or a traditionalist rejection of, modernity.

In another Anancy-spirited poem, Bennett juxtaposes Jamaican folk tradition and Western "development" to deconstruct the teleology of Western narratives of modernization. "Jamaica Oman" takes to task the notion that Third World women need to be liberated by the West:

"long before Oman Lib bruck out / Over foreign lan," she declares, "Jamaica female wasa work / Her liberated plan!" (21–23). Questioning the developmental set of assumptions that casts the West as export model for other regions, Bennett shows Jamaican women to have modernized themselves long before the modernization of Western gender relations. Exemplifying an indigenous feminism, Jamaican women are presented as warriors (heroic Nanny, who is said to have made bullets ricochet off her buttocks to kill her enemies) and intellectual achievers (the spelling bee champion, who in the Caribbean gained access to further academic opportunities). Their strength and physical skill, their cleverness and intellectual resourcefulness, defy outside presuppositions that they are in need of liberation by the First World. While they may trick men into thinking they are demure, Jamaican women energetically guide and support, fearlessly push and prod men, even "lick sense eena man head," says the speaker. This dramatic pile-up of verbs to suggest oman's agency and her frenetic, varied activity recurs in a subsequent quatrain, where five transitive verbs appear in three lines — "Ban [band]," "bite," "Ketch," "put," "dig." Playing on the biblical story of Eve's emergence from Adam's rib, Bennett transforms a bone indicative of female subordination into an emblem of genuine strength: "While man a call her 'soso rib' / Oman a tun backbone!" According to Bennett, Jamaican women need not look for salvation to "Oman Lib," since they already control the finances, the social and familial life, and other aspects of the Jamaican "yard." The poem's verbal wit and rhetorical vigor are immediate evidence of these claims for oman's cunning.

As this and other poems indicate, Third World poets cast doubt on Western triumphalist narrative of global "development," in which an exported program of modernization is imagined as helping "developing" nations "advance" and become more like "developed" nations in economics, politics, social relations, technology, and culture. Bennett's ebullient humor sets her apart from other poets, but her ironic and irreverent laughter in the face of the invasiveness of modernity is the other side of the coin of the fear, grief, and anger in the work of Soyinka, Ali, Walcott, Brathwaite, and Okot p'Bitek, and others, as well as in modern Western poetry. In this rich postcolonial ambivalence, laughter or anxiety combines with a readiness to indigenize modernity. Poets often represent their local cultural resources as outlasting an externally imposed modernity by hybridizing with and thus transforming it.

The postcolonial ambivalence toward modernity resembles but is not the same as that of the Euromodernists. Because African,

Caribbean, and South Asian writers more often associate modernity with the ruptures of colonization, and because the geotemporal disjunctions between their experience of modernity and tradition are more acute, they sometimes represent modernity as even more violent than did the Euromodernists. At the same time, like poets of the Irish, Harlem, and Scottish renaissances, postcolonial poets link their desire to transvalue the forces of modernity with the writerly effort to remake the master's verbal and formal tools. Because poets of the global South encounter Western modernity from across even greater social and geographical differences than do poets of the British Isles and African American poets, they tend to represent it as an even stranger and more estranging force, and refuse to surrender "native" forms, vocabularies, and myths to a homogenizing Western model. Even so, they recognize that modernity cannot be naïvely screened out without consigning their poetry to the nostalgic amber of nativism — itself, in part, a defensive reaction to colonialism and modernity.[28] So they respond to and harness the forces of modernity in fashioning a postcolonial poetics that includes discordantly literal translation (Awoonor), anticompensatory elegizing (Ali), mythical syncretism (Soyinka), cross-cultural genres (Okot), technically facilitated visuality and orality (Brathwaite), and comically updated archetypes (Bennett). Even as they refuse to let modernity erase their cultural inheritances, even as they associate modernity with colonialism's violence, these poets modernize the indigenous and indigenize the modern.

2. Modernist Alienation or Subaltern Solidarity?

In definitions of modernism, "alienation" is one of the most frequently invoked categories of experience, understood as the marginalized writer's predicament in a bustling, commercially driven, late capitalist modernity that has little use for bards or shamans. As Raymond Williams sees it, alienated modernists turned to a preoccupation with their formal materials; in the absence of meaningful social bonds, they "found the only community available to them: a community of the medium; of their own practices."[29] How do postcolonial poets of Africa, Asia, and the Caribbean imagine their relation to their audiences, their societies, their new nations? Do they see their poetry as marginal or central? Do they represent themselves as alienated from, or integral to, emergent, postcolonized collectivities? Can we specify the dynamics of postcolonial poetry's social imaginary through further triangulated comparisons with Euromodernist and Harlem Renaissance poetries?

Among the most famous personifications of modernist social alienation are, of course, T. S. Eliot's painfully self-conscious Prufrock, who feels in company as if his nerves have been projected on a screen, and the protagonist of Ezra Pound's *Hugh Selwyn Mauberley,* who, repulsed by mass-produced art and writing, looks within for authentic feeling and creativity. By contrast, an iconic poem of the Harlem Renaissance, Langston Hughes's "The Negro Speaks of Rivers," purports to speak, as seen in chapter 3's discussion of traveling poetry, from within a transhistorical and translocational black and "human" experience.[30] Many Harlem Renaissance poets look to "folk" or oral forms for inspiration, implicitly joining their expressive capacity to that of African American common people — whether absorbing the rhetorical structures and narrative style of the sermon, like James Weldon Johnson, or the structure and imagery of the blues, spirituals, and tall tales, like Langston Hughes and Sterling Brown. Spurning and being spurned by what Yeats calls "the noisy set / Of bankers, schoolmasters, and clergymen,"[31] Euromodernist poets develop an art that — in its arcane mythologies, scholarly allusions, learned polyglossia, and private references — both reproduces and reinforces the very estrangement it mourns. Sometimes this social alienation turns rhetorically violent, as when Pound in his "Hell Cantos" unleashes a torrent of invective — "slow rot, fœtid combustion" — toward politicians, bankers, clergymen, and other pillars of modern society.[32]

This binary schema needs, however, to be complicated. As an Anglo-Irishman bestriding the divide between colonizer and colonized, Yeats also tries to reclaim indigenous resources for a nation-shaping poetry, and Eliot and Pound betray a fascination with the mass culture seemingly scorned in their often elitist references to advertising, consumerism, and popular ditties.[33] For the purposes of this chapter, a still more important qualification pertains to Harlem Renaissance poets, whose alienation, like that of postcolonial poets, should not be overlooked, despite their eschewal in most cases of the public-estranging ferocity of high modernist diction, rhetoric, and reference. In its Janus-faced form, diction, and persona, Hughes's "The Weary Blues" probes the dividing line between the poet, writing for a literary audience, and the blues singer, more closely affiliated with the poor masses.[34] When in his manifesto "The Negro Artist and the Racial Mountain" Hughes embraces the common folk as the rightful source of forms and materials for the black artist, his idealization of "the low-down folks" betrays at least some difference: "Their joy runs, bang! into ecstasy. Their religion soars to a shout. Work maybe a little today, rest a little tomorrow. Play awhile. Sing awhile. O, let's dance!"[35] As poets articulating emergent cultural and social identities and straddling dominant and historically oppressed social collectivities, Harlem Renaissance writers resemble those of decolonizing nations as poets of in-betweenness — between middle-class black audiences and the poor creators of the blues, between white patrons and the African American "folk" experience.

"Postcoloniality," writes Kwame Anthony Appiah, "is the condition of what we might ungenerously call a comprador intelligentsia: of a relatively small, Western-style, Western-trained, group of writers and thinkers," mediating between the Third World and the West through cultural goods.[36] The interstitiality of postcolonial writers, like that of Harlem Renaissance poets, necessarily involves some distance from their communities of origin, even as postcolonial poets attempt to epitomize and speak for the nation or region, to engage their home audience as members of the same social world. Sometimes the sense of apartness becomes so intense that poets of the global South more nearly resemble the Euromodernist example of diffident withdrawal from, and hostility toward, the larger social world, however exaggerated that sense of apartness may be; sometimes it recalls instead Harlem Renaissance examples of greater identification with, and participation in, a communal identity, however troubled and complex that solidarity may be; and at other times, postcolonial poetry shuttles productively between these poles.

That the social distance most evident in the attitudes and forms of white modernist poetry could bear comparison with the work of postcolonial poets may be surprising. Yet some postcolonial poets represent themselves as no less alienated from their societies than do the Euromodernists from theirs. Christopher Okigbo clearly recalls Euromodernist inwardness and estrangement, especially in his early poetry, if not in the manner of his death, fighting among Igbo secessionists for an independent Biafra. Though he died in a blaze of public solidarity, Okigbo had grown up a member of the tiny stream of students who attended elite secondary and higher educational institutions under British colonialism, his father being a Catholic mission teacher in Igboland. His poetry does not disguise his distance and difference from Nigerian society at large, from what he calls "the people."[37] Despite the antiphonal structure of some poems, the persona of Okigbo's poetry is characteristically solitary, speaking for and often to himself, exploring a penumbral state of consciousness between dream and waking. Even when he purports to reclaim his African roots, his language evokes intense isolation and perpetual "exile" ("Newcomer" in *Heavensgate*, 17): "I was the sole witness of my homecoming" ("Distances" I, 53). Poetry arises not from collectivism but from an inward, agonized quest, as in his adaptation of Psalms 5 and 130: "out of the depths my cry" ("The Passage" in *Heavensgate*, 3). Only through communion with his or her innermost self, Okigbo's verse seems to suggest, can the poet discover lasting truths and reveal mythopoeic visions. Like the high modernists, Okigbo mythologizes the quest within and dons a depersonalizing mask, though as an African he needs to explain his mask in contradistinction to the ritual object: "Mask over my face — // my own mask, not ancestral — I sign" ("Newcomer" in *Heavensgate*, 17). To inscribe this mask, as emphasized by the syntactic inversion ("Mask . . . I sign"), is to appropriate for himself a cultural inheritance with a dual pedigree in both high modernist and Igbo mythologies. In the African context, he remakes a ritual object saturated with social significance into a tool of paradoxically depersonalized personal expression.

The dreamy inwardness of Okigbo's poetry sometimes coincides with bitterly satiric attacks on society at large, making abrupt tonal swings between inward brooding and outward assaults. Okigbo denounces many of the same social groups decried by the Euromodernists: "fanatics and priests and popes, / organizing secretaries and / party managers," all of whom exploit the society they pretend to serve, keeping in place colonialism's structures of domination ("Initiations" in *Heavensgate*, 7). Put together an inward-questing poet and a society corrupted by "vendors princes negritude / politicians" ("Distances" III, 56), and the result is an image of the poet, as in much high modernist verse, as martyr or even scapegoat. At times Okigbo compares himself to Orpheus, Tammuz, and other dying gods. Elsewhere he identifies with historical victims, such as the assassinated Congolese leader Patrice Lumumba, who is part Shakespeare's betrayed Caesar, part Eliot's drowned Phlebas: "They struck him in the ear they struck him in the eye; / They picked his bones for scavenging" ("Lament of the Silent Sisters" II in "Silences," 40). Okigbo worries that his poetry likewise puts him at risk: "If I don't learn to shut my mouth I'll soon go to hell" ("Hurrah for Thunder," 67). Even without the many allusions scattered through his verse to Eliot, Pound, and Yeats, Okigbo's poetry can be said to bring into expression specifically postcolonial estrangement by indigenizing the alienated social structure and language of modernist verse.

At the other end of the social spectrum are poets of the global South, who more nearly resemble Harlem Renaissance writers in their efforts to summon the voices, forms, and language of the people, however troubled may be their acts of poetic identification. Kofi Anyidoho of Ghana seems to have poets like Okigbo in mind when he disavows the merely "private dreams of poets" and "pampered dreams of poets."[38] For Syl Cheney-Coker of Sierra Leone, it is not enough to be read in English honors class — "my country I do not want that!" — but rather "to be the breakfast of the peasants who read" and "to help the fishermen bring in their catch."[39] Seldom, if ever, has this ideal fusion been realized, but it is especially alluring in societies where material and collective needs are pressing and massive, often making poets feel guilty about their individualist and apparently useless aesthetic pursuits. Still, such a synthesis may not be altogether impossible; a few postcolonial poets can at least claim to have garnered a national or regional audience, including Okot p'Bitek, whose *Song of Lawino* enjoyed widespread popular as well as critical esteem in East Africa and beyond, and Bennett, whose multimedia dissemination of her Creole poetry helped valorize the use of West Indian English.

Often performed to musical accompaniment, Johnson's dub poetry represents a determined effort to write from within and to the specifically defined community of "black Britn."[40] In "New Craas Massakah," Johnson grounds his relation to this collectivity in a shared experience of racial victimization:

wi did know seh it couda happn
yu know — anytime, anywhe
far dont it happn to wi
an di Asians dem aready?[41]

This poem attempts to merge "wi" and "yu," speaker and audience, poet and microsociety, delimiting a separate sphere of collectivity in opposition to violent racists, an indifferent police, and a white British public at large.

Most postcolonial poets move between these poles, recognizing their status as members of a small, highly educated, literary elite, like the Euromodernists, yet aspiring, like the Harlem Renaissance poets, to announce, define, and participate in an emergent cultural identity. Even the individualist dreamer Okigbo sees himself as a "town-crier," and even the collectivist Johnson mourns personal losses and writes to his "own sense a time."[42] This in-betweenness both vitalizes and vexes postcolonial poetry. Poetry's function in the postcolonial imaginary has often been, at least in part, to mediate between the antinomies of isolated apartness and communal solidarity. This is true even of popular poets whose relation to the local people may seem to be direct and unambiguous. Bennett recalled writing her first Creole poem in the 1930s, as Mervyn Morris explains, after she boarded a crowded tramcar as a well-dressed teenager and heard one of the country women, required to sit in the back with baskets, say they should spread out to keep the middle-class interloper from sitting down:

> Pread out yuhself deh Liza, one
> Dress-oman dah look like seh
> She see di li space side-a we
> And waan foce herself een deh.[43]

The well-dressed young woman, as Carolyn Cooper observes, "cannot violate the social space that the ostracized market-women have come to claim as their own."[44] Bennett's scene of initiation into becoming a dialect poet is predicated on her donning the persona of a woman who belongs to a lower social class than her own, who sees a person of Bennett's class as an intruder at the back of the tramcar. Poetry extends across the class antagonisms and social frictions that separate the poet from the people for whom she is a spokesperson. Although Bennett is often seen as a quintessentially local and authentically Jamaican popular poet—a view reinforced by her extraordinarily favorable reception among West Indians of varied social classes—even this most gleefully national poetry, with its empathic adoption of the people's voice, reflects within its fissured social structure a relation of desire for, and distance from, "the people."

The overdetermined slide of pronouns between first person singular and plural in a poem such as the Nigerian Ben Okri's "On Edge of Time Future" is similarly illustrative of these social fractures and ambiguities: "I remember the history well," begins this poem, referring one strophe later to "our history" as Africans, only to shift again from "I remember" to "We emerged from our rubbish mounds."[45] By poem's end, the speaker is referring "To us // Who remember the history well," claiming that he is writing for the collective, national project of restoration and healing: "We shall spin silk from rubbish / And frame time with our resolve."[46] Although poetry is affirmed as playing a vital role in imagining a new future created from the detritus of colonial and post-colonial history, the pronominal instabilities of the poem hint at the difficulty of fusing the individuated poetic self to the larger national aspiration.

Walcott's high diction and rhetoric, his use of European literary forms, his self-identification with Western poets — all would seem to place him squarely on the side of alienated, introspective, modernist elitism. And, indeed, as recalled at the beginning of chapter 1, the hero of "The Schooner *Flight*" declares, after abandoning and being abandoned by both whites and blacks in the Caribbean, "I had no nation now but the imagination."[47] Yet in this same Odyssean tale, poetry is figured as saturated by its environment, much as the poet's verb forms are inflected by West Indian Creole: "when I write / this poem, each phrase go be soaked in salt; / I go draw and knot every line as tight / as ropes in this rigging."[48] The formal interstitiality of metaphor (the poem *as* and *as not* a wave, a boat, rigging) and of linguistic register (between Creole and Standard English) instantiates the poem's social ambiguity and ambivalence, its mixture of communal longing and melancholy separation. The stinging recognition that his poetry is not at one with the Caribbean common people recurs in Walcott's poetry. In "The Light of the World," he writes of taking a public minibus or "transport" to his hotel, and of a beautiful local woman humming to a Bob Marley song on the van's stereo: "I had abandoned them," he reflects, feeling the painful contrast between the assimilation of Marley's songs into everyday Caribbean life and his own apartness as an elite poet frequently living abroad, with nothing to offer the common folk except a poem such as "The Light of the World," which they will likely never read or hear.[49] The hope of Walcott's poetry is that even with this gulf between poet and the people, he can help summon into literary existence the dignity of Caribbean identity — mongrelized, polyglot, burdened with multiple inheritances, yet born afresh out of imperial and postimperial violence, racism, and rot.

The tension between estrangement from postcolonial community and the longing to serve and give expression to emerging national and social collectivities was discomfiting but generative for poets like Walcott and Okigbo who came of age during the post–World War II decolonization of the British Empire. It continues to animate the work of postcolonial writers born twenty years later, such as Agha Shahid Ali and Lorna Goodison, who give voice to profound uncertainty about their relation to ex-colonial societies. For these poets, migration to the metropole has exacerbated issues of communal affiliation and identity. The sense of the privileged intellectual's social isolation, already evident in Okigbo's and (even the pre-émigré) Walcott's verse, is only intensified by the geographic displacement of poets in the postcolonial diaspora. The fraught imagery of connection yet disconnection in Ali's poems, such as the title poem of his 1997 collection *The Country without a Post Office*, exemplifies the struggle to honor one's birthplace (for him, Kashmir) and community of origin (South Asian Muslims), while frankly conceding the solitary condition of the postcolonial expatriate. Having learned about the conflagration that destroyed the Kashmiri town and shrine of Chrar-e-Sharif while he was living in the United States, Ali vividly imagines the ruin — a minaret is entombed, houses burn and are buried, a wall of fire caves in — but at the same time signals his geographical and social distance from his traumatized homeland in images of writing that redounds on itself: seemingly unreadable messages are "scratched on planets"; stamps are canceled but "blank," with no nation; addresses are written but "doomed"; there is a strange "card lying on the street"; envelopes have "vanished"; the speaker's cries are "like dead letters." "My words go out in huge packages of rain," laments the poet, "go there, to addresses, across the oceans," but never seem to arrive at their destination.[50] "These words may never reach you," plaintively cries a prisoner's letter. Undelivered or unreadable, misfired or self-canceling, the letters in Ali's poem suggest the frustration of writing to and for a community from which the poet knows he stands apart. As for many South Asian writers who compose in English rather than Urdu, Hindi, Tamil, or other indigenous languages, writing poetry in a Western language used by an elite minority, literally unreadable by most members of his homeland, further exacerbates the poet's estrangement. This sense of isolation in an expatriated conscience and language is formally embodied in the poem's mirrorlike or palindromic rhyme scheme, each octave structured in an *abcddcba* pattern. Pronouns suggest both a desire to reach the poet's community of origin and an elegiac admission of inevitable failure. "Again I've returned to this country," begins the poem, and this "I" soon morphs into a hopeful "us," "our," and "we," eventually splitting into self-address ("Phantom heart") and into self-accusing address to a Kashmiri other: "Then be pitiless you whom I could not save." The ambiguity and instability of Ali's address, now to himself and now to an imagined Kashmiri interlocutor, as well as of tone, now frantically yearning and now skeptically mournful, embodies the postcolonial expatriate's fragile sense of poetic identity as alienated from, yet longing

to reconnect with, a community of origin—in this case, one still struggling to define its political destiny.

The poems of Lorna Goodison's collection *Controlling the Silver*
(2005), largely set in Jamaica but written after years of living in North
America, also make frequent use of second-person address in ways that
similarly encapsulate the interstitiality of the postcolonial expatriate. "Island Aubade" begins by describing in the third person a morning in Jamaica, but soon the voice has shifted to insistent and intimate
second-person address: "Come drink this cup of Blue Mountain coffee /
stirred with a brown suede stick of cinnamon."[51] Deploying the second
person to ground herself in her recuperated homeland, the poet seems
continually to be inviting the reader in, as a host introducing outsiders
to her (former) social world: "Don't shake hands with the wicked, eat
greens, abase / and abound."[52] In "Ode to the Watchman," the desire to
form imaginative community steers the gracious shift from third-person
description of an exhausted night watchman who has kept even ghosts,
or "rolling calves," at bay ("evidence of his vigilance against nocturnal /
furies red in his eyeballs") to second-person address: "All praise to you
O beneficent watchman // for keeping guard over us while we slept."
The watchman becomes a more intimate "watchie" at the height of the
poem's willed communion, before he is surrendered to the more formal
"kind" and finally "good watchman" as blessing turns to imagined ca-
maraderie and then to decathectic farewell.[53] The speaker would turn
her connection with the watchman into a dialogic, "I-Thou" relation,
but her use of apostrophe also records the absence and unavailability
of the relation it conjures into being. Goodison's poetry represents itself as extending ever outward, ever desirous, into a world that may or
may not receive it. Its continual apostrophic gestures embody both fe-
rocious hope and elegiac melancholy over the possibilities of solidarity,
with both her imagined international reader and with her community
of origin. The grammar of address and the mercurial pronouns in her
poetry, the shifts in register between Creole and Standard English, and
in tone between melancholy and blessing, form the tissue of a longingly
inclusive yet inevitably fissured identity-in-community.

"Triple exile" is Ali's self-description, as "exile" from Kashmir to India to the United States. Edward Said characterizes exiles in terms of
a "plurality of vision," since life and language in one environment play
against memories of other cultural spaces, giving "rise to an awareness of
simultaneous dimensions."[54] Such double- or triple-visioned awareness
lends itself to poetry's prismatic perspectivism, as embodied in its met-

aphoric richness and layered forms. A fundamental source of creativity for the displaced Euromodernists, "exile" is no less so for doubly or sometimes triply "exilic" poets such as Walcott, Ali, and Goodison. Indeed, the complexities of their affiliations may even exceed those of the expatriate modernists, for the geographic and cultural distances crossed are still greater, and, to the extent that they belong to a "comprador intelligentsia," these postcolonial poets write out of divided allegiances to local or "native" communities and to the cultures and languages of colonization, even when they don't emigrate. We might assume comfortable and tightly knit relations between poets and the decolonizing societies for and to which they (partly) speak, as if they were the loudspeakers of their emergent nations, at least by comparison with First World poets, whose alienation from modern capitalist societies is more readily presupposed. And indeed, many postcolonial poets, like poets of the Harlem Renaissance, aspire intensely to reconnect with and help shape their often fluid national or regional communities of origin. Yet whether styling themselves nativists or cosmopolitans, poets of the global South are often set apart by their education, literary inheritances, language, class status, and geographic mobility, as well as their cultural function as intermediaries between First and Third worlds. This is true even of many "native" poets, such as the Creole-performing Jamaican localist Bennett, trained at the Royal Academy of Dramatic Art in London on a British Council scholarship; the proverb-wielding Acoli poet Okot p'Bitek, schooled in anthropology at Oxford; and the dub poet Johnson, educated in sociology at Goldsmiths College, University of London — a poet who half-mockingly concedes his professional aspiration to be counted a "tap-natch poet / like Chris Okigbo / Derek Walcot / ar T. S. Eliot."[55] Still more clearly for postcolonial poets such as Goodison, Ali, Walcott, and Okri, poetry plays across the fractures between experiential and remembered, national and transnational, solitary and communal worlds.

* * *

If modernist poetry is, bluntly put, poetry that responds to modernity, then surely postcolonial poets of Africa, South Asia, and the Caribbean belong in the company of the modernists, even though most of the major postcolonial poets emerged much later, did not write in what are usually seen in the West as "experimental" styles, and explored in their verse sharply different geographic and cultural inflections of modernity and alienation — as revealed by a transnationally comparative approach. Still, modernity makes it difficult to hold the lines between North and South, colonizer and colonized, modern and contemporary securely in place, because the acceleration of human mobility across national and regional boundaries has partly eroded them. As we have seen, the migrancy associated with Western modernists such as Eliot, Pound, Stein, Loy, H.D., and Auden — poets in search of aesthetic stimulation and publishing prospects abroad — is no less characteristic of postcolonial poets such as McKay, Walcott, Brathwaite, Goodison, Ali, Ramanujan, and Soyinka, who have traversed an even greater geo-economic divide for academic, financial, and publishing opportunities in North America and the British Isles. "Exile is the first significant feature of Anglophone Caribbean writing," writes Brathwaite, citing McKay at the start; "it is the need — or the imagined need — to emigrate to metropolitan centres in order to exist as writers."[56] Postcolonial poets have thus written out of the disjunctions and layerings of transgeographic experience, even when they have been fiercely attached to the local soil. As such, they have created a transnational poetry that is often a cacophony of discrepant idioms and genres, landscapes and images. In its cross-hemispheric reach, its intercultural bearings, and its melancholy alienation, such poetry recalls the work of the Euromodernists, emergent during an earlier stage of globalization. But as in the poetry of the Irish, Scottish, and Harlem renaissances, this transnational heterogeneity has helped postcolonial poets fashion not discordant requiems for a dying elite culture but nativity odes — however conflicted — to cultural identities still emerging and changing in the wake of colonialism and modernity.

POETRY AND DECOLONIZATION

Few transnational political processes were more central to twentieth-century history than the advent of a global modernity traced in the last chapter and what Edward Said calls "the great movement of decolonization all across the Third World," with the resultant withdrawal of Western imperial powers — notably Great Britain, France, Belgium, Portugal, Italy, Spain — from their former colonies.[1] In 1914, 85 percent of the earth's surface was under European control.[2] At the end of World War II, a third of the world's population still lived in non-self-governing territories. Fewer than two million do today.[3] This momentous shift from colonial to postcolonial status, though far from complete, is reflected in the emergence of the word "decolonization": while the word "colonization" goes back to Edmund Burke's use of it in the imperial eighteenth century, "decolonization" was coined only in the 1930s; it gained wide currency in the 1960s, when many African, Caribbean, and Asian nations were winning independence.[4] Most of the eighty new nations listed by the United Nations Decolonization Unit had been colonies of Great Britain — "in an imperial class by itself," as Said remarks, "bigger, grander, more imposing than any other" modern empire.[5]

The work of Edward Said, seen by many as the founder of postcolonial studies, is especially helpful in understanding the relation between poetry and decolonization. Hence, the second part of this chapter seeks to develop Said's insights into the transnational affiliations that form the basis, sometimes paradoxically, for anticolonial poetic solidarities. In the first part of the chapter I reflect on what might be termed a global poetics of decolonization, asking by what strategies decolonization has been imagined and named, announced and even satirized. How have

poets from new postcolonial nations and from the imperial center represented the sublimity of decolonization, yet also its unfulfilled promise?

To explore the poetry and poetics of decolonization in the postwar period, this chapter continues to build on the insights of Kwame Anthony Appiah, Homi Bhabha, and Gayatri Spivak with respect to postcolonial writers who straddle native and imperial worlds, colonial and ex-colonial temporalities.[6] Informed by postcolonial studies, it also makes use of the analytic tools of poetry studies to investigate how poems fashion postcolonial histories, selves, and collectivities. Alert to what Derek Walcott calls "Adam's task of giving things their names,"[7] poetry helps illuminate the colonizing and potentially decolonizing force of naming and renaming in the (post)colonial context. And because of its compressed tessellation, its articulation of multiple and often contending affiliations, transnational poetry also helps reveal the ambiguities of emergent social identities in the wake of decolonization.

1. Imagining Decolonization

To evoke the magnitude of decolonization, Resolution 1514 of the United Nations General Assembly, the Declaration on the Granting of Independence to Colonial Countries and Peoples, occasionally reaches toward "the poetic": it conveys its meaning in part by its rhetorical elevation and its syntactic patterning, by its vast scope ("Recognizing that the peoples of the world ardently desire the end of colonialism in all its manifestations") and its identification with "the passionate yearning for freedom in all dependent peoples," and by its idealistic assertion "that the process of liberation is irresistible and irreversible."[8] Adopted in 1960, the year of Nigeria's and Cyprus's independence, and coming just after the decolonization of Ghana, Malaysia, and Sri Lanka and just before that of numerous African, Caribbean, and Asian nations, the Declaration on Decolonization summons a verbal power and urgency that seem meant both to reflect and to advance the eruption of many states out of a few, the thunderous collapse of a political system built on "alien subjugation, domination and exploitation."[9]

Other documents on decolonization share these and additional "poetic" qualities. Even the UN's blandly matter-of-fact list of decolonized nations ironically resembles one of the most ancient forms of poetry: the list poem or catalog verse. In the West, the topos is familiar from Homer's list of ships, the genealogies of the Bible, catalogs in Chaucer,

Shakespeare, Milton, and Whitman, up to Marianne Moore and Kenneth Koch; but it is also widespread in the non-European world — in lists of place-names, for example, in Polynesian and Abyssinian verse,[10] or more recently in the poetic songs of Okot p'Bitek. The United Nations lists under the United Kingdom names that are no longer subordinate possessions but, at least formally, sovereign equals:

Aden Colony and Protectorate	Independence as South Yemen	1967
Bahamas	Independence	1973
Barbados	Independence	1966
Basutoland	Independence as Lesotho	1966
Bechuanaland Protectorate	Independence as Botswana	1966
British Guiana	Independence as Guyana	1966
British Honduras	Independence as Belize	1981
British Somaliland	Independence as Somalia (joined with Italian Somaliland)	1960
Brunei	Independence Now Brunei Darussalam	1984
Cyprus	Independence	1960

The ABCs of British decolonization extend on and on, to the Z's of Zambia, Zanzibar, and Zimbabwe.[11] The catalog structurally imputes commonality to these names, which nevertheless display a stunning geographic and linguistic variety. Like Kant's "mathematical sublime," a seemingly endless repetitive series,[12] so too the awesome incremental series in the history of decolonization — first India and Pakistan, then Ghana, Malaysia, and Sri Lanka, then Cyprus and Nigeria, then the unstoppable flood of Sierra Leone, Tanzania, Jamaica, Trinidad and Tobago, Uganda, Kenya, Malawi, Zambia, Singapore, and so forth — might be thought of as a "postcolonial sublime." Yet the UN's heading of its list of former British colonies by the name of the "administering state," or empire, circumscribes the catalog's potential sublimity, raising the perennial question in postcolonial studies of whether, after formal decolonization, the former colonies remain in the grips of an officially absent yet persistent neocolonialism.

Poems of the decolonizing world often list the names of liberated nations and dependent territories. Empires colonize territories not only through bullets and battleships but also, as Brian Friel's play *Translations* memorably demonstrates and Said's *Culture and Imperialism* argues, through the verbal process of renaming and remapping the land.[13]

Consequently, imaginative writers often make use of the decolonizing list to invert this process, repossessing multinationed regions through toponym-studded poems. Derek Walcott's "A Sea-Chantey," in his 1962 volume *In a Green Night*, twins the repetitive structure of prayer with the secular incantations of a work song at sea, as if by the verbal magic and labor of nomination to reclaim the islands of the Lesser Antilles in a north-to-south arc:

> The litany of islands,
> The rosary of archipelagoes,
> Anguilla, Antigua,
> Virgin of Guadeloupe,
> And stone-white Grenada
> Of sunlight and pigeons. . . .[14]

Similarly, Kamau Brathwaite's "Calypso" (1967) begins with a creation myth in which Caribbean islands are formed by a rock-skipping game:

> The stone had skidded arc'd and bloomed into islands:
> Cuba and San Domingo
> Jamaica and Puerto Rico
> Grenada Guadeloupe Bonaire. . . .[15]

In a collapse of temporalities, the original emergence of geologically discrete islands in the Caribbean is made to foretell their political self-definition millions of years later. Here again, the equalizing syntactic structure of the list is counterbalanced by the diversifying effect of toponymic heterogeneity. These and other postcolonial lists transvalue names that Europeans once invoked to demonstrate the boundless reach and might of empires on which the sun would never set. By their number, range, and geographic diversity, such transnational catalogs of place-names assert a sublime heterogeneity that can no longer be contained in an imperial treasure box.

The multiplicity of emerging national and regional identities, central to these poems of the 1960s, is occasionally internalized in later poems, which revel in the toponymic variety to be found even within a single decolonizing nation. Lorna Goodison's "To Us, All Flowers Are Roses" plays on postcolonial Jamaica's multifarious place-names as the linguistic deposits left by colonization, the slave trade, and indigenous peoples:

There is everywhere here.
There is Alps and Lapland and Berlin.
Armagh, Carrick Fergus, Malvern
Rhine and Calabar, Askenish
where freed slaves went to claim
what was left of the Africa within,
staging secret woodland ceremonies.[16]

Rejecting the colonial image of the West Indies as a peripheral back-water, with "no people there in the true sense of the word,"[17] Goodison uncovers in Jamaica's transnational toponyms a vibrant cosmopolitanism, spanning Europe and Africa, Northern and Southern hemispheres. Highlighting African survivals, such as the Nigerian place-name Calabar, Goodison etymologically links Accompong to the history of Jamaica's ex-slave rebels, or maroons:

Accompong is Ashanti, root, Nyamekopon
appropriate name Accompong, meaning
warrior or lone one.[18]

The linguistic deposits in a place-name bespeak a buried history of transcontinental slave transport and rebellion, a history largely suppressed under British colonialism and now made visible by topographic and linguistic decolonization. Poets thus marshal toponymic sprawl, whether concentrated within a single nation or distributed across islands and regions, to signify the sublimity of decolonization, awesome and yet, in Kant's phrase, "without any dominion over us"[19] — the unleashing of a cultural and national multiplicity once squelched by the homogenizing force of empire.

If transnational poetic lists are one kind of literary gathering meant to evoke the global ungathering of decolonization, a national anthology of poems, plays, and stories is another kind — etymologically a flower gathering (*anthos* + *logia*) — and it often accompanies decolonization on the assumption that a literature of one's own helps prove a people's right to a country of their own. *The Independence Anthology of Jamaican Literature* (1962), published in the year of that country's official decolonization, instances this attempt at national self-legitimization.[20] Dedicated to "THE FREE PEOPLE OF JAMAICA" and published by a committee of the Jamaican Ministry of Development and Welfare, the volume includes poems meant to justify political self-sufficiency through poetic self-representation and self-nomination. Poem titles such as "Jamaica Market," "Jamaica Symphony," "Jamaica Fisherman," and simply "Jamaica" establish the nation's self-identity by locating a corresponding self-identity in the sphere of culture.

Just as postcolonial poets rename and reclaim their formerly colonized lands in lists, litanies, and anthologies, so too black British poets, such as Linton Kwesi Johnson, Grace Nichols, and Bernardine Evaristo, rechart the space of the imperial center, undoing the image of a supremely civilized "mother country." Johnson's work, as John McLeod points out, which is often centered in the African Caribbean community of Brixton, "offers an alternative inventory of place-names wholly devoid of mythical charm and rewrites the map of London to reflect a sombre geography of the city's realities that is grounded in the experiences of British-born or -raised black youth."[21] To help decolonize metropolitan space, Johnson represents it as a site not of monumental beauty and civilization but of systemic oppression and determined resistance. In his verse, "Landan toun" in particular and England in general are seen as having reimported and internalized the colonial divide — between black and white, colonizer and colonized. In the refrain of one of his most famous poems, he declares:

> Inglan is a bitch
> dere's no escapin it
> Inglan is a bitch
> dere's no runin whe fram it[22]

There is no escaping it in a double sense. There is no escaping the truth of England's exploitation of people such as the West Indian migrant to London, described as shuttled from one demeaning job to another — underground worker to dish washer, ditch digger to factory worker and finally the dole. And there is no running away from England, a prison that lures and then confines peoples from lands it once colonized. Immigrants find themselves worked hard for meager pay and then repeatedly fired, and yet their countries of origin, still in the grip of the ravaging and impoverishing aftermath of colonialism and now economic neocolonialism, can offer few alternatives.

If, as Johnson suggests, colonialism persists in new guises both within Britain and in the former colonies, then what happened to the exalted expectations of formal decolonization? Already at the time of independence, poets such as Louise Bennett, a key influence on Johnson, were raising questions about the promise of decolonization, in wily poems such as Bennett's "Independence Dignity," "Jamaica Elevate," and "Independance." Bennett's verse sometimes seems to greet decolonization as heroic accession, as in "Independence Dignity":

It was a sight fi cure sore yeye,
A time fi live fi see:[23]
Jamaica Independence
Celebration dignity.[24]

Yet this bundling of Jamaica with a list of three seemingly triumphal nouns comes at the end of a poem that has earlier mocked the commodification of the nation's birth in a listing of souvenirs:

Independence pen an pencil,
Cup an saucer, glass an tray;
Down to Independence baby bawn
Pon Independence Day.[25]

Abruptly shifting from commodities to a baby, Bennett's poem deploys the list not to celebrate a new multiplicity unleashed by decolonization but to poke fun at the homogenizing use of the new nation's identity to brand everything, from pens and pencils to babies. While celebrating and even attempting to enact decolonization through rites of naming, postcolonial poets such as Bennett also playfully satirize representations of the nation-state as the sole arbiter of worth.

Writing in the heyday of African independence movements, Okot p'Bitek more sternly questions the sufficiency of political decolonization, even as he supports an African cultural revolution. Although *Song of Lawino* affirms indigenous cultural values, it cannot be reduced to a literary cheer for decolonization without ignoring its critique of the viciously feuding political parties that supposedly fight for Uhuru in Uganda and elsewhere in Africa. For these groups, self-interest is paramount:

Someone said
Independence falls like a bull buffalo
And the hunters
Rush to it with drawn knives,
Sharp shining knives

> For carving the carcass.
> And if your chest
> Is small, bony and weak
> They push you off,
> And if your knife is blunt
> You get the dung on your elbow,
> You come home empty-handed
> And the dogs bark at you!
>
> . . . .
>
> And the other men
> Carry large pieces of fatty beef,
> You hear their horns loud and proud![26]

Like the native bourgeoisie that Frantz Fanon feared would protect its entrenched interests after the revolution,[27] these party leaders and their families seize on independence as an opportunity for gorging themselves, as sonically emphasized here by the assonance of "loud" and "proud." Instead of imagining decolonization as the triumph of the weak over the strong, the rising up of a newly empowered collectivity, Okot's Lawino says "Independence falls," as if an animal felled by the strong for the strong.

Political decolonization, moreover, seems to bring little change to lives of the dispossessed:

> . . . the hip bones of the voters
> Grow painful
> Sleeping on the same earth
> They slept
> Before Uhuru!
> And they cover the ulcers
> On their legs
> With animal skins.[28]

Formal decolonization may be a desirable aim, but if it fails to help the dispossessed, it can have scant meaning and may even deepen despair. Being able to vote — from the Latin *votum*, vow or wish — can turn into a cruelly ironic betrayal of vows and wishes. A "bullfrog bellowing for the vote" is Walcott's satiric epithet for the postcolonial politician in "The Sea Is History."[29] Toward the end of Walcott's poem, the political decolonization of the West Indies — "each rock broke into its own nation"—fails to meet hopes for genuine rebirth. In the form of a beast fable, Walcott mocks the froglike politicians, flylike clerics, batlike ambassadors, and buglike police and judges who assume control in postcolonial societies, betraying the promise of a sublime eruption of a new "History," a fresh "beginning," after centuries of colonial subjugation (367). In brief, while postcolonial poets often celebrate the creation of new nations—multiple, sublimely heterogeneous, freed from the grip of imperial domination—they also question and even ridicule expectations that political independence will transform the economic, social, or geopolitical order. Nationality can become a fetish with little genuine meaning, one of modernity's many chimeras, if neither the formerly colonized nor their colonizers fundamentally alter economic and political structures of exploitation. Even so, disillusioned independence poetry—Bennett's ebullient self-mockery, Okot's angry accusations, Walcott's fabulistic satire, even Johnson's militant critique—does not extinguish all hope for "History, really beginning," as Walcott puts it in the last words of his poem (367). Indeed, these witty responses to the failures of decolonization can be seen as caustic poetic efforts to help spur emancipatory alternatives to failed promises and despair, to the misplaced priorities and entrenched interests of the status quo.

*   *   *

Within a transnational and cross-cultural framework of analysis, we need also ask, how does the decolonization of British territories look to poets on the other side of the colonial divide? As we might expect, the global rupture of decolonization is not always a cheering spectacle, let alone sublime. After the Suez Crisis of 1956, Britain's confidence in the imperial project dwindled, and by the 1960s, after the decolonization of much of the empire, the British government decided to draw down troops east of Suez. Philip Larkin's "Homage to a Government" (1969) laments the diminishment of the British Empire and satirizes its shrinkage for the sake of monetary savings:

> The places are a long way off, not here,
> Which is all right, and from what we hear
> The soldiers there only made trouble happen.[30]

Larkin's coupling of the homonyms "here" and "hear" suggests, as does his restriction of rhyme to three repeated words in each six-line stanza (*home/home*, *right/right*, *orderly/orderly*, etc.), the claustrophobia of an empire that is folding in upon itself. His poem contrasts sharply with the rhetoric of the postcolonial sublime, whether in poems or UN documents, and while its deflative tone has more in common with satiric poems on decolonization, those postcolonial poems retain, in contrast to Larkin's bleakness, a sense of emergent possibility. The sonic and tonal detumescence of Larkin's lament for "Little England" bespeaks an anxious somnolence, a bored disquiet, about the sameness (and indeed "same" is one of the repeated rhyme words in the last stanza) of a "country" (another repeated word) without overseas possessions and with little expectation of reversing the decline in its world status. The antisublimity of a poem with a narrowly limited verbal, tonal, and sonic palette becomes emblematic of a nation deprived of the reach and resources of the *imperium*.

But just as the response to decolonization was mixed among poets of the decolonizing world, not all white British poets greeted decolonization with sourness or melancholy. In the empire's waning years, one Englishman turned on its head the triumphant roll call of British territories on which the sun would never set. In his song "Mad Dogs and Englishmen" (1932), Noël Coward ranges from Burma to Hong Kong, Bangkok to Bengal, invoking geographic and cultural variety to satirize Britain's attempt to force uniformity on the world:

> In the Malay States
> There are hats like plates
> Which the Britishers won't wear.
> At twelve noon
> The natives swoon
> And no further work is done.
> But mad dogs and Englishmen
> Go out in the midday sun.[31]

Although Coward's verse is shot through with British imperial attitudes, this song wryly lists colonial sites that refuse conformity with an inflexible British custom. As in the toponymic lists of postcolonial poetry, the place-names themselves indicate an ungovernable heterogeneity. But whereas postcolonial lists often evoke the uncontainable sublimity of decolonization, Coward's rigidly boundary-setting versification and jauntily insistent rhyme risk echoing the imperial limits that the toponyms and varied cultural attitudes are meant to unsettle.

cott, Goodison, Brathwaite, Ramanujan, Soyinka, and other poets, as in the examples cited earlier, can be seen as participating in a central task of cultural decolonization — not, as we might expect, angrily taunting or satirizing the colonizer, but renaming and remapping topography. "If there is anything that radically distinguishes the imagination of anti-imperialism," says Said, sounding much like Frantz Fanon, "it is the primacy of the geographical element. Imperialism after all is an act of geographical violence," which begins experientially, for the colonized, with "loss of the locality to the outsider" (225). But whereas Fanon gives violence an almost mystical role in forming communal identity,[41] Said's emphasis is instead on reimagining geography, the *poiesis* of giving places their names.

A second key task of cultural decolonization, according to Said's analysis, is the process of re-creating and reclaiming a communal history, and in this respect Said again builds on Fanon's *Wretched of the Earth*. Much as the empire has expropriated the land, displacing native names, myths, and attachments, so too it has marginalized and disfigured indigenous narratives of the past, subordinating them to "the Western powers' monumental histories" (215).[42] Decolonization involves reimagining and reintegrating a mythical and historical past for the indigenous community, repopulating that past with a different cast of heroes, heroines, and perhaps even villains. Among anglophone poets, Yeats revives mythical Irish histories, Ramanujan traces the fantastically heterogeneous elements of the past that circulate through him and other South Asians, and Goodison thinks back through her family history to her enslaved great-grandmother:

a guinea woman
wide eyes turning
the corners of her face
could see behind her. . . .[43]

To enable the emergence of freshly reconstituted communities and national identities, decolonization thus requires nothing less than the imaginative remaking of both space — the once expropriated topography — and time — the collective historical experience of that place.

This account of cultural decolonization may well seem to overlap substantially with nativist and nationalist views; indeed, Said is loath to underestimate the importance of such formations in resisting colonialism and breaking the grip of empire. Yet at the heart of his description of cultural decolonization, Said also emphasizes, perhaps surprisingly, a transnational humanism — what he calls the pervasive and "noticeable pull away from separatist nationalism toward a more integrative view of human community and human liberation" (216). Echoing elsewhere Fanon's critique of nationalist "separatism and mock autonomy" as internalizing colonialist oppression, Said cites Césaire's *Cahier* to urge that postcolonial independence be considered no more than a starting point on the way to the "real work": "nothing less than the reintegration of all those people and cultures, once confined and reduced to peripheral status, with the rest of the human race."[44] Decolonization is in Said's view crippled, narrow, and insufficient, unless it "refuses the short-term blandishments of separatist and triumphalist slogans in favor of the larger, more generous human realities of community *among* cultures, peoples, and societies" (217, emphasis in original). Decolonization requires both the actual and the poetic repossession of a land and a history, but to succeed, this struggle must be recognized as participating in a larger, transnational, human struggle, which crosses boundaries among colonized populations and even between colonizer and colonized. Said witheringly condemns "remaining trapped in the emotional self-indulgence of celebrating one's own identity" (229). Despite the many postcolonial critiques of a humanist "universalism" as cloaking Eurocentrism, by Chinua Achebe and others, despite localist anxieties that it risks effacing cultural specificity, Said asserts that transnational secular humanism is crucial to "a more generous and pluralistic vision of the world" (230). He exhorts us to "acknowledge the massively knotted and complex histories of special but nevertheless overlapping and interconnected experiences" (32).

This knotting can be theorized along two vectors. First is the horizontal vector of connections and affiliations among different decolonizing groups: fundamental to cultural and political resistance are reciprocal recognitions and affiliations across cultural and national lines (196), and such recognitions can be considered at base "poetic" insofar as they involve the figurative construction of likeness, of similitude. Indeed, the work of many postcolonial poets bears out Said's analysis. Walcott horizontally identifies the ambivalent Caribbean cultural struggle against empire with that of the Irish — in his words, "colonials with the same kind of problems that existed in the Caribbean. They were the niggers of Britain" (ten years before the more famous remark of Roddy Doyle's character in *The Commitments*, "The Irish are the niggers of Europe").[45] So too Goodison builds poems around the transnational affinities between South African and Jamaican feminisms; Agha Shahid Ali sees the mirror image of South American atrocities and disappearances in those of Kashmir;[46] and, as we have seen, Harrison identifies the blackness of his working-class boots with Césaire's negritude.

Second, Said accentuates the vertical entanglements between colonizer and colonized, which are so extensive that their cultures, histories, realities are ultimately inseparable. As seen in chapter 5, poets such as Ali, Brathwaite, Soyinka, Goodison, and Okigbo redeploy core modernist strategies — translocalism, mythical syncretism, heteroglossia, apocalypticism — for their decolonizing struggles against local cultural hegemonies. Mocking "tribalism" and other identitarian views that require, for example, "Arabs to read Arab books, use Arab methods, and the like," Said approvingly cites the view of one of his intellectual heroes, C. L. R. James, that "Beethoven belongs as much to West Indians as he does to Germans, since his music is now part of the human heritage" (xxv).

As we might expect from the terms of his praise for Darwish, when Said discusses particular instances of the literature of decolonization, he shies away from patriotic huzzah, and he avoids placing some writers on the side of heroic and revolutionary resistance, while viewing others as its antithesis. His most extended discussion of a "poet of decolonization" is hesitant and conflicted. Said's Yeats sometimes leans more in the "nativist" and "nationalist" direction, his early work standing "at a threshold it cannot cross," even his later work stopping "short of imagining full political liberation" (234, 238). At other times Yeats is hailed for his cross-national affinities with other poets of decolonization — Tagore, Senghor, Césaire, Darwish, Neruda — and seems to exemplify, especially in his later work, a movement "beyond national consciousness" toward a fuller, transnational conception of "liberation" (230). Yeats's ambivalently decolonizing work, according to this reading, cannot be limited either to nativism or to its supposed antithesis.[47]

Said is sometimes caricatured as a shrilly one-dimensional and partisan writer, but as a theorist of decolonizing cultural resistance, the reverse is true. The complexity of his thinking becomes all the more evident when we compare it with other critical statements on the poetry of decolonization, unmentioned by Said. According to the authors of the influential *Toward the Decolonization of African Literature*, again a useful point of reference, the task of cultural decolonization is to throw off all European influences and paradigms, "to end all foreign domination of African culture, to systematically destroy all encrustations of colonial and slave mentality."[48] Chinweizu and his coauthors condemn poets such as Soyinka, J. P. Clark, and the early Okigbo for having "assiduously aped" European models, importing foreign imagery, diction, forms, and attitudes (163, 170). At the same time, they praise poets such as Okot p'Bitek, Kofi Awoonor, and the later Okigbo for using authentic African imagery, genres, and models (195), and thus helping to build a distinctive African national consciousness, based in "the separate and autonomous status of African literature," purged of foreign contaminants (10). For Said, by contrast, cross-cultural affiliations and identifications are central to the poetry of decolonization. When he writes of Césaire, for example, he claims that the core of the poet's work is not the *ressentiment* of an overzealous nativism but "affectionate contention" with Western precursors.[49] Citing Fanon's warning that nativist resistance risks replicating the old colonial order in reverse, Said states: "The dangers of chauvinism and xenophobia ('Africa for the Africans') are very real. It is best when Caliban sees his own history as an aspect of the history of *all* subjugated men and women, and comprehends the complex truth of his own social and historical situation."[50]

Another important book on the subject, frequently cited in earlier chapters, Brathwaite's *History of the Voice* more subtly attacks assimilated writers for retarding cultural decolonization, while hailing nativist writers for advancing it. Poets who have been unfaithful to West Indian forms and experience include Claude McKay, one of whose sonnets "could have been written by a European," George Campbell, whose ode lacks "any unique element in terms of the Caribbean environment," and even Louise Bennett, whose Creole poetry uses a "Scots tune" for rhythm.[51] Although Brathwaite argues that a poetry of decolonization must be rooted in native rhythms and the local environment, he offers, ironically, cogent evidence for an alternative view when he cites, as discussed in chapter 5 above, the decisive influence of T. S. Eliot's recorded voice in awakening West Indian poets like himself to their own Caribbean speech rhythms.[52] By this measure, colonial importation and literary decolonization, instead of being steps in a linear movement toward liberation, are entangled and even inextricable. Said, who in *Culture and Imperialism* openly adapts Eliot's model of the pastness and yet presence of the past from "Tradition and the Individual Talent," writes that "to ignore or otherwise discount the overlapping experience of Westerners and Orientals, the interdependence of cultural terrains in which colonizer and colonized co-existed and battled each other through projections as well as rival geographies, narratives, and histories, is to miss what is essential about the world in the past century."[53]

Said's cross-national, cross-cultural, cross-hemispheric vision of decolonization thus helps illuminate the ambivalences and hybrid texture of postcolonial poetry. Walcott, for example, can rage at England's Renaissance writers as "Ancestral murderers and poets," attack them for their complicity in an empire guilty of "the abuse / Of ignorance by Bible and by sword," while also recognizing "That Albion too was once / A colony like ours."[54] Similarly, in "The Stranglehold of English Lit.," the Malawian poet Felix Mnthali launches an angry critique of a canonical British novelist, anticipating Said's more nuanced reading of her in *Culture and Imperialism*:

> Your elegance of deceit,
> Jane Austen,
> lulled the sons and daughters
> of the dispossessed
> into a calf-love
> with irony and satire
> around imaginary people.[55]

Slavery "made Jane Austen's people / wealthy beyond compare!" but, from Mnthali's perspective, Austen's sly fiction has blinded modern Africans to the ravages of empire. In attacking Austen, however, Mnthali's poem draws on a more recent European paradigm — the agonistic, modernist apostrophe to a dead canonical writer, such as Pound's to the "detested," "pig-headed" Whitman in "A Pact."[56] Like Walcott's lyric, Mnthali's Janus-faced poem instances the often resistive relation of postcolonial poets to writers seen as cultural agents of British imperial expansion and, as seen in chapter 5, their more affiliative, if still revisionary, relationship with modernist poets — Pound, Eliot, Yeats — whose ambivalent response to the earlier British canon helps enable their own.

Further, Said's transnationalist view can help us understand and embrace a wide range of poets of decolonization, whether nativists or cosmopolitans; whether writers in Standard English or writers in creoles, pidgins, and local vernaculars; whether decolonizers of genre, meter, and form or decolonizers of historical and political content. "The extraordinary formal precision and virtuosity of these poems," said Said of *The Country without a Post Office*, "as well as their often searing imagery, derive from Agha Shahid Ali's responses to Kashmir's agony. But this is poetry whose appeal is universal, its voice unerringly eloquent."[57] Like many other poets of decolonization, Ali wrote in both Western forms, such as the canzone and free verse, and in non-Western forms, such as the ghazal, one of which was dedicated to Said and used Darwish's phrase "after the last sky" in an epigraph and within the poem. This ghazal, "By Exiles," ends each couplet with the *radif* or refrain "by exiles" and intricately interconnects Said's fate as a Palestinian exile with Ali's as a Kashmiri exile — "two destinies at last reconciled by exiles." In the echoic repetitions of this form, the exilic destinies of a poet and a critic from two embattled, non-self-governing homelands are made to rhyme. The image of a shawl seen draped on Said's piano — "By the Hudson lies Kashmir, brought from Palestine" — punningly enacts a double geographic displacement (Kashmir is surreally translocated to New York via Palestine) and serves as the intimate basis for this ghazal's linkage of Kashmiri and Palestinian exile.[58] The personal and the public interlock, as Said indicates of Darwish; in other poems, Ali achieves what Said calls, also in reference to Darwish, "a harassing amalgam of poetry and collective memory," Ali mourning both the military ravages of Kashmir and the more private agonies of a lover's or a mother's death. Western and non-Western forms, public and private griefs, converge when Ali closes "Lenox Hill" with the defiant claim that his private mourning for the loss of his mother exceeds even Kashmir's collective, national grief — a distinction that further intertwines the two kinds of bereavement:

> For compared to my grief for you, what are those of Kashmir,
> and what (I close the ledger) are the griefs of the universe
> when I remember you — beyond all accounting — O my mother?[59]

"Lenox Hill" hypnotically circulates its rhyme words in accordance with the dictates of the Italian form of the canzone, yet this sonic and verbal repetition also recalls Ali's use of the *radif* in his many poems following the conventions of the Urdu and Persian versions of the ghazal. An elegy, the poem invokes the Western tradition of poetic mourning, yet Ali also, as we've seen, habitually associated the elegiac with Urdu poetry and culture — even as he also found it in Eliot's *Waste Land*. "Partly because of empire," Said writes, "all cultures are involved in one another; none is single and pure, all are hybrid, heterogeneous, extraordinarily differentiated, and unmonolithic" (xxv).

Said's nuanced attention to the "hybrid" and "heterogeneous" texture of literary works, instead of being a distraction from the geopolitical analysis for which he is best known — not poems but politics, not culture but coercion — made him all the more alert to the brutal simplifications of imperial policy. Take, for example, this prescient statement on American self-deception in *Culture and Imperialism*, written more than a decade before the U.S.-led invasion of Iraq. The U.S. government's supposedly well-intentioned schemes to "make the world safe for democracy," "especially in the Middle East," never succeed, Said states, "because they trap the planners in more illusions of omnipotence and misleading self-satisfaction (as in Vietnam), and because by their very nature they falsify the evidence."[60] In the posthumously published *Humanism and Democratic Criticism*, Said cites Cavafy's famous poem about how an empire needs "barbarians" to construct its identity and legitimacy, even if this requires the illusory deformation of reality: "the regretful last line of Cavafy's splendid poem 'Waiting for the Barbarians,' suggests, in its lapidary irony, how useful a hostile Other is in such circumstances — 'they were, those people, a kind of solution.'"[61] Regrettably, some recent policymakers — far from recognizing that "all cultures are involved in one another," "hybrid, heterogeneous," "unmonolithic" — have split the world into civilization and barbarism, terrorists and democratizers, here and over there. We are reminded of what is torn and shredded by such ideological machinery when we explore, with Said's guidance, the subtly interwoven and ineluctably cross-cultural fabric of the poetry of decolonization.

* * *

While enormously promising at mid-twentieth century, decolonization is far from a finished process. As indicated by poets such as Bennett, Okot, and Walcott, native regimes have perpetuated a held-over colonialism within many Third World nations. For poets such as Linton Kwesi Johnson, an internal colonization of immigrant communities persists within Britain, where non-European peoples often face a version of the economic and racial barriers that divided European colonial territories. And global corporate neocolonialism has held in place enormous economic imbalances between "developed" nations and much of the "developing" world. Decolonization has certainly fallen short of the changes resonantly proclaimed by the UN — the end of colonial "subjugation, domination and exploitation"; yet the ending of direct

European rule in many parts of the world, the withdrawal of armies and district commissioners, and the reclamation of lands once occupied and cultural resources once denigrated and suppressed under colonialism should not be cynically dismissed. Decolonization is incomplete, but it began with national and transnational resistance to direct foreign domination, the transfer of sovereignty from European powers, and the sublime eruption of multiple nationalities, cultures, identities. Keenly aware of the limitations of nationalism as a salvific response to colonialism, poets have nevertheless participated vigorously in the momentous process of decolonization. Working along vertical and horizontal axes of transnational affiliation, they have renamed and recharted both native spaces and centers of metropolitan power, have satirically wrestled with pseudo-decolonization that perpetuates the imperial status quo, and have articulated emergent postcolonized identities and their own vexed relations to these collective formations. This is not to say that literary decolonization has been able to lift forever the yoke of European influences and attitudes, as advocated by the authors of *Toward the Decolonization of African Literature*;[62] indeed, the continuing transnational interrelations between colonizer and once colonized — both cultural and material — complicate the teleology embedded in the very concept of decolonization and render improbable any final decolonization of the mind.[63] Yet poetry helps remind us that decolonization is not only a political and military process but also an imaginative one — an enunciation of new possibilities and collectivities, new names and identities, new structures of thought and feeling. Just as the imposition of British poems and novels on subaltern peoples played a role in colonization, both at home and abroad, so too the imaginative labor of articulating an experience and a world after independence — in its sameness to and difference from what came before — continues to play a part in decolonization. If decolonization seems a diminished thing, it would be all the more so without the rich self-divisions and split affiliations, the imaginative exuberance and bracing skepticism, the cross-cultural forms and transnational solidarities of postcolonial poetry.

CHAPTER 8

POETRY AND
THE TRANSLOCAL:
BLACKENING BRITAIN

"Wherever I hang me knickers — that's my home," declares the Guy-anese British poet Grace Nichols. Immersed in the sensory present of London and yet vividly remembering her former life in the Carib-bean, she gives utterance to a diasporic sensibility, "divided to de ocean / Divided to de bone." Her poem enacts these split affinities in code-switching between Guyanese Creole ("where I belaang") and Standard English ("my home") and shuttling imagistically between the Caribbe-an's "humming-bird splendour" and London's "misty greyness."[1] In mod-ern and contemporary poetry studies, place is sometimes conceived as indefinite and abstract: modernist poetry, as we've recalled, can be un-derstood as arising out of collisions between tradition and moderniza-tion. At the same time, regionally defined poetries — for example, the poetry of Northern Ireland or the New York school — are often seen as springing from the soil of a specific location. Yet neither the Aeolian model of poetry as airborne and placeless nor the Antaean model of po-etry as drawing strength from a particular earthly plot can adequately explain the poetry of geographic and cultural displacement — the trans-national poetry of multiple "positionings," in Stuart Hall's term.[2] Hav-ing considered the poetic repercussions of global modernity and decol-onization in chapters 6 and 7, I conclude by narrowing the focus to a specific body of poetry — namely, black British poetry as it reconceives widely disparate geocultural spaces and histories in relation to one an-other. The poetry of the African diaspora in Britain, I argue, is neither homebound nor homeless, neither rooted nor rootless, but, in James Clifford's words, both "rooted and routed in particular landscapes, re-gional and interregional networks."[3] Like other postcolonial, diasporic, and migrant poetries, black British poetry gives expression and shape to a cross-geographic experience, enjambed between the (post)colonies and the Western metropole.

"The Western metropole must confront its postcolonial history," writes Homi Bhabha, "told by its influx of postwar migrants and refugees."[4] On June 21, 1948, the arrival of 492 West Indians aboard the *Empire Windrush* at Tilbury Docks, near London, began a large-scale immigration by peoples of African (and later Asian) descent into Britain. These migrant British subjects, most of them in search of economic and educational opportunities, were permitted to enter "the mother country" as citizens by the 1948 British Nationality Act, many more arriving after 1952, when the McCarran-Walter Act restricted West Indian immigration into the United States. In 1962, the Commonwealth Immigrants Act held immigration from the Commonwealth into England to thirty thousand a year, and the 1968 Commonwealth Immigrants Act limited it further to British citizens of British (that is, white) family origin. Still, by then the demographic change was substantial and irreversible. By 1970, nearly half a million West Indians had settled in Britain, and by 1991, British citizens of color made up just under 5.5 percent of the total population.[5]

How has the poetry of African Caribbean and African migrants and their children represented "the mother country"? How has it both absorbed and contested colonially disseminated images of an ideal England? And how has it imaginatively mediated between the writers' former or ancestral lands and the English metropolis? These are among the questions that will animate this chapter's readings of a handful of prominent poems and songs written early in the twentieth century by the Jamaican Claude McKay; at mid-century by the Jamaican Louise Bennett, the Trinidadian Lord Kitchener, and the Nigerian Wole Soyinka; and in the late twentieth and early twenty-first century by the Anglo-Jamaican Linton Kwesi Johnson, the Anglo-Guyanese Grace Nichols, and the Anglo-Nigerian Bernardine Evaristo. Because poetry lives in its nuances and luminous particulars, this small but heterogeneous sampling allows close analysis, though many of the ideas pursued here also bear on the work of Una Marson, Derek Walcott, Kamau Brathwaite, Edward Markham, John Agard, David Dabydeen, Jean Binta Breeze, Benjamin Zephaniah, Fred D'Aguiar, Jackie Kay, and Patience Agbabi, among other notable poets. The designation "black British" has often been used to include Asian and other British peoples of non-European origin — usage that would have covered even my Persian grandfather, who immigrated to Britain in the 1920s and there met my English grandmother. But this chapter, reflecting the more recent circumscription of the term, focuses on poets with African Caribbean and African backgrounds, who have played a crucial role in the early and sustained blackening of British poetry.[6]

1.

By disseminating across the colonies the phantasmal space "England," the British Empire helped legitimize its domination of other, putatively uncivilized spaces. Poets of non-European backgrounds have had to grapple especially with the glorious "London" of monuments and palaces as the quintessence of English civilization.[7] In so doing, they have reconceived the site from which many of the empire's rulers, militaries, and missionaries once set sail. Though often "located" in London, their poems are "translocal" in that they see the metropolis afresh through the lenses of nonmetropolitan history, language, and power, and shuttle across and unsettle imperial hierarchies of center and periphery, mother country and colonial offspring, North and South. In short, they dislocate the local into translocation. Interleaving European and non-European cultures, histories, and topographies, these poems are based on what Stuart Hall calls "unstable points of identification and suture"; "diaspora identities" are defined "by the recognition of a necessary heterogeneity and diversity; by a conception of 'identity' which lives with and through, not despite, difference; by *hybridity*."[8]

Near the beginning of the twentieth century, well before the mass postcolonial migrations to Britain after World War II, a young West Indian poet embarked on an imaginary voyage to the empire's chimerical capital, some years before he actually traveled to London. At first blush, Claude McKay's "Old England" (1912) seems to bow to London's symbolic force as synecdoche for the empire's glorious sights, monuments, and history. Elsewhere in *Songs of Jamaica* (1912) and *Constab Ballads* (1912), two volumes of poetry written in Jamaican English, McKay more obviously wrestles with British governance in Jamaica—the courts, the police, the colonial administrators. Here the speaker professes a yearning to walk London's streets and averts his gaze from the fact that "de homeland England" has ruled and exploited Jamaica and other Caribbean colonies for hundreds of years.[9] The word "conquer" in the poem's first line, instead of referring to Jamaica's colonial history, signifies lifelong entrapment within colonial desire: "I've a longin' in me dept's of heart dat I can conquer not, / 'Tis a wish dat I've been havin' from since

I could form a t'o't." Similarly, the words "beat" and "roar" are used to describe not the Middle Passage but ocean waves during the journey to England, the final leg of the triangular route by which the speaker's enslaved ancestors were brought to the Caribbean. Unlike later, black British poems more adequate to Paul Gilroy's concept of the "black Atlantic"—African diasporic culture haunted by the memory of slavery—McKay's lyric seems to whitewash the Atlantic.[10] Imagining himself at Saint Paul's Cathedral listening to the "massive organ soun'," the speaker surrenders to the imperial sublime: "I would ope me mout' wid wonder." Stylistically, his light Creole and British ballad meter (seven-stress lines that combine ballad's alternating four- and three-beat lines) also pay deference to imperial norms.

Yet even this early twentieth-century imaginative journey, despite what Kamau Brathwaite calls its "literary colonialism" and "primordial (?) anglicanism," affords murmurs of a postcolonial critique, born of cross-geocultural contact and friction.[11] Although the speaker gushes over the "solemn sacred beauty" of London's tourist sites, what he first sees and mentions are "de fact'ry chimneys pourin' smoke" and "matches-children" passing by. Looking upon London from the vantage point of a preindustrial Jamaica, he notes casualties of industrial modernity, such as the girl who freezes to death on New Year's Eve, in both Hans Christian Andersen's short story "The Little Match-Seller" and William McGonagall's poem "The Little Match Girl." Although planning to visit Saint Paul's and the City Temple, McKay's speaker feels they house but the "relics of old fait'," as spaces "where de old fait' is a wreck" ("wreck" ironically echoing "relics"). And although he pays homage to "Missis Queen, Victoria de Good," under whose reign slaves were freed in the West Indies, his description of royal British power is far from flattering: each monarch passes on "when all de vanity is done." While he pays tribute to London's poetic, musical, and architectural beauty—above all, poetry by "de great souls buried" in Poets' Corner of Westminster Abbey—McKay is also alert to the contradictions between the imperial capital's aesthetics and underlying inequities, and he identifies the economic, religious, and political underpinnings of British colonialism. When McKay physically traveled to England and lived in London, from 1919 to 1921, his experience of English racial prejudice shocked and disenchanted him, as he indicates in A Long Way from Home (1937). Although "Old England" is far more sanguine, even this early, self-divided poem both idealizes London and defamiliarizes it from the viewpoint of a British colony, fingering tensions that will emerge ever more clearly in later poets' remappings of metropolitan space.

Nearly half a century later, McKay's foremost Jamaican heir, Louise Bennett, presents not one person's imaginative journey but the mass migration into England that began in 1948. Bennett witnessed Britain's demographic change firsthand, having lived in Britain just before and just after the first influx of West Indians, when from 1945 to 1947 she attended the Royal Academy of Dramatic Art in London and from 1950 to 1953 acted in British theaters and worked on a special Caribbean program for the BBC. In the early 1950s, between one thousand and three thousand colonial migrants were entering Britain each year, and by the time she published "Colonization in Reverse" in 1957, more than forty thousand a year were arriving.[12] Although migrants of African descent had lived in Britain since antiquity, this postwar migration began England's transformation into a more thoroughly multiracial nation, as West Indians, deflected from the United States, flocked to England to fill the postwar demand for labor:

> By de hundred, by de tousan,
> From country an from town,
> By de ship-load, by de plane-load,
> Jamaica is Englan boun.[13]

Impeded by caesurae in the first and third lines, then released in the second and fourth, the syntax and rhythms of Bennett's ballad stanza enact the onward tumbling rush of this great migration. Relishing the irony that "Jamaica people colonizin / Englan in reverse," Bennett's poem wryly overlays the northward migration atop centuries of southbound colonization, while colonizing in reverse Britain's ballad stanza and its language of colonization.

Unlike McKay's awed, if subtly critical, visitor, who opens his "mout' wid wonder," Bennett's immigrants "box bread / Out a English people mout"; and her poem's ebullient tone, Creole diction, and wordplay could be said to snatch poetry out of the mouths of the English. Instead of traveling to England like McKay's voyager in search of venerable aesthetic glories, these migrants are attracted by the prospect of material gain, though some, such as Bennett's dole-kept couch-potato Jane, merely exploit Britain's largesse. Bennett excised her unflattering portrait of a welfare cheat when she performed the poem in 1980s London; once a shrewd self-critique, it had come uncomfortably close to

racist British depictions of immigrants of Caribbean origin — views stridently espoused and legitimized by politicians such as Enoch Powell in
the 1960s and 1970s.[14] Indeed, the intensification of such hostilities first
became apparent the year after the poem's publication, when whites attacked blacks in the 1958 "race riots" in Nottingham and Notting Hill.

2.

Among other poetic sites in which criss-crossed imaginings of London — both imperial and subtropical — were negotiated at mid-century
was calypso, "the first popular music transported directly from the West
Indies," in Stuart Hall's words, which included the vocal music initially
recorded in 1950s Britain on the Melodisc label and circulated transatlantically.[15] Derived from Trinidadian Carnival, calypso songs were
topical and often satiric, wittily commenting on politics, race, sex, and
other matters of the moment. They marked for West Indians, according
to Brathwaite, "the first major change in consciousness," a "folk" poetry
that departed from English formal, literary, and phonetic norms instilled
by a colonial education.[16] In London, the songs proved as responsive to
the local as in Trinidad, while also extending to encompass Ghanaian
independence, African American jazz, and Jamaican hurricanes. Even
without these overtly international, black Atlantic excursions, British
calypso is translocal, encountering the metropolis through African Caribbean deprivations and aspirations, sung in West Indian English to an
exuberant, duple-metered rhythm.

The most celebrated calypsonian in 1950s Britain, the Trinidadian
Lord Kitchener composed "London Is the Place for Me" on board the
Empire Windrush en route to England in 1948 and performed it on arrival at Tilbury Docks. The recorded song, book-ended by a rendering
of Big Ben's chimes on the piano, idealizes London as a most welcom-
ing social space:

> To live in London you really comfortable,
> Because the English people are very much sociable.
> They take you here and they take you there,
> And they make you feel like a millionaire.[17]

Even this reverent song reconceives the imperial center through the aesthetics and viewpoint of the West Indies. The utopian hope that the English would embrace West Indians and guide them around the "mother

country" creolizes England culturally by attributing to it a Caribbean hospitality, while also creolizing it linguistically (e.g., the West Indian ellipsis in "you really comfortable") and musically (a buoyantly syncopated sound new to London). Anglocentric but with a destabilizing difference, the song exemplifies what Bhabha calls "the *ambivalence* of mimicry": its vision of an ideal London "is almost the same, *but not quite*" as through English eyes.[18] Kitchener imagines spaces such as Shaftesbury Avenue as free, open, and permeable, intimating this view musically by buoyant percussive rhythms and clarinet solos, and poetically by his use of polysyndeton and long-vowel rhyme: "There you will laugh and talk and enjoy the breeze, / And admire the beautiful sceneries." Drawing on calypso's carnivalesque inversion of power structures, Kitchener declares at the end: "I have every comfort and every sport, / And my residence is at Hampton Court." These final lines humorously unveil the song's fantastical premise: surely "life in London is really magnificent" when one ascends to royal status, but of course it was in Brixton, not in Hampton Court, that black Britons settled. True, some West Indian immigrants prospered in England, including the popular Kitchener, at least until rock and roll sent him back to Trinidad in the early 1960s. But since racial prejudices, social hierarchies, and spatial strictures typically limited the prospects of the new black Britons, Kitchener, performing and recording this song in 1950s England, sang an egalitarian standard against which to measure these inequities.

In contrast to "London Is the Place for Me," Kitchener's "My Landlady's Too Rude" (1956) details the black British scrabble to survive discriminatory housing conditions. Hampton Court is replaced by a cramped, underfurnished, overpriced rental flat, and generous English hosts are supplanted by a mean-spirited, money-grubbing landlady, "worse than the landlord from Trinidad." Threatening and badgering, spying and persecuting, she nosily intrudes at all hours of the night, posts signs restricting visitors, provides inadequate hot water and bedding, and cares nothing about her tenant save her weekly demand — the refrain sardonically intoned by the chorus: "Mister give me me rent." Empire and colony seem to have been relocated and internalized within the metropole. Hapless, embattled, querulous, Kitchener's tone, accentuated by the twanging guitar solos, bears little resemblance to his earlier jubilance. In the similarly disillusioned "If You're Not White You're Black," Kitchener belies myths of easy congress and interracial permeability: in race-bound Britain, any attempt to blur racial lines is doomed to fail, whether you socialize with whites, put on airs, adopt a

Cambridge accent, or even, in one of Kitchener's funniest rhymes, "You use all sorts of Vaseline / To make out you a European." Yet both Kitchener's utopian and dystopian songs reenvision London translocally, reconsidering the urban ideal circulated in the West Indies and then reimported into Britain.

During this period, when for the first time large numbers of African Caribbean migrants were bringing their Londons of the mind into direct contact with Londons of daily life, expressions of reverence for the mother country often exist in poetry and song alongside, and jostle with, other impulses. Young Tiger, another calypsonian from Trinidad, gazes "rapturously" at the sublimely global yet minutely local spectacle of a multinational procession in "I Was There (At the Coronation)"—that of Queen Elizabeth II in 1953. Taking up a position the night before at Marble Arch and tenaciously holding it in the cold "like a young creole," or tough West Indian, he creolizes the heart of the empire by his physical presence. His response to the queen ("really divine") and the Duke of Edinburgh ("dignified and neat") may seem fawning, but his deep-toned refrain casts his relation to them in a language of equivalence: "She was there. / I was there"; "He was there. / I was there." Syntactic parallelism and deictis horizontally reconfigure the relation of sovereign to colonial subject. "Mix Up Matrimony" by *Windrush*-voyager Lord Beginner, a courageously utopian exaltation of racial mixture, also uses mirroring poetic devices such as epanalepsis and insistent rhyme to criss-cross the color line: mixed couples were once a rarity, but now lovers, realizing that a "race is a race," are choosing partners of every background and kind. "Marriage is a fixing / And the races are mixing," Beginner proclaims, advising in his refrain, as he claims preachers do, "Please cooperate / And amalgamate." Calling for the full miscegenation of Britain, which would leave it looking ethnically more like the West Indies, this song, like British calypso more generally, enacts in its music, diction, intonation, and racial politics an aesthetic version of the hybridization it gleefully hymns.

As sometimes indicated by these and other songs and poems, many immigrants to Britain from the late 1940s into the 1960s, believing the mother country would receive them as full-fledged British subjects, instead found themselves unwelcome. Most black British immigrants were forced to take jobs below their skill level, and widespread housing discrimination was reflected in signs such as "Rooms to Let: No dogs, no coloureds."[19] But if the non-slum spaces of London were often marked off against black immigrants, translocal texts, such as

Wole Soyinka's 1960 poem "Telephone Conversation," were vehicles by which to question, erode, even overrun these boundaries. Written just a few years after Kitchener's London songs, Soyinka's poem still more boldly confronts the racial delimitation of urban English space. From 1954 to 1960, Soyinka had lived in Britain, attending the University of Leeds on an undergraduate scholarship and working as a play reader, actor, and director with the Royal Court Theatre in London. In his dramatic poem, an English landlady asks her prospective African tenant about his skin color: "HOW DARK?" and "ARE YOU LIGHT / OR VERY DARK?"[20] His black body the object of interrogation, the African — trapped, panicked — feels pressed in upon by quintessentially red British sights, including a double-decker bus that suggestively bears down on the black road: "Red booth. Red pillar-box. Red double-tiered / Omnibus squelching tar. It *was* real!" When his painterly self-description as a man whose skin is "West African sepia" baffles the landlady, he switches to a hair color terminology she is more likely to understand:

'Facially, I am brunette, but madam, you should see
'The rest of me. Palm of my hand, soles of my feet
'Are a peroxide blonde. Friction, caused —
'Foolishly madam — by sitting down, has turned
'My bottom raven black — . . . .

Pushing the logic of racist attention to skin color so hard that he unmakes it, the speaker deconstructs racial binarism, revealing his skin to display a spectrum of colors, from "peroxide blonde" to "brunette" to "raven black." Ironically, it is his sitting down, presumably to nurture an intellect that the landlady's views on English racial superiority cannot acknowledge, that has blackened his bottom. His final plea to the literally and figuratively unseeing landlady — "Wouldn't you rather / See for yourself?" — straddles the line between taunt (wouldn't you rather see my black bottom for yourself?) and plaintive appeal (wouldn't you rather encounter my full humanity for yourself?). Giving the lie to any such racial gauge of human value, the poem satirically contrasts her befuddled single-mindedness with the African's mental agility, with his metaphorical, syntactic, and tonal resourcefulness, and with the poet's deft redeployment of English literary forms, such as blank verse and Jacobean verbal extravagance. Though formally couched, this counterassault marks a turning point in the poetic relations between migrant and metropole, away from accommodation and toward more active resistance.

3.

Whether utopian or dystopian, musical or literary, Creole or Standard English, African or African Caribbean, these postcolonial reimaginings dislocate England from itself by casting it into translocational conversation with its "others." From early to mid-century, the poetic reverse colonizers of England took, as we have seen, an ever more skeptical, if conflicted and often humorous, approach to the empire's capital, where racist, xenophobic, and imperialist attitudes frequently greeted migrants of color. By the 1970s and '80s, after British politicians and neofascists had fomented racist attitudes, and also after black Britons inspired by decolonization, the civil rights movement, and Black Power had mobilized resistance, poets of African descent in England began to reimagine the colonial metropolis still more assertively. In the reggae or dub poetry of Linton Kwesi Johnson, who arrived from Jamaica at the age of eleven and as a teenager joined a London-based wing of the Black Panthers, the internal colonization of immigrants and their descendants within Britain meets with fierce resistance. His verse contrasts sharply with that of McKay and the calypsonians. Drawing on reggae, mento, ska, and other African Caribbean oral music and on the militancy and musicality of the U.S. Black Arts movement's poetry, Johnson declares, in a 1970s poem (cited in chapter 7), "Inglan is a Bitch."[21] Dispensing with calypso's more standardized diction and light-hearted rhythms, he drops the grinning mask to assail imperial norms. He often performs to reggae's heavy, four-beat rhythm and transcribes the orality of his Jamaican Creole, or patois, to destandardize even standard words (e.g., "fyah" for "fire"). As John Agard indicates in another poem of the period, "Listen Mr Oxford don" (1985), the attack on the empire's literary, grammatical, and orthographic norms — "mugging de Queen's English," "inciting rhyme to riot," "assault / on de Oxford dictionary" — is central to black British poetry's effort to reconfigure the politics of race in 1970s and '80s Britain.[22]

Whereas tourist sites define London in McKay's and Kitchener's verse, Johnson situates his more defiant poetry primarily in African Caribbean neighborhoods in and around Brixton. "New Craas Massakah,"[23] for example, commemorates the 1981 death by fire of thirteen young Afro-Britons attending a sixteenth birthday party in New

Cross, near Brixton, under circumstances that led many to suspect a racially motivated arson attack; the incident sparked riots in Brixton and other immigrant communities across Britain a few months later.[24] In this poem, London is no longer a place where peoples of African descent expect to be warmly welcomed: they know they may be brutally attacked ("wi did know seh it couda happn"). But the event itself is no less traumatic for that knowledge, and the poem's refrain repeatedly replays the transformation of a dance party — captured in loosely anapestic cadences and sensual description — into fiery death, as if to make sense of the senseless:

first di comin
an di goin
in and out af di pawty

di dubbin
an di rubbin
an di rackin to di riddim

di dancin
an di scankin
an di pawty really swingin

den di crash
an di bang
an di flames staat fi trang

di heat
an di smoke
an di people staat fi choke

di screamin
an di cryin
an di diein in di fyah[25]

To mark the tear in narrative time ("first," "den"), the poem switches from syncopated rhythms and gerundive feminine rhymes (*dubbin/rubbin*, *dancin/scankin/swingin*) to abrupt, bottled, monosyllabic masculine rhymes (*bang/trang*, *smoke/choke*). Because the partygoers are at first doing what the poet is doing — "di dubbin / an di rubbin / an di rackin to di riddim"—the poem intimately enmeshes the speaker in the African Caribbean London he describes. It switches back and forth between these songlike refrains—short-lined and intensely rhythmic—and more prosaic, longer-lined, retrospective ruminations on the event's implications and the people's collective response, described in apocalyptic terms: "how di whole a black Britn did rack wid rage / how di whole a black Britn tun a fiery red." Britain is not a white space into which migrants of color struggle to insert themselves: as indicated by Johnson's aggressively antitraditional style, "black Britn" is a distinct social sphere, claimed by the poem's audience-and-author connecting "we" and defined in stark contrast to white Englishness.

Despite the rage and grief firing Johnson's and much other poetry of the time, the trajectory of postcolonial and black British poetry cannot be reduced to a linear movement from passive acquiescence to militant defiance. Even in the 1970s and '80s, some black British poets favored humor as a strategy for creolizing the heart of the empire. In *The Fat Black Woman's Poems* (1984), Grace Nichols, who grew up in Guyana and moved to the United Kingdom in her twenties, playfully reimagines England's capital with a fat Caribbean woman translocated to its center. Celebrated and affirmed, this migrant body inverts metropolitan norms of femininity: "Beauty / is a fat black woman."[26] But when the fat Caribbean woman goes shopping for clothes in London, she discovers—amid the cold, thin, white mannequins—that "the choice is lean // Nothing much beyond size 14," in a characteristically humorous rhyme.[27] Despite these restrictions, a London where a fat black woman has shopped and taken the tube, has loved and cursed, has longed for tropical fruit and danced the limbo, is a changed space, nonhierarchically intermapped with Caribbean spaces once ruled by Britannia.

Stereoscopically conjoining the British metropolis and the West Indian experience, Nichols often uses translocal conjunctures to contrastive effect. A man from a Caribbean island wakes daily "to the sound of blue surf / in his head," hearing the crash of waves and the clamor of seabirds in his groggy morning state, only to discover that here in London he wakes "to surge of wheels / to dull North Circular roar."[28] Although "Island Man" is built around geocultural difference, its pivot—the phrase "his small emerald island"—encompasses not only his sun-basking Caribbean island but also the rainy island where he now lives. In another poem of translocal juncture and friction, "Tropical Death," the fat black woman contrasts Northern European "quiet," "polite," abbreviated rites of mourning with the loud "bawl" and "sleepless droning" night after night at a tropical wake.²⁹ Although the woman situates herself within metropolitan England, she decries death "in some North Europe far/forlorn"—a region that can be described as "far" only if her psychic attachment to the tropics is so strong that she still imaginatively dwells there. Geography is thus, in this diasporic poem and others in *The Fat Black Woman's Poems*, transhemipherically pleated. In Nichols's later poetry, some of these contrasts blur. The speaker of "Wherever I Hang" misses her sunny Caribbean home amid life in London but is gradually shedding her "calypso ways"—visits without warning or not waiting in line—a shedding she performs linguistically in shifting from "me home" in the poem's first line to "my home" in its last. Nichols's speaker shows herself to be at "home" in both Creole and Standard English and thus both in the West Indies and in England. She is, in Bhabha's phrase, a "vernacular cosmopolitan," "moving in-between cultural traditions and revealing hybrid forms of life and art that do not have a prior existence within the discrete world of any single culture or language."³⁰ She exists in between cultures that, by virtue of such intercultural negotiation, become "intricately and intimately interleaved with one another."³¹

4.

Bernardine Evaristo's novel-in-verse *The Emperor's Babe* (2001) startlingly traces this vernacular cosmopolitanism eighteen centuries back to Roman-occupied Londinium in the year 211. Like other black British poets, Evaristo knows that to reimagine the metropole is to reimagine its history, and, indeed, the epigraph to her book is Oscar Wilde's statement, "The one duty we owe history is to rewrite it."³² Countering views of Britain as racially homogeneous before 1948, recovering ancient precursors for post-*Windrush* black Britons, Evaristo represents Britain as already richly multicultural in ancient times, as exemplified by her African-born protagonist Zuleika. She and Evaristo's other characters have come to Londinium from Africa, Asia, and Europe and thus speak a vibrant mixture of languages and dialects, including Latin (*"How nunc brown vacca"* [204]), cockney ("wot 'adn't mastered the lingua Latin proper" [176]), Scots ("Mammy an Faither were chieftens, ye ken" [57]), Jamaican Creole ("likkle"), and urban slang ("innit," "wassup"). Looking backward and forward in time, the poem's heteroglossia is emblematic of ancient and contemporary creolization in the British Isles. Unlike the migrant writers discussed so far, Evaristo was born in London, to an

English mother and a Nigerian father; like Zadie Smith and other recent black British writers, she takes a cross-racial, polyglot England to be fundamental and is less interested than some poets of the 1970s and '80s in championing a separate black experience. Literary classicism is as much hers as jive talk; the third century is as alive to her as the urban present; slave owning is as much her past as enslavement.

Delving backward in time, Evaristo's poem humorously provincializes London, representing it not as the energizing hub of empire but, in the Roman scheme of things, as peripheral and marginal, an underdeveloped backwater to the imperial center. Energetically translocational and transhistorical, Evaristo's verse novel plays on the ironic differences in the layers of its topographical palimpsest. London's past implicitly jangles against its present in descriptions of "the wheatfields of Hyde Park" (218), "the wild sloping grassland of Mayfair" (217), "the jungle of Notting Hill" (158), "the mud flats of Southwark" (236), "the forests of Greenwich" (163), and the "impenetrable swamps of Thamesmead" (169). Fields, grassland, jungle, mud flats, forests, swamps — London oddly comes to resemble the far-off outposts that it later subjugates, defamiliarized through the vocabulary later associated with the Third World. Zuleika's aristocratic husband talks of making London "my far-western base" (15), and her Sudanese immigrant parents had "heard / of Londinium, way out in the wild west" (26). Instead of being the center against which east and west are measured, London is a place on the fringe. Evaristo puts flesh on Walcott's declaration in "Ruins of a Great House" "That Albion too was once / A colony like ours."[33] In so doing, she destabilizes the relations between colonizer and colonized, center and periphery, showing them to be temporary, historically contingent, hence subject to strange and unexpected reversals.

If London is paradoxically made to seem akin to territories conquered by Britain, then the colonization of Britain has two antithetical resonances in *The Emperor's Babe,* as indicated by the emperor Septimius Severus's imperial plans. According to various orators, the emperor "would surely one day visit Britannia, / this far-flung northern outpost of empire" and violently quell all resisters, "colonize their terra firma, make them speak // our lingo, impose taxes, yay! And thus / bring Pax Romana to this our blessed island."[34] Indeed, the historical Severus died at York trying to subdue Britain. In Evaristo's book, the language of forcible occupation, linguistic imposition, and economic exploitation is eerily made to anticipate Britain's subsequent colonization of much of the world in its supposed quest of a Pax Britannia. Yet because the emperor is African-born and speaks with a strong *"Leeebyan"* (i.e., African) accent (53), this colonization of Britain is also made to look ahead to the reverse colonization of Britain by its former empire. When Zuleika's parents decide to migrate to Londinium, this migration sounds uncannily like that of many later colonial subjects to London: "a sea to cross, a man / could make millions of denarii" (26). As in Louise Bennett's "Colonization in Reverse," which jauntily overlays British colonization and the economically motivated counter-"colonization" by Third World migrants, Evaristo develops a humorously stereoscopic vision of London as both colonizing and colonized. *The Emperor's Babe* thus casts doubt on sharply drawn moral and political boundaries between centers and peripheries — positionalities that unpredictably reverse, blur, or merge over time.

In rewriting the past, Evaristo vigorously reimagines the present. Her representation of London's past as racially mixed, ethnically mongrelized, linguistically creolized — long before the post-1948 migration — is also, inescapably and funnily, a representation of its multicultural present. A Gallic brothel owner offensively propositions Zuleika: "I 'ave a Woppy, a Chinky, a Honky, a Paki, / a Gingery, an Araby, now all I need is a Blackie" (45). Seamen sport tattoos that span a similarly transcultural spectrum of libidinal investments:

> *I Luv Mei Ling*
>   *Zindiwe IV Me*
>   *Yazmin, Mi Numero Uno Futuo*
>   *Doris: Mi & Tu: IV Ever II Gether* (104)

In both lists, the Eurocentric norm — "Honky," *"Doris"* — assumes a diminished part as but one color in a multicultural rainbow. Sex and love are not the only causes of transnational mixing. Economic globalization is shown to go back millennia. In his shops, Zuleika's father employs "all sorts" — "a Syrian, Tunisian, Jew, Persian, // hopefuls just off the olive barge from Gaul" (4). All of these peoples bring different dialects and languages into London and into the verse novel, such as "pidgin-Latin" of Zuleika's father (57), the "strange pidgin" of Zuleika's Caledonian slaves (57), and Severus's "thick African accent" (144). Ancient music and poetry, too, are represented as thoroughly intercultural. The band Nu Vox features

Little Rex on antelope drums,
Prince Mahmood III on the lyre,

Puff Daddy Fabius on the tuba
and Madd Marcia on caterwauling vocals. . . . (117)

In these proper names and instruments, Evaristo locates ancient precedents for today's multicultural London and knowingly winks as she does so. In contrast to the identity-founding gestures of Johnson's and other 1970s and '80s poems, identity in this and many later black British poems "becomes a noun of process," as cultural theorist Paul Gilroy writes more generally. "Its openness provides a timely alternative to the clockwork solidarity based on outmoded notions of 'race' and disputed ideas of national belonging."[35]

The self-reflexivity in Evaristo's construction of a multicultural past intensifies when Zuleika, hoping to show off her achievement as versifier, organizes a poetry reading that degenerates into a chaotic orgy before she can take the stage. The star of the show turns out to be a precursor of today's identity poet, Hrrathaghervood, "the very real Authentic Pict"[36] who fulminates against his oppressors and enemies, taking in the audience with "the exotic charm of his Pictish patois" (196), and "how brilliantly he *did* Anger" (196). Making love to him, Zuleika's transvestite friend Venus discovers that "he's not a real Pict" at all but was born south of the Antonine Wall (212). So much for his performance of collective victimization, his bearing of past scars and speaking in a "posh accent" (213). Evaristo satirizes the exoticization of subaltern identity in black British poetry, similarly mocking a poet named "Manumittio X" whose every poem ends "*I just wanna be free*" (198). Through the lens of the ancient past, Evaristo skeptically judges such monoculturalist performed identities to be self-serving and self-essentializing.

But agonizingly divided poetic identities are also shown to rely on hypostatized identity constructs. Questions of poetry and identity come to a head when, with scarcely anyone listening, a dispirited Zuleika recites her poem "Identity Crisis: Who is she?" Parodying the cross-cutting allegiances and vexed self-questionings of Derek Walcott's "A Far Cry from Africa" ("I who am poisoned with the blood of both, / Where shall I turn, divided to the vein?") and the poem with which we began this book, "The Schooner *Flight*" ("I have Dutch, nigger, and English in me, / and either I'm nobody, or I'm a nation"),[37] Zuleika asks,

Do I feel a sense of lack
Because I am swarthy?
Or am I just a groovy chick
Living in the lap of luxury?
Am I a slave or a slave-owner?
Am I a Londinio or a Nubian?[38]

As if the poem were not self-deflating enough by virtue of its diction
("*swarthy*," "*groovy chick*") and its mechanical syntactic parallels, the "un-
controllable yawns" of her only auditor further ironize this self-pitying
precursor to the tragic "mulatto/a poem."

Even so, Evaristo also highlights in this set piece the complexity of
Zuleika's identity within the racial-power-gender nexus of Londinium,
making use of the social fabric knotted into the form of the verse novel
to contextualize identities and historicize experiences. Zuleika is a slave
owner living in luxury, but as a woman trapped within her husband's
house, forbidden to leave, ultimately poisoned for her sexual infidelity,
she also has some things in common with her powerless slaves. At some
level, she is like any other Roman citizen ("Civis Romana sum" [54]), her
citizenship defined in part by her typically Roman fear that "to leave //
the city wall was to risk unknown horrors" (242). To her surprise, she
finds herself speaking and "sounding like every magniloqua / matrona I'd
ever had the misfortune to meet" (204). Indeed, as a slave-owning aristo-
crat, she treats her Caledonian slaves like chained animals. Interpellated
within Roman institutions of power, she declares to her slaves, even as
she feels some sympathetic correspondences between their wounds and
hers: "'You will have your manumission when I die.' // Where did that
come from?" (60). Still, her sense of being spoken through and by power
also indicates her difference from other elite Romans. Feeling "all this
is mine but I am a stranger / here" (33), Zuleika knows that the power
speaking through her body is hers, yet alien.

When Zuleika attends a Greenwich amphitheater called The Conqueror ("embodying // the very ethos of empire: to conquer," 168), she
is horrified by the gruesome spectacle of lions eating pregnant women
("surrounded by bloody meat on the bone, / clumps of hair sticking out
of mouths," 179). Despite this alienation, she feels increasingly at one
with the crowds as the emotional intensity of witnessing gratuitous
slaughter builds. "None of us is guilty / each of us took part," she summarizes, in an aphorism that blurs the hard lines that in some black British poetry once separated victimizer from victimized, colonizer from

colonized (184). "What had I become? But a composite," affirms Zuleika, her character's complicities and ambiguities complicating the racial and power divide that may have once seemed intractable (204).

*   *   *

Just as British imperialism reversed the Londinium-era migration of Africans and other peoples into Britain, so too the displacement of post–World War II non-Europeans into England turned around centuries of human movement from the British Isles into the colonies. These demographic flows brought cultural flows. If the empire once transplanted Wordsworth's lyric daffodils and Anglocentric representations of London from England into the tropics, where no real daffodils grew, poets of the African diaspora in Britain have borne black bodies and creoles, calypso and reggae, to London, along with idealistic, skeptical, and humorous attitudes toward the imperial center. At different times, their emphasis has been more accommodating or more resistant, but whether angry or idealistic or both, whether in the form of lyric, calypso, dramatic verse, reggae performance, or novel-in-verse, poetry has been a multifaceted resource by which migrants to Britain and their children have enacted their creolization of Britain and Britain's creolization of themselves. Black British and postcolonial writers have used the musical, tonal, and imagistic richness of poetry to help produce and reproduce themselves, to reimagine themselves as both "rooted and routed" in and through London to Africa and the Caribbean — living and writing, like other transnational poets, between styles, between histories, between hemispheres.

NOTES

1. Poetry, Modernity, and Globalization

1. Derek Walcott, "The Schooner *Flight*," *Collected Poems, 1948–1984* (New York: Farrar, Straus and Giroux, 1986), 346.

2. James Anthony Froude, *The English in the West Indies; or, The Bow of Ulysses* (1887; New York: Charles Scribner's Sons, 1897), 347.

3. Homer, *The Odyssey*, book 9; Emily Dickinson, "I'm Nobody, Who Are You?" (#288), *The Poems of Emily Dickinson*, ed. Thomas H. Johnson (Cambridge, MA: Belknap–Harvard University Press, 1963), 206–7; Sylvia Plath, "Tulips," *The Collected Poems*, ed. Ted Hughes (New York: Harper and Row, 1981), 160–62.

4. Walcott, *Collected Poems*, 350.

5. I use the term "transnational" for poems and other cultural works that cross national borders, whether stylistically, topographically, intellectually, or otherwise; hence this book's emphasis on some exemplary clusters of transnational poetry. Some poems are more obviously "transnational" than others in this sense of the term — say, T. S. Eliot's more than William Carlos Williams's, or Christopher Okigbo's more than Okot p'Bitek's. I also apply the term to the hermeneutic lens through which the nation-traversing qualities of poetry can be revealed and examined. In this second sense, a still wider array of different kinds of poetry, whether more locally or globally oriented, can be revealed as bearing transnational traces and filiations. My use of "transnational" is meant to highlight flows and affiliations not among static national entities, as sometimes suggested by "international," but across the borders of nation-states, regions, and cultures. Even so, there are no perfect terms: contextual uses of "transnational," "international," "global," "planetary," "cosmopolitan," "cross-cultural," "world," and related terms with various shades of meaning are meant to bring out different aspects of the extranational poetics I seek to explore. The similarly imperfect vocabulary I use for cross-cultural processes includes "hybridization," "creolization," "interculturation," "indigenization," and so forth; I define and defend "hybridity" in Jahan Ramazani, *The Hybrid Muse: Postcolonial Poetry in English* (Chicago: University of Chicago Press, 2001), 179–84.

6. T. S. Eliot, "Little Gidding," *Four Quartets* (London: Faber and Faber, 1959), 53.

7. Mina Loy, "Anglo-Mongrels and the Rose," *The Lost Lunar Baedeker*, ed. Roger L. Conover (Highlands: Jargon Society, 1982), 109–72.

8. Langston Hughes, "Theme for English B," *The Collected Poems of Langston Hughes*, ed. Arnold Rampersad and David Roessel (New York: Knopf, 1997), 410.

9. Bernardine Evaristo, *The Emperor's Babe* (London: Penguin, 2001), 201.

10. Marilyn Chin, "How I Got That Name," *The Phoenix Gone, the Terrace Empty* (Minneapolis: Milkweed Editions, 1994), 16–18.

11. Martha Nussbaum, *Cultivating Humanity* (Cambridge, MA: Harvard University Press, 1997), 85–112. For two contrastive views on fiction and cosmopolitanism, see Rebecca Walkowitz, *Cosmopolitan Style: Modernism beyond the Nation* (New York: Columbia University Press, 2006), and Timothy Brennan, *At Home in the World: Cosmopolitanism Now* (Cambridge, MA: Harvard University Press, 1997). See also the narrative emphasis in two special issues published in the same year: "Anglophone Literature and Global Culture," *South Atlantic Quarterly* 100, no. 3 (2001) and "Globalizing Literary Study," *PMLA* 116, no. 1 (2001).

12. T. S. Eliot, "The Social Function of Poetry," *On Poetry and Poets* (New York: Farrar, Straus and Giroux, 1957), 8. W. H. Auden, "Writing," *The Dyer's Hand and Other Essays* (New York: Vintage–Random House, 1968), 23.

13. Robert Eric Livingston, "Glocal Knowledges: Agency and Place in Literary Studies," *PMLA* 116 (2001): 151, 150. Livingston insightfully engages theories of globalization.

14. M. M. Bakhtin, *The Dialogic Imagination: Four Essays*, ed. Michael Holquist, trans. Caryl Emerson and Michael Holquist (Austin: University of Texas Press, 1981), 272–73.

15. See Michael Eskin, "Bakhtin on Poetry," *Poetics Today* 21, no. 2 (2000): 384–86.

16. Bakhtin, *Dialogic Imagination*, 358.

17. Christopher Okigbo, *Heavensgate* (1962), rpt. and rev. in *Labyrinths, with Path of Thunder* (London: Heinemann, 1971), 3. Critical collections on Okigbo's poetry include *Critical Essays on Christopher Okigbo*, ed. Uzoma Esonwanne (New York: G. K. Hall, 2000), and *Critical Perspectives on Christopher Okigbo*, ed. Donatus Ibe Nwoga (Washington, DC: Three Continents Press, 1984). Two useful introductory essays are Robert Fraser, "The Achievement of Christopher Okigbo," *West African Poetry* (Cambridge: Cambridge University Press, 1986), 104–37, and David Richards, "The Poetry of Christopher Okigbo," in *Debating Twentieth-Century Literature, 1900–1960*, ed. Richard Danson Brown and Suman Gupta (New York: Routledge, 2005). I have also benefited from an unpublished manuscript by Chukwuma Azuonye, "Christopher Okigbo at Work: Towards a Pilot Study and Critical Edition of His Previously Unpublished Poems, 1957–1967."

18. "Give ear to my words, O Lord. . . . Hearken unto the voice of my cry" (Psalm 5) and "Out of the depths have I cried unto thee, O Lord" (Psalm 130).

19. Okigbo, *Heavensgate*, 3 (ellipsis in original).

20. Okigbo, "Introduction," *Labyrinths*, xi.

21. Marjory Whitelaw, "Interview with Christopher Okigbo" (1965/1970), rpt. in *Critical Essays on Christopher Okigbo*, ed. Esonwanne, 55.

22. Anthony Giddens, *The Consequences of Modernity* (Stanford: Stanford University Press, 1990), 63, 177.

23. Giddens, *Consequences,* 63–64.

24. Okot p'Bitek, *"Song of Lawino" and "Song of Ocol"* (London: Heinemann, 1984), 41.

25. Okot, *"Song of Lawino,"* 45.

26. See the chapter on the poem in Ramazani, *Hybrid Muse*, 141–78.

27. Derek Walcott, *Omeros* (New York: Farrar, Straus and Giroux, 1990), 289.

28. Walcott, *Omeros,* 3, 4.

29. Homi K. Bhabha, *The Location of Culture* (New York: Routledge, 1994), 218.

30. Andreas Huyssen, "Geographies of Modernism in a Globalizing World," in *Geographies of Modernism: Literatures, Cultures, Spaces,* ed. Peter Brooker and Andrew Thacker (New York: Routledge, 2005), 9, 13.

31. Fredric Jameson, "Notes on Globalization as a Philosophical Issue," in *The Cultures of Globalization,* ed. Jameson and Masao Miyoshi (Durham: Duke University Press, 1998), 63, and *A Singular Modernity* (New York: Verso, 2002).

32. The word "destroyed" is from Jameson, "Notes," 63; Stephen Owen, "World Poetry," *New Republic*, November 19, 1990, 28–32; see also his "Stepping Forward and Back: Issues and Possibilities for 'World' Poetry," *Modern Philology* 100 (2003): 532–48.

33. Chinweizu, Onwuchekwa Jemie, and Ihechukwu Madubuike, *Toward the Decolonization of African Literature* (Washington, DC: Howard University Press, 1983).

34. David Held et al., *Global Transformations: Politics, Economics, and Culture* (Stanford: Stanford University Press, 1999), 2.

35. Stuart Hall, "The Local and the Global: Globalization and Ethnicity," *Culture, Globalization and the World-System,* ed. Anthony D. King (London: Macmillan, 1991), 34.

36. Arjun Appadurai, *Modernity at Large: Cultural Dimensions of Globalization* (Minneapolis: University of Minnesota Press, 1996), 32.

37. Ulf Hannerz, "Scenarios for Peripheral Cultures," and Janet Abu-Lughod, "Going beyond Global Babble," both in *Culture, Globalization and the World-System,* ed. King, 124, 133.

38. Revathi Krishnaswamy, "Postcolonial and Globalization Studies: Connections, Conflicts, Complicities," in *The Postcolonial and the Global*, ed. Revathi Krishnaswamy and John C. Hawley (Minneapolis: University of Minnesota Press, 2008), 11. On the overlap and difference between the humanities-based (postcolonial) and social science-based (globalization) areas of study, see also Simon Gikandi, "Globalization and the Claims of Postcoloniality," *South Atlantic Quarterly* 100, no. 3 (2001): 627–58.

39. Kwame Anthony Appiah, *Cosmopolitanism: Ethics in a World of Strangers* (New York: Norton, 2006), 101, 103. See Appiah's description of how foreign television shows are absorbed within local cultural contexts that change their meanings (108–11), by contrast with Jameson's account of the global "Americanization or standardi-

zation of culture, the destruction of local differences," as instanced by the effects of exported American television programs (Jameson, "Notes," 57–58, 70).

40. Édouard Glissant, *Caribbean Discourse: Selected Essays*, trans. J. Michael Dash (Charlottesville: University Press of Virginia, 1989), 14–26; *Le Discours antillais* (Paris: Éditions du Seuil, 1981), 28–36. Dash translates these terms "diversion" and "reversion."

41. On Pound's early belief that East Asian poetic imagery was presentational, nonallusive, and free of convention, see Ming Xie, *Ezra Pound and the Appropriation of Chinese Poetry* (New York: Garland, 1999), 41, 69, 223. For a defense of Pound's Chinese "misunderstanding" and "misreading" as generative, see Xiaomei Chen, "Rediscovering Ezra Pound: A Postcolonial 'Misreading' of a Western Legacy," *Paideuma* 22, nos. 2–3 (1994): 81–105, among other critical works on the subject usefully surveyed in Eric Hayot, "Critical Dreams: Orientalism, Modernism, and the Meaning of Pound's China," *Twentieth-Century Literature* 45, no. 4 (1999): 511–33.

42. Edward [Kamau] Brathwaite, "Calypso," *The Arrivants* (New York: Oxford University Press, 1973), 49. On Pound's American ambitions, see Josephine Nock-Hee Park, *Apparitions of Asia: Modernist Form and Asian American Poetics* (New York: Oxford University Press, 2008), 23–56.

43. Kirsten Peterson, "Okot p'Bitek: Interview," *Kunapipi* 1, no. 1 (1979): 89; Bernth Lindfors, "An Interview with Okot p'Bitek," *World Literature Written in English* 16 (1977): 282–83.

44. Edward W. Said, *Orientalism* (New York: Pantheon, 1978).

45. See, for example, Mariana Torgovnik, *Gone Primitive: Savage Intellects, Modern Lives* (Chicago: University of Chicago Press, 1990), and Edward Marx, *The Idea of a Colony: Cross-Culturalism in Modern Poetry* (Toronto: University of Toronto Press, 2004). See also Marjorie Perloff's critique of such approaches in "Tolerance and Taboo: Modernist Primitivisms and Postmodernist Pieties," in *Prehistories of the Future: The Primitivist Project and the Culture of Modernism*, ed. Elazar Barkan and Ronald Bush (Stanford University Press, 1995), 339–54.

46. Dennis Porter, "*Orientalism* and Its Problems," rpt. in *Colonial Discourse and Post-Colonial Theory: A Reader*, ed. Patrick Williams and Laura Chrisman (New York: Columbia University Press, 1994), 153–54, 155.

47. For a thoughtful critique of Picasso's African appropriations, see Simon Gikandi, "Picasso, Africa, and the Schemata of Difference," *Modernism/Modernity* 10, no. 3 (2003): 455–80.

48. Samuel P. Huntington, *The Clash of Civilizations and the Remaking of World Order* (New York: Simon and Schuster, 1996).

49. Pascale Casanova, "Literature as a World," *New Left Review* 31 (2005): 81.

50. Gikandi, "Globalization and the Claims of Postcoloniality," 632.

51. My use of the term "translocal (not global or universal)" is indebted to James Clifford, *Routes: Travel and Translation in the Late Twentieth Century* (Cambridge, MA: Harvard University Press, 1997), 7.

52. Giddens, *Consequences*, 64.

53. Fredric Jameson, "Modernism and Imperialism," in Jameson et al., *Nationalism, Colonialism, and Literature* (Minneapolis: University of Minnesota Press, 1990), 51, 57. Despite this convergence between Jameson and Giddens, it should be noted that Jameson sees his Marxist framework as incompatible with Giddens's sociology of globalization and attacks Giddens as an "ideologue of 'modernity'" in *A Singular Modernity*, 11.

54. Jameson, "Modernism and Imperialism," 50, 52.

55. Les Murray, "The Powerline Incarnation," *Learning Human: Selected Poems* (New York: Farrar, Straus and Giroux, 2000), 20–21.

56. Louise Bennett, "South Parade Peddler," *Selected Poems*, ed. Mervyn Morris (Kingston: Sangster's Book Stores, 1983), 83–84.

57. Laura Doyle and Laura Winkiel, "Introduction: The Global Horizons of Modernism," in *Geomodernisms: Race, Modernism, Modernity*, ed. Doyle and Winkiel (Bloomington: Indiana University Press, 2005), 3. Among other useful essay collections seeking to open the "global horizons of modernism," see also *Geographies of Modernism*, ed. Brooker and Thacker; the special issue on "Modernism and Transnationalisms," ed. Simon Gikandi, of *Modernism/Modernity* 13, no. 3 (2006); and the forthcoming *Oxford Handbook of Global Modernisms*, ed. Mark Wollaeger (Oxford: Oxford University Press). In influential essays, Susan Stanford Friedman has been arguing for opening up modernism's period as well as spatial boundaries, including "Periodizing Modernism: Postcolonial Modernities and the Space/Time Borders of Modernist Studies," *Modernism/Modernity* 13, no. 3 (2006): 425–43; "Modernism in a Transnational Landscape: Spatial Poetics, Postcolonialism, and Gender in Césaire's *Cahier/Notebook* and Cha's *Dictée*," *Paideuma* 32, nos. 1–3 (2003): 39–74; and "Definitional Excursions: The Meanings of *Modern/Modernity/Modernism*," *Modernism/Modernity* 8, no. 3 (2001): 493–514. On modernism and globalization, see also Melba Cuddy-Keane, "Modernism, Geopolitics, Globalization," *Modernism/Modernity* 10, no. 3 (2003): 539–58. On the transnational turn in modernist studies, see Douglas Mao and Rebecca L. Walkowitz, "The New Modernist Studies," *PMLA* 123, no. 3 (2008): 737–48.

58. Lord Kitchener, "London Is the Place for Me," *London Is the Place for Me: Trinidadian Calypso in London, 1950–56*, compact disc (Honest Jons Records, 2002).

59. Bruce Robbins, "Comparative Cosmopolitanisms," in *Cosmopolitics: Thinking and Feeling beyond the Nation*, ed. Pheng Cheah and Robbins (Minneapolis: University of Minnesota Press, 1998), 250.

60. Hughes, "Theme for English B," *Collected Poems*, 409–10.

61. David Harvey, *The Condition of Postmodernity* (Oxford: Blackwell, 1989), 260–307.

62. W. H. Auden, "Prologue at Sixty," *Selected Poems: New Edition*, ed. Edward Mendelson (New York: Vintage–Random House, 1979), 286, and Derek Walcott, "The Fortunate Traveller," *Collected Poems*, 458.

63. Mike Featherstone, *Undoing Culture: Globalization, Postmodernism and Identity* (London: Sage, 1995), 92.

64. Seamus Heaney, "Alphabets," *The Haw Lantern* (New York: Farrar, Straus and Giroux, 1987), 3.

65. See Glissant, *Caribbean Discourse*, xii, 134–44; *Discours antillais*, 28–36.

66. Clifford, *Routes*, 36.

67. Heaney, "Alphabets," 3.

68. Gayatri Chakravorty Spivak, *Death of a Discipline* (New York: Columbia University Press, 2003), 73.

69. Spivak, *Death,* 72.

70. Held et al., *Global Transformations,* 2.

71. Bruce Robbins, "Actually Existing Cosmopolitanism," in *Cosmopolitics*, ed. Cheah and Robbins, 1, 2–3. On hyphenated world citizenship, see Mitchell Cohen, "Rooted Cosmopolitanism," in *Toward a Global Civil Society*, ed. Michael Walzer (Providence: Berghahn, 1995), 223–40.

72. See Gerard Delanty, *Citizenship in a Global Age* (Buckingham, UK: Open University Press, 2000), 5, 143, 145.

73. Li-Young Lee, "Persimmons," *Rose* (Brockport, NY: Boa Editions, 1986) 19.

74. Spivak, *Death,* 9; Jonathan Arac, "Anglo-Globalism?" *New Left Review* 16 (2002): 35–45. Yet while exhorting more immersion in the "languages of the global South" (languages, it should be noted, often also used in the global North), Spivak acknowledges that linguistic specificity often takes priority over the national: "The verbal text is jealous of its linguistic signature but impatient of national identity" (Spivak, *Death*, 9).

75. Joshua A. Fishman, "The New Linguistic Order," in *Globalization and the Challenges of a New Century*, ed. Patrick O'Meara, Howard Mehlinger, and Matthew Krain (Bloomington: Indiana University Press, 2000), 434–46.

76. See "Poetry and Other Englishes," ed. David Buuck and Juliana Spahr, *Boundary 2* 33, no. 2 (2006): 1–49; *Rotten English: A Literary Anthology*, ed. Dohra Ahmad (New York: Norton, 2007); and Rob Jackaman, *Broken English / Breaking English: A Study of Contemporary Poetries in English* (Madison, NJ: Farleigh Dickinson University Press, 2003).

77. Charles Baudelaire, "L'Invitation au voyage," *Les Fleurs du mal* (Paris: Librarie Larousse, 1959), 42–43.

78. Auden, "Writing," 32.

79. Wai Chee Dimock, *Through Other Continents: American Literature across Deep Time* (Princeton: Princeton University Press, 2006), 3.

80. Cf. Bakhtin's distinction between "intentional" and "organic" hybridity in *Dialogic Imagination*, 258–62.

81. T. S. Eliot, "Tradition and the Individual Talent," *Selected Prose of T. S. Eliot*, ed. Frank Kermode (New York: Farrar, Straus and Giroux, 1975), 39.

2. A Transnational Poetics

1. Gertrude Stein, "An American and France" (1936), *What Are Masterpieces* (1940; New York: Pitman Publishing, 1970), 61.

2. Étienne Balibar, "World Borders, Political Borders," trans. Erin M. Williams, *PMLA* 117, no.1 (2002): 76.

3. Benedict Anderson, *Imagined Communities: Reflections on the Origin and Spread of Nationalism* (London: New Left, 1983).

4. On the transnational poetic avant-garde, see *Assembling Alternatives: Reading Postmodern Poetries Transnationally*, ed. Romana Huk (Middletown, CT: Wesleyan University Press, 2003) and Charles Bernstein, "Poetics of the Americas," *Modernism/Modernity* 3, no.3 (1996): 1–23.

5. Werner Sollors, "Introduction: The Invention of Ethnicity," *The Invention of Ethnicity*, ed. Sollors (New York: Oxford University Press, 1989), xiii–xiv.

6. Edward W. Said, "Reflections on Exile," *Reflections on Exile and Other Essays* (Cambridge, MA: Harvard University Press, 2000), 173.

7. Raymond Williams, "Metropolitan Perceptions and the Emergence of Modernism," *The Politics of Modernism: Against the New Conformists* (London: Verso, 1989), 45.

8. Terry Eagleton, *Exiles and Émigrés: Studies in Modern Literature* (New York: Shocken, 1970), 15.

9. Ezra Pound, "The Renaissance," *The Literary Essays of Ezra Pound*, ed. T. S. Eliot (London: Faber and Faber, 1954), 214.

10. Susan Stewart, *Poetry and the Fate of the Senses* (Chicago: University of Chicago Press, 2002), 250.

11. Michael North, *Reading 1922: A Return to the Scene of the Modern* (New York: Oxford University Press, 1999), 15, 19. See North's analysis of literary modernism's cultural contexts of globalization.

12. This assessment of critical production is based on the critical bibliographies compiled for *The Norton Anthology of Modern and Contemporary Poetry*, 3rd ed., ed. Jahan Ramazani, Richard Ellmann, and Robert O'Clair, 2 vols. (New York: Norton, 2003). Most recently published anthologies in the field have been nation based; see, for example, the many fine anthologies of modern American poetry published since 2000, including *American Poetry: The Twentieth Century* (New York: Literary Classics of the United States, 2000), 2 vols.; *Anthology of Modern American Poetry*, ed. Cary Nelson (New York: Oxford University Press, 2000); *Modern American Poetry*, ed. Joseph Coulson, Peter Temes, and Jim Baldwin (Chicago: Great Books Foundation, 2002); *Twentieth-Century American Poetry*, ed. Dana Gioia, David Mason, and Meg Schoerke (New York: McGraw-Hill, 2004); *The New Anthology of American Poetry*, vol. 2: *Modernisms, 1900–1950*, ed. Steven Gould Axelrod, Camille Roman, and Thomas Travisano (New Brunswick: Rutgers University Press, 2005); and *The Oxford Book of American Poetry*, ed. David Lehman (New York: Oxford University Press, 2006). Transnational literary forums include the inherently cross-national field of postcolonial studies, the Modernist Studies Association, the journals *Modernism/Modernity* and *Twentieth-Century Literature*, and the collection of essays *Something We Have That They Don't: British and American Poetic Relations*, ed. Steve Clark and Mark Ford (Iowa City: University of Iowa Press, 2004). For a prescient critique of national literary classifications, see Reed Way Dasenbrock's "English Department Geography: Interpreting the MLA Bibliography," in *Pedagogy Is Politics: Literary Theory and Critical Teaching*, ed. Maria-Regina Kecht (Urbana: University of Illinois Press, 1992), 193–214.

13. Arjun Appadurai, *Modernity at Large: Cultural Dimensions of Globalization* (Minneapolis: University of Minnesota Press, 1996), 188.

14. Alex Davis and Lee M. Jenkins, "Locating Modernisms: An Overview," in *Locations of Literary Modernism: Region and Nation in British and American Modernist Poetry*, ed. Davis and Jenkins (Cambridge: Cambridge University Press, 2000), 3.

15. C. Barry Chabot, *Writers for the New Nation: American Literary Modernism* (Tuscaloosa: University of Alabama Press, 1997), 4, 10.

16. Angus Fletcher, *A New Theory for American Poetry: Democracy, the Environment, and the Future of the Imagination* (Cambridge, MA: Harvard University Press, 2004).

17. Walter Benn Michaels, *Our America: Nativism, Modernism, and Pluralism* (Durham: Duke University Press, 1995), 2.

18. Robert Crawford, *Devolving English Literature* (New York: Oxford University Press, 1992), 270. In 2000, the second edition was published by Edinburgh University Press. (Ensuing references to the first edition appear in text.) In a subsequent work, while arguing that modern poets construct themselves in association with particular territories, Crawford concedes that they create their "territorial voices" typically by looking abroad, and he acknowledges the "fluid" and "dialogic" nature of poetic identities; see *Identifying Poets: Self and Territory in Twentieth-Century Poetry* (Edinburgh: Edinburgh University Press, 1993), 13.

19. See Harish Trivedi, "'Ganga Was Sunken': T. S. Eliot's Use of India," in *The Fire and the Rose: New Essays on T. S. Eliot*, ed. Vinod Sena and Rajiva Verma (Delhi: Oxford University Press, 1992), 44–62. On Pound and China, see Eric Hayot, "Critical Dreams: Orientalism, Modernism, and the Meaning of Pound's China," *Twentieth-Century Literature* 45, no. 4 (1999): 511–33; Robert Kern, *Orientalism, Modernism, and the American Poem* (Cambridge: Cambridge University Press, 1996); and Zhaoming Qian, *Orientalism and Modernism: The Legacy of China in Pound and Williams* (Durham: Duke University Press, 1995), and *The Modernist Response to Chinese Art: Pound, Moore, Stevens* (Charlottesville: University of Virginia Press, 2003). On Eliot in transnational contexts, see Anita Patterson, *Race, American Literature and Transnational Modernisms* (Cambridge: Cambridge University Press, 2008), and *The International Reception of T. S. Eliot*, ed. Elisabeth Däumer and Shyamal Bagchee (New York: Continuum, 2007).

20. James Clifford, *Routes: Travel and Translation in the Late Twentieth Century* (Cambridge, MA: Harvard University Press, 1997), 19, 8, 27.

21. Clifford, *Routes*, 3.

22. See, e.g., Samuel P. Huntington's division of the world into discrete and conflictual civilizations (Western, Confucian, Islamic, and so forth) in *The Clash of Civilizations and the Remaking of World Order* (New York: Simon and Schuster, 1996).

23. On McKay's exclusion from the United States and the British colonies, including Jamaica, because of his Soviet "pilgrimage" and communist activities, see William J. Maxwell, "Introduction" to Claude McKay, *Complete Poems*, ed. Maxwell (Urbana: University of Illinois Press, 2004), xvi–xvii. In his "Global Poetics and State-Sponsored Transnationalism: A Reply to Jahan Ramazani," *American Literary History*

18, no. 2 (2006): 360–64, Maxwell cites McKay's political exclusion as the basis for the claim that such transnationalism is sponsored by the nation-state. While appreciating this irony, I would suggest that without modernity's accelerated mobility of ideas (communism) and transnational travel (a Jamaican in the Soviet Union), the issue of whether to exclude McKay and others like him would never have arisen.

24. Michael North, *The Dialect of Modernism* (New York: Oxford University Press, 1994), 100–16, and Bernstein, "Poetics of the Americas," 10–14. North delineates a "trap" (102), or double-bind, that befell Harlem Renaissance poets such as McKay and Jean Toomer: if they used dialect and oral genres, they met official verse culture's primitivist expectations; if they turned to Standard English or Euromodernism, they capitulated to dominant norms. See also the chapter on McKay's vernacular and Standard English poetry in Lee M. Jenkins, *The Language of Caribbean Poetry* (Gainesville: University Press of Florida, 2004), 13–67.

25. Claude McKay, "A Midnight Woman to the Bobby," *Complete Poems*, 51–52.

26. Walter Jekyll, Preface to Claude McKay, *Songs of Jamaica* (1912), rpt. in *The Dialect Poetry of Claude McKay*, ed. Wayne Cooper (Freeport, NY: Books for Libraries Press, 1972), 5.

27. Édouard Glissant, *Caribbean Discourse: Selected Essays*, trans. J. Michael Dash (Charlottesville: University Press of Virginia, 1989), 125; David Dabydeen, "On Not Being Milton: Nigger Talk in England Today," in *The State of the Language*, ed. Christopher Ricks and Leonard Michaels (London: Faber and Faber, 1990), 6, 11–12.

28. The dialogic framework of my reading is indebted to M. M. Bakhtin, *The Dialogic Imagination: Four Essays*, ed. Michael Holquist, trans. Caryl Emerson and Michael Holquist (Austin: University of Texas Press, 1981).

29. McKay, "Outcast," *Complete Poems*, 173.

30. McKay, "America," *Complete Poems*, 153.

31. Kamau Brathwaite, *History of the Voice: The Development of Nation Language in Anglophone Caribbean Poetry* (1984), rev. and rpt. in *Roots* (Ann Arbor: University of Michigan Press, 1993), 274 (the phrase does not appear in Brathwaite's 1984 text).

32. McKay, "If We Must Die," *Complete Poems*, 177–78. See Lee M. Jenkins, "'If We Must Die': Winston Churchill and Claude McKay," *Notes and Queries* 50, no. 3 (2003): 333–37.

33. Aihwa Ong, "Experiments with Freedom: Milieus of the Human," *American Literary History* 18, no. 2 (2006): 229–44. See also the critiques of transnationalism in *The Cultures of Globalization,* ed. Fredric Jameson and Masao Miyoshi (Durham: Duke University Press, 1998).

34. See Jahan Ramazani, *The Hybrid Muse: Postcolonial Poetry in English* (Chicago: University of Chicago Press, 2001), 21–48.

35. Mina Loy, "Anglo-Mongrels and the Rose," in *The Last Lunar Baedeker*, ed. Roger L. Conover (Highlands, NC: Jargon Society, 1982), 126. On the poem's hybridity, see Rachel Blau DuPlessis, *Genders, Races and Religious Cultures in Modern American Poetry, 1908–1934* (Cambridge: Cambridge University Press, 2001), 160–66, and

Marjorie Perloff, "English as a 'Second' Language: Mina Loy's *Anglo-Mongrels and the Rose*,'" in *Mina Loy: Woman and Poet*, ed. Maeera Shreiber and Keith Tuma (Orono, ME: National Poetry Foundation, 1998), 131–48.

36. D. H. Lawrence, "The Poetry of the Present," *Playboy,* nos. 4 and 5 (1919): 7–8. On Whitman's global influences, see *Walt Whitman and the World*, ed. Gay Wilson Allen and Ed Folsom (Iowa City: University of Iowa Press, 1995).

37. "D. H. Lawrence was the hero of these years," according to Robert Creeley. Cited by Robert Adamson in "Robert Creeley, 1926–2005," http://jacketmagazine .com/26/adam-creeley.html (accessed 22 January 2006).

38. H.D., *The Walls Do Not Fall, Collected Poems*, ed. Louis L. Martz (New York: New Directions, 1983), 509–11.

39. Laura (Riding) Jackson, "The Map of Places," *The Poems of Laura Riding* (1938; New York: Persea Books, 1980), 87.

40. W. H. Auden, "In Memory of W. B. Yeats," *Selected Poems: New Edition*, ed. Edward Mendelson (New York: Vintage–Random House, 1979), 80–83.

41. W. H. Auden, "Prologue at Sixty," *Selected Poems,* 284–87. On Auden as a "postnational" poet, see Nicholas Jenkins, "Writing 'Without Roots': Auden, Eliot, and Post-national Poetry," *Something We Have That They Don't,* 75–97.

42. William Carlos Williams, Prologue to *Kora in Hell: Improvisations* (Boston: Four Seas Company, 1920), 27, 26. On Williams's Puerto Rican heritage, see Julio Marzán, *The Spanish American Roots of William Carlos Williams* (Austin: University of Texas Press, 1994).

43. Ann Douglas, *Terrible Honesty: Mongrel Manhattan in the 1920s* (New York: Farrar, Straus and Giroux, 1995).

44. Williams, Prologue to *Kora in Hell*, 12.

45. See Gertrude Stein, "A Transatlantic Interview," *A Primer for the Gradual Understanding of Gertrude Stein*, ed. Robert Bartlett Haas (Los Angeles: Black Sparrow Press, 1971), 15–35.

46. *The New Princeton Encyclopedia of Poetry and Poetics*, 2nd ed., ed. Alex Preminger and T. V. F. Brogan (Princeton: Princeton University Press, 1993), 57.

47. *New Princeton Encyclopedia*, 350.

48. See Paul Giles, "American Literature in English Translation: Denise Levertov and Others," *PMLA* 119 (2004): 31–41.

49. Donald E. Pease, "National Narratives, Postnational Narration," *Modern Fiction Studies* 43, no. 1 (1997): 18.

50. See Philip Larkin, *Required Writing* (New York: Farrar, Straus and Giroux, 1983), 80–82, 286–98.

51. Charles Tomlinson, *The Poem as Initiation* (Hamilton, NY: Colgate University Press, 1968).

52. See Langdon Hammer, "The American Poetry of Thom Gunn and Geoffrey Hill," *Something We Have That They Don't,* 118–36.

53. See Aidan Wasley, "The 'Gay Apprentice': Auden, Ashbery, and a Portrait of the Artist as a Young Critic," *Contemporary Literature* 43, no. 4 (2002): 667–708, and

Bonnie Costello, "'A Whole Climate of Opinion': Auden's Influence on Bishop," in *Something We Have That They Don't*, 98–117.

54. Terence Brown, *Ireland: A Social and Cultural History, 1922 to the Present* (Ithaca: Cornell University Press, 1985), 54.

55. Praising him as "an Irish writer," Crawford dismisses the idea of Heaney as a "cosmopolitan" (*Devolving*, 292). David Lloyd accuses Heaney of Romantic reterritorialization; see "'Pap for the Dispossessed': Seamus Heaney and the Poetics of Identity" (1985), rpt. in *Seamus Heaney: A Collection of Critical Essays*, ed. Elmer Andrews (London: Macmillan, 1992), 95. For a contrasting view of Irish poetry, see Edna Longley, "'Atlantic's Premises': American Influences on Northern Irish Poetry in the 1960s," *Poetry and Posterity* (Highgreen, Tarset, Northumberland [UK]: Bloodaxe Books, 2000), 259–79. See also the transnational and cross-cultural paradigm developed in Cheryl Herr's *Critical Regionalism and Cultural Studies: From Ireland to the American Midwest* (Gainesville: University of Florida Press, 1996).

56. Seamus Heaney, "Bogland," *Poems, 1965–1975* (1980; New York: Noonday–Farrar, Straus and Giroux, 1988), 85–86.

57. Heaney, "The Tollund Man," *Poems*, 125–26.

58. Heaney, "Bog Queen," *Poems*, 187–89.

59. Richard Kearney, "Heaney and Homecoming," *Transitions: Narratives in Modern Irish Culture* (Dublin: Wolfhound Press, 1988), 101.

60. Seamus Heaney, "In Memoriam Francis Ledwidge," *Field Work* (1979; New York: Noonday–Farrar, Straus and Giroux, 1989), 59–60; *"Anything Can Happen": A Poem and Essay* (Dublin: TownHouse, 2004), 11; "Electric Light," *Electric Light* (New York: Farrar, Straus and Giroux, 2001), 96–98.

61. Paul Muldoon, "7, Middagh Street," *Poems, 1968–1998* (New York: Farrar, Straus and Giroux, 2001), 175–80. On exilic "transits" in Muldoon's poetry, see John Kerrigan, "Paul Muldoon's Transits: Muddling through after *Madoc*," in *Paul Muldoon: Critical Essays*, ed. Tim Kendall and Peter McDonald (Liverpool: Liverpool University Press, 2004), 125–49. On Muldoon's intermapping of Irish and Native American identities, see Omaar Hena, "Playing Indian / Disintegrating Irishness: Globalization and Cross-Cultural Identity in Paul Muldoon's 'Madoc; A Mystery,'" *Contemporary Literature* 49, no. 2 (2008).

62. Sigmund Freud, *Civilization and Its Discontents*, trans. and ed. James Strachey (New York: Norton, 1961), 61.

63. Paul Muldoon, "The Grand Conversation," *Moy Sand and Gravel* (New York: Farrar, Straus and Giroux, 2002), 45–46.

64. Eavan Boland, "Anorexic" and "Mise Eire," *An Origin like Water: Collected Poems, 1967–1987* (New York: Norton, 1988), 96–97, 156–57. See Victor Luftig, "'Something Will Happen to You Who Read': Adrienne Rich, Eavan Boland," *Irish University Review* 23, no. 1 (1993): 57–66.

65. Medbh McGuckian, "The Dream-Language of Fergus," *On Ballycastle Beach* (Oxford: Oxford University Press, 1988), 48–49.

66. Derek Mahon, "Afterlives," *Selected Poems* (New York: Penguin, 1991), 50–51.

67. See, for example, Chinweizu, Onwuchekwa Jemie, and Ihechukwu Madubuike, *Toward the Decolonization of African Literature* (Washington, DC: Howard University Press, 1983), 163, 259.

68. Derek Walcott, *Omeros* (New York: Farrar, Straus and Giroux, 1990), 3.

69. Louise Bennett, "Bans a Killin," *Selected Poems*, ed. Mervyn Morris (Kingston: Sangster's Book Stores, 1983), 4–5.

70. Melvin Tolson, "Mu," *"Harlem Gallery," and Other Poems*, ed. Raymond Nelson (Charlottesville: University Press of Virginia, 1999), 263.

71. On Baraka in cross-racial contexts, see Andrew Epstein, *Beautiful Enemies: Friendship and Postwar American Poetry* (Oxford: Oxford University Press, 2006).

72. George Oppen, "Psalm," *New Collected Poems,* ed. Michael Davidson (New York: New Directions, 2002), 99. On Jewish American poetry, see Norman Finkelstein, *Not One of Them in Place: Modern Poetry and Jewish American Identity* (Albany: State University of New York Press, 2001), and Maeera Y. Shreiber, *Singing in a Strange Land: A Jewish American Poetics* (Stanford: Stanford University Press, 2007).

73. Charles Bernstein, "The Lives of the Toll Takers," *Dark City* (Los Angeles: Sun and Moon Press, 1994), 23.

74. McKay, "Outcast," *Complete Poems,* 174.

75. Jean Toomer, "Portrait in Georgia" (1923), *Cane: A Norton Critical Edition*, ed. Darwin T. Turner (New York: Norton, 1988), 29.

76. Louis Zukofsky, "Poem Beginning 'The,'" *Complete Short Poetry* (Baltimore: Johns Hopkins University Press, 1991), 17.

77. Salman Rushdie, "In Good Faith," *Imaginary Homelands: Essays and Criticism 1981–1991* (London: Granta Books, 1991), 394.

78. T. S. Eliot, "Gerontion," *The Complete Poems and Plays of T. S. Eliot* (London: Faber and Faber, 1969), 38.

79. Meredith McGill, "Introduction: The Traffic in Poems," *The Traffic in Poems: Nineteenth-Century Poetry and Transatlantic Exchange*, ed. McGill (New Brunswick: Rutgers University Press, 2008), 2.

80. See A. O. Amoko, "The Problem with English Literature: Canonicity, Citizenship, and the Idea of Africa," *Research in African Literatures* 32, no. 4 (2001): 19–43, and Simon Gikandi, "Globalization and the Claims of Postcoloniality," *South Atlantic Quarterly* 100, no. 3 (2001): 627–58.

81. Edward W. Said, *Culture and Imperialism* (New York: Knopf, 1993), 331.

3. Traveling Poetry

1. Ezra Pound, Canto 81, *The Cantos of Ezra Pound* (New York: New Directions, 1972), 517.

2. Edward W. Said, "Traveling Theory," *The World, the Text, and the Critic* (Cambridge, MA: Harvard University Press, 1983), 226–47; James Clifford, "Traveling Cultures," *Routes: Travel and Translation in the Late Twentieth Century* (Cambridge, MA: Harvard University Press, 1997), 17–46.

3. Clifford, *Routes,* 39, 3, 27–28.

4. Robert von Hallberg, "Tourists," *American Poetry and Culture, 1945–1980* (Cambridge, MA: Harvard University Press, 1985), 62–92, and Jeffrey Gray, *Mastery's End: Travel and Postwar American Poetry* (Athens, GA: University of Georgia Press, 2005).

5. Pound, *Cantos,* 513.

6. W. H. Auden, "Introduction," *The Poet's Tongue,* ed. W. H. Auden and John Garrett (London: G. Bell and Sons, 1935), v–x.

7. Arjun Appadurai, *Modernity at Large: Cultural Dimensions of Globalization* (Minneapolis: University of Minnesota Press, 1996), 37.

8. Brian Musgrove, "Travel and Unsettlement: Freud on Vacation," in *Travel Writing and Empire: Postcolonial Theory in Transit,* ed. Steve Clark (London: Zed Books; New York: St. Martin's Press, 1999), 31. On the travel in travel writing, see the other essays in this collection and in *The Cambridge Companion to Travel Writing,* ed. Peter Hulme and Tim Youngs (Cambridge: Cambridge University Press, 2002).

9. Regarding this poem's self-consciousness about its literary tourism, see Sarah Brouillette, *Postcolonial Writers in the Global Literary Marketplace* (Basingstoke, UK: Palgrave, 2007), 33–40.

10. Frank O'Hara, "The Day Lady Died," *The Collected Poems of Frank O'Hara,* ed. Donald Allen (Berkeley: University of California Press, 1995), 325.

11. Mary Louise Pratt, *Imperial Eyes: Travel Writing and Transculturation* (New York: Routledge, 1992), 6–7.

12. W. B. Yeats, "Vacillation," *The Poems,* rev. ed., ed. Richard J. Finneran, vol. 1 of *The Collected Works of W. B. Yeats,* ed. Finneran and George Mills Harper (New York: Macmillan, 1989), 249–53.

13. Melvin B. Tolson, *"Harlem Gallery," and Other Poems,* ed. Raymond Nelson (Charlottesville: University Press of Virginia, 1999), 279.

14. Derek Walcott, *Omeros* (New York: Farrar, Straus and Giroux, 1990), 75.

15. Wallace Stevens, "Bantams in Pine-Woods," *The Collected Poems* (New York: Random House, 1982), 75–76. See Ann Mikkelson, "'Fat! Fat! Fat!'—Wallace Stevens's Figurations of Masculinity," *Journal of Modern Literature* 27, no. 1 (2003): 106–13, and Rachel Blau DuPlessis, *Genders, Races and Religious Cultures in Modern American Poetry, 1908–1934* (Cambridge: Cambridge University Press, 2001), 95–97, which adds another intercultural subtext by arguing that the poem responds to the threat of Vachel Lindsay's racial impersonation in "The Congo."

16. Thomas Hardy, "Drummer Hodge," *The Complete Poetical Works of Thomas Hardy,* ed. Samuel Hynes, 5 vols. (Oxford: Clarendon Press, 1982–85), 1:122.

17. Rupert Brooke, "The Soldier," *The Collected Poems of Rupert Brooke,* ed. George Edward Woodberry (1915; New York: John Lane, 1918), 111.

18. Gwendolyn Brooks, "The Rites for Cousin Vit," *Selected Poems* (New York: Harper and Row, 1963), 58.

19. Brooks, "A Song in the Front Yard," *Selected Poems,* 6.

20. William Carlos Williams, *The Collected Poems of William Carlos Williams,* ed.

A. Walton Litz and Christopher MacGowan, 2 vols. (New York: New Directions, 1986–88), 1:58.

21. Amy Clampitt, "A Procession at Candlemas," *The Kingfisher* (New York: Knopf, 1985), 22.

22. Bonnie Costello, "Amy Clampitt: Nomad Exquisite," *Shifting Ground: Reinventing Landscape in Modern American Poetry* (Cambridge, MA: Harvard University Press, 2003), 118–19.

23. Sylvia Plath, "Cut," *The Collected Poems*, ed. Ted Hughes (New York: Harper and Row, 1981), 235–36.

24. Seamus Heaney, *The Government of the Tongue: Selected Prose, 1978–1987* (New York: Farrar, Straus and Giroux, 1989), 165.

25. Ted Hughes, "Out," *Collected Poems*, ed. Paul Keegan (New York: Farrar, Straus and Giroux, 2003), 165.

26. Sterling Brown, "Memphis Blues," *The Collected Poems of Sterling A. Brown*, ed. Michael S. Harper (Evanston, IL: Triquarterly Books, 1996), 60.

27. Sherman Alexie, "Crow Testament," *One Stick Song* (Brooklyn, NY: Hanging Loose Press, 2000), 26.

28. Susan Howe, "Rückenfigur," *Pierce-Arrow* (New York: New Directions, 1999), 129.

29. Howe, "Rückenfigur," 131.

30. Anthony Giddens, *The Consequences of Modernity* (Stanford: Stanford University Press, 1990), 64.

31. Among the theoretical works informing this general view of cross-cultural globalism are Salman Rushdie, "In Good Faith," *Imaginary Homelands: Essays and Criticism 1981–1991* (London: Granta Books, 1991), 393–414; Édouard Glissant, *Caribbean Discourse: Selected Essays*, trans. J. Michael Dash (Charlottesville: University Press of Virginia, 1989), 120–57; Paul Gilroy, *The Black Atlantic: Modernity and Double Consciousness* (Cambridge, MA: Harvard University Press, 1993), 1–40; Homi K. Bhabha, *The Location of Culture* (London: Routledge, 1994); Clifford, *Routes*, 1–46; Michael F. Brown, *Who Owns Native Culture?* (Cambridge, MA: Harvard University Press, 2003), 43–68; and Kwame Anthony Appiah, *Cosmopolitanism: Ethics in a World of Strangers* (New York: Norton, 2006), 101–35.

32. Langston Hughes, *The Big Sea: An Autobiography* (New York: Knopf, 1940), 55, and Arnold Rampersad, *The Life of Langston Hughes*, 2 vols. (New York: Oxford University Press, 1986), 1:39–40.

33. Langston Hughes, "The Negro Speaks of Rivers," *The Collected Poems of Langston Hughes,* ed. Arnold Rampersad and David Roessel (New York: Knopf, 1997), 23.

34. M. M. Bakhtin, *The Dialogic Imagination: Four Essays*, ed. Michael Holquist, trans. Caryl Emerson and Michael Holquist (Austin: University of Texas Press, 1981), 272–73.

35. Walter Benn Michaels, "American Modernism and the Poetics of Identity," *Modernism/Modernity* 1, no. 1 (1994): 51.

36. Jeff Westover, "Africa/America: Fragmentation and Diaspora in the Work of Langston Hughes," *Callaloo* 25, no. 4 (2002): 1221; Brent Hayes Edwards, *The Practice*

of Diaspora: Literature, Translation, and the Rise of Black Internationalism (Cambridge, MA: Harvard University Press, 2003), 59–68, and "Langston Hughes and the Futures of Diaspora," *American Literary History* 19, no. 3 (2007): 689–711.

37. On the poem's going back to a "pre-'racial' dawn" and its avoidance of "racial essentialism," see George Hutchinson, *The Harlem Renaissance in Black and White* (Cambridge, MA: Belknap–Harvard University Press, 1995), 415.

38. Mutlu Konuk Blasing, *American Poetry — The Rhetoric of Its Forms* (New Haven: Yale University Press, 1987), 114.

39. Lee Edelman, "The Geography of Gender: Elizabeth Bishop's 'In the Waiting Room,'" *Contemporary Literature* 26, no. 2 (1985): 179–96. For a wide-ranging discussion of imaginative travel in Bishop's work, see Bonnie Costello, "Excursive Sight," *Elizabeth Bishop: Questions of Mastery* (Cambridge, MA: Harvard University Press, 1991), 127–74.

40. Elizabeth Bishop, "In the Waiting Room," *The Complete Poems* (New York: Farrar, Straus and Giroux, 1983), 159–61.

41. Appadurai, *Modernity at Large*, 53.

42. Giddens, *Consequences of Modernity*, 21.

43. Gayatri Chakravorty Spivak, "Three Women's Texts and a Critique of Imperialism," *Critical Inquiry* 12.1 (1985): 245. (Ensuing references appear in text.)

44. Elizabeth Bishop as quoted by George Starbuck, "'The Work!': A Conversation with Elizabeth Bishop," in *Elizabeth Bishop and Her Art*, ed. Lloyd Schwartz and Sybil P. Estess (Ann Arbor: University of Michigan Press, 1983), 318.

45. Osa Johnson, *I Married Adventure: The Lives and Adventures of Martin and Osa Johnson* (Philadelphia: Lippincott, 1940), 151, Edelman, "Geography," 191.

46. See the photograph of a "Tribal Chief and His Favourite Wife," in which the wife, though fully clothed, has many brass rings around her neck, and of a woman with multiple horsehair and bead necklaces, "Rendille Belle on the Northern Frontier," in Osa Johnson, *Four Years in Paradise* (London: Hutchinson, 1941), plates following pages 16 and 128. Photographs of a "longhead" mother whose arms largely cover her naked breasts and of Osa Johnson amid many bare-breasted "Pygmies," one of whom she lifts, are in *I Married Adventure*, plates following pages 112 and 328.

47. Okot p'Bitek, *"Song of Lawino" and "Song of Ocol"* (London: Heinemann, 1984), 39. (Ensuing references appear in text.)

48. Arthur Rimbaud to Georges Izambard (13) May 1871, *Oeuvres*, ed. Suzanne Bernard (Paris: Éditions Garnier Frères, 1960), 344.

49. Paul de Man, "Autobiography as De-Facement," *The Rhetoric of Romanticism* (New York: Columbia University Press, 1984), 67–81.

50. Dionisio D. Martínez, "Hysteria," *Bad Alchemy* (New York: Norton, 1995), 26–27.

4. Nationalism, Transnationalism, and the Poetry of Mourning

1. On "historical poetics" and "the new lyric studies," see the cluster of essays on "The New Lyric Studies" in *PMLA* 123, no. 1 (2008): 181–234. Elsewhere, I have ar-

gued for a historicized transhistorical approach to genre, contextualizing in particular the modern elegy's transformation of inherited conventions in relation to Western modernity's social suppression of mourning (Jahan Ramazani, *Poetry of Mourning: The Modern Elegy from Hardy to Heaney* [Chicago: University of Chicago Press, 1994]).

2. Wilfred Owen, Preface, *The Poems of Wilfred Owen*, ed. Jon Stallworthy (New York: Norton, 1985), 192.

3. Benedict Anderson, *Imagined Communities: Reflections on the Origin and Spread of Nationalism* (London: New Left, 1983), 9.

4. Jahan Ramazani, "Afterword: 'When There Are So Many We Shall Have to Mourn,'" in *Modernism and Mourning*, ed. Patricia Rae (Lewisburg, PA: Bucknell University Press, 2007), 286–95.

5. Rupert Brooke, "The Soldier," *The Collected Poems of Rupert Brooke*, ed. George Edward Woodberry (1915; New York: John Lane, 1918), 111.

6. Amiri Baraka [Leroi Jones], "A Poem for Black Hearts," *Black Magic: Collected Poetry, 1961–67* (Indianapolis: Bobbs-Merrill, 1969), 112.

7. Lawrence Lipking, "The Genius of the Shore: Lycidas, Adamastor, and the Poetics of Nationalism," *PMLA* 111, no. 2 (1996): 205–21.

8. See Jay Surdukowski, "Is Poetry a War Crime? Reckoning for Radovan Karadzic, the Poet-Warrior," *Michigan Journal of International Law* 26, no. 673 (2005): 1–27.

9. Vamik Volkan, "Large-Group Identity and Chosen Trauma," *Psychoanalysis Downunder* 6 (Dec. 2005), http://www.psychoanalysis.asn.au/downunder/backissues/6/427/large_group_vv (accessed 30 Nov. 2007).

10. Anderson, *Imagined Communities*, 141.

11. Anderson, *Imagined Communities*, 145.

12. Roman Jakobson, "Linguistics and Poetics," *Language in Literature*, ed. Krystyna Pomorska and Stephen Rudy (Cambridge, MA: Belknap–Harvard University Press, 1987), 69.

13. Anderson, *Imagined Communities*, 146.

14. Anderson, *Imagined Communities*, 145.

15. Alfred Lord Tennyson, "Ode on the Death of the Duke of Wellington," *Tennyson's Poetry*, ed. Robert W. Hill, Jr. (New York: Norton, 1999), 294.

16. Tennyson, "Ode," 299.

17. Tennyson, "Ode," 294.

18. W. B. Yeats, "Mourn—and Then Onward," *The Poems*, rev. ed., ed. Richard J. Finneran, vol. 1 of *The Collected Works of W. B. Yeats*, ed. Finneran and George Mills Harper (New York: Macmillan, 1989), 531.

19. Tennyson, "Ode," 297.

20. Yeats, "Easter, 1916," *Poems*, 180–82. On the poem, see R. F. Foster, "Yeats at War: Poetic Strategies and Political Reconstruction from the Easter Rising to the Free State," *Transactions of the Royal Historical Society*, 6, no. 11 (2001): 127–33; Marjorie Perloff, "'Easter, 1916': Yeats's World War I Poem," in *The Oxford Handbook of British and Irish War Poetry*, ed. Tim Kendall (Oxford: Oxford University Press, 2007),

227–41; Helen Vendler, *Our Secret Discipline: Yeats and Lyric Form* (Cambridge, MA: Belknap–Harvard University Press, 2007), 16–26.

21. Anderson, *Imagined Communities*, 11.

22. Judith Butler, *Precarious Life: The Powers of Mourning and Violence* (London: Verso, 2004), 23.

23. Richard Danson Brown, "Neutrality and Commitment: MacNeice, Yeats, Ireland, and the Second World War," *Journal of Modern Literature* 28, no. 3 (2005): 120.

24. Maud Gonne, MG to WBY, 8 November 1916, *The Gonne-Yeats Letters 1893–1938*, ed. Anna MacBride White and A. Norman Jeffares (New York: Norton, 1993), 385.

25. Jahan Ramazani, *Yeats and the Poetry of Death: Elegy, Self-Elegy, and the Sublime* (New Haven: Yale University Press, 1990), 59–64.

26. Yeats, "An Irish Airman Foresees His Death," *Poems,* 135.

27. Yeats, "In Memory of Eva Gore-Booth and Con Markievicz," *Poems,* 233–34.

28. Edmund Spenser, "Two Cantos of Mutabilitie," 7.58.515, 7.59.525. I refer here to Spenser's call for Irish extermination in his *View of the Present State of Ireland.*

29. W. H. Auden, "In Memory of W. B. Yeats," *Selected Poems: New Edition*, ed. Edward Mendelson (New York: Vintage–Random House, 1979), 80–83.

30. Butler, *Precarious Life*, 22–23.

31. Ramazani, *Poetry of Mourning*, 182–91. On the poem's transnationalism, see also Lawrence Lipking, *The Life of the Poet: Beginning and Ending Poetic Careers* (Chicago: University of Chicago Press, 1981), 151–60, and Edward Mendelson, *Later Auden* (New York: Farrar, Straus and Giroux, 1999), 3–13.

32. Butler, *Precarious Life*, 22 (emphasis in original).

33. Owen, Preface, "Strange Meeting," *Poems,* 192, 125.

34. Auden, "In Memory of Sigmund Freud," *Selected Poems,* 91–95.

35. Butler, *Precarious Life*, 21.

36. Owen, "Strange Meeting," 125–26.

37. Owen, Preface, *Poems,* 192.

38. Geoffrey Hill, "September Song," *Collected Poems* (New York: Oxford University Press, 1986), 67.

39. Mina Loy, "The Widow's Jazz," *The Lost Lunar Baedeker*, ed. Roger L. Conover (New York: Farrar, Straus and Giroux, 1996), 95–97.

40. Denise Levertov, "Olga Poems," *Poems 1960–1967* (New York: New Directions, 1983), 209.

41. Levertov, "Olga Poems," 209.

42. Levertov, "Olga Poems," 210.

43. Kamau Brathwaite, "Hawk," *Born to Slow Horses* (Middletown, CT: Wesleyan University Press, 2005), 99.

44. Ellipsis in original, a note presented in small type; Brathwaite, "Hawk," 105.

45. James Wright, "A Centenary Ode: Inscribed to Little Crow, Leader of the Sioux Rebellion in Minnesota, 1862," *Collected Poems* (Hanover, NH: Wesleyan University Press, 1971), 181.

46. Simonides' epitaph famously also appears in Herodotus, *The History*, trans. David Grene (Chicago: University of Chicago Press, 1987), 552.

47. Rudyard Kipling, "Epitaphs of the War," *Rudyard Kipling's Verse* (New York: Doubleday, Doran, 1940), 384–90.

48. Franco Moretti, *Graphs, Maps, Trees* (London: Verso, 2005).

49. Kipling, "Epitaphs of the War," 385.

50. Kipling, "Epitaphs of the War," 389.

51. T. S. Eliot, *The Complete Poems and Plays of T. S. Eliot* (London: Faber and Faber, 1969), 11.

52. Ezra Pound, *Hugh Selwyn Mauberley, Poems 1918–21, including Three Portraits and Four Cantos* (New York: Boni and Liveright, 1921), 56.

53. Sylvia Plath, "Daddy," *The Collected Poems*, ed. Ted Hughes (New York: Harper and Row, 1981), 222.

54. Marilyn Chin, *Rhapsody in Plain Yellow* (New York: Norton, 2002), 105.

55. Agha Shahid Ali, "Lenox Hill," *Rooms Are Never Finished* (New York: Norton, 2002), 17.

56. Wallace Stevens, "The Death of a Soldier," *The Collected Poems* (New York: Vintage–Random House, 1982), 97. I interpret the poem in the context of earlier critical readings in *Poetry of Mourning*, 98–100.

57. Stevens, "To an Old Philosopher in Rome," *Collected Poems*, 508.

58. Stevens, "To an Old Philosopher in Rome" (ellipsis in original), 508.

59. Percy Bysshe Shelley, *Adonais, Shelley's Poetry and Prose*, ed. Donald H. Reiman and Sharon B. Powers (New York: Norton, 1977), 406.

60. Stevens, "To an Old Philosopher in Rome," 509.

61. Stevens, "To an Old Philosopher in Rome," 510.

62. Stevens, "The Snow Man," *Collected Poems*, 9–10.

63. Butler, *Precarious Life*, xi–xv.

64. Butler, *Precarious Life*, 37.

5. Modernist Bricolage, Postcolonial Hybridity

1. Lorna Goodison, "Country, Sligoville," *Turn Thanks* (Urbana and Chicago: University of Illinois Press, 1999), 47. See Michael Malouf's richly historical reading of the poem in "Duppy Poetics: Yeats, Memory, and Place in Lorna Goodison's 'Country, Sligoville,'" in *Ireland and Transatlantic Poetics: Essays in Honor of Denis Donoghue*, ed. Brian G. Caraher and Robert Mahony (Newark: University of Delaware Press, 2007), 191–204.

2. Édouard Glissant, *Caribbean Discourse: Selected Essays*, trans. J. Michael Dash (Charlottesville: University Press of Virginia, 1989), xii, 134–44.

3. Simon Gikandi, *Writing in Limbo: Modernism and Caribbean Literature* (Ithaca: Cornell University Press, 1992), 4–5. In subsequent work, Gikandi has seen more continuity between modernism and postcolonialism; see his *Maps of Englishness: Writing Identity in the Culture of Colonialism* (New York: Columbia University Press, 1996), 158–62.

4. Chinweizu, Onwuchekwa Jemie, and Ihechukwu Madubuike, *Toward the Decolonization of African Literature* (1980; Washington, DC: Howard University Press, 1983), 2–3; on the necessity of freeing African poetry from Euromodernism, see chapter 3, 163–238.

5. Fredric Jameson, "Modernism and Imperialism," in Jameson et al., *Nationalism, Colonialism, and Literature* (Minneapolis: University of Minnesota Press, 1990), 64.

6. Bill Ashcroft and John Salter, "Modernism's Empire: Australia and the Cultural Imperialism of Style," in *Modernism and Empire*, ed. Howard J. Booth and Nigel Rigby (Manchester: Manchester University Press, 2000), 293.

7. Kamau Brathwaite, *History of the Voice: The Development of Nation Language in Anglophone Caribbean Poetry* (1984), rev. and rpt. in *Roots* (Ann Arbor: University of Michigan Press, 1993), 286–87. Discussions of Brathwaite's statement include Gikandi, *Maps of Englishness*, 158; Charles Bernstein, "Poetics of the Americas," *Modernism/Modernity* 3, no. 3 (1996): 1–23; Neil ten Kortenaar, "Where the Atlantic Meets the Caribbean: Kamau Brathwaite's *The Arrivants* and T. S. Eliot's *The Waste Land*," *Research in African Literatures* 27, no. 4 (1996): 15–27; and Matthew Hart, "Tradition and the Postcolonial Talent: T. S. Eliot *versus* Edward Kamau Brathwaite," in *The International Reception of T. S. Eliot*, ed. Elisabeth Däumer and Shyamal Bagchee (New York: Continuum, 2007), 5–35.

8. Charles Olson, "Projective Verse," *Collected Prose*, ed. Donald Allen and Benjamin Friedlander (Berkeley: University of California Press, 1997), 248.

9. As Xiaomei Chen argues in another context — that of post-Mao China — occidentalist affiliations can "sometimes be used as a locally marginal or peripheral discourse against the centrality of the internal dominant power." See her *Occidentalism: A Theory of Counter-Discourse in Post-Mao China* (New York: Oxford University Press, 1995), 8–9.

10. Derek Walcott, "Prelude," *Collected Poems, 1948–1984* (New York: Farrar, Straus and Giroux, 1986), 3–4.

11. See Terry Eagleton, *Exiles and Émigrés: Studies in Modern Literature* (New York: Shocken Books, 1970). On modernism's continuities with postcolonialism, see Gikandi, *Maps of Englishness*, 158–62; Elleke Boehmer, *Empire, the National, and the Postcolonial, 1890–1920* (New York: Oxford University Press, 2002), 169–77, and her *Colonial and Postcolonial Literature* (New York: Oxford University Press, 1995), 123–33, 144–47; and Reed Way Dasenbrock, "Why the Post in Post-Colonial Is Not the Post in Post-Modern: Homer, Dante, Pound, Walcott," in *Ezra Pound and African American Modernism*, ed. Michael Coyle (Orono: National Poetry Foundation, 2001), 111–22. Three books on U.S. and Caribbean poetry that further explore the continuities are Charles W. Pollard, *New World Modernisms: T. S. Eliot, Derek Walcott, and Kamau Brathwaite* (Charlottesville: University of Virginia Press, 2004); Lee M. Jenkins, *The Language of Caribbean Poetry: Boundaries of Expression* (Gainesville: University of Florida Press, 2004); and Anita Patterson, *Race, American Literature and Transnational Modernisms* (Cambridge: Cambridge University Press, 2008).

12. Brathwaite, *History of the Voice,* 263–64, 297.

13. Dasenbrock, "Why the Post," 115; in other respects, I agree with Dasenbrock's excellent piece.

14. James Clifford, *Routes: Travel and Translation in the Late Twentieth Century* (Cambridge, MA: Harvard University Press, 1997), 36.

15. Claude Lévi-Strauss, *The Savage Mind* (Chicago: University of Chicago Press, 1966), 17.

16. A. K. Ramanujan, *The Collected Poems of A. K. Ramanujan* (Delhi: Oxford University Press, 1995), 186.

17. A. K. Ramanujan, "Afterword," *Poems of Love and War*, trans. Ramanujan (New York: Columbia University Press, 1984), 246, 287. Ezra Pound, *Gaudier-Brzeska: A Memoir* (1916; New York: New Directions, 1970), 89. Pound layers Mount Taishan and a Pisan mountain near the Disciplinary Training Center in *The Pisan Cantos*.

18. Salman Rushdie, "In Good Faith," *Imaginary Homelands* (New York: Granta–Penguin, 1991), 394. As migrants, the Euromodernists traversed lesser inequities of power or differences of culture in the Northern hemisphere.

19. Marjory Whitelaw, "Interview with Christopher Okigbo" (1965/1970), rpt. in *Critical Essays on Christopher Okigbo*, ed. Uzoma Esonwanne (New York: G. K. Hall, 2000), 55.

20. Christopher Okigbo, "Lament of the Masks," in *W. B. Yeats 1865–1965: Centenary Essays on the Art of W. B. Yeats*, ed. D. E. S. Maxwell and S. B. Bushrui (Ibadan: Ibadan University Press, 1965), xiii–xv.

21. See Molara Ogundipe-Leslie, "The Poetry of Christopher Okigbo: Its Evolution and Significance" (1973), rpt. in *Critical Essays on Christopher Okigbo*, 185–86.

22. *W. B. Yeats*, ed. Maxwell and Bushrui, 245.

23. Okigbo is echoing Canto 8 in "Limits 3," *Labyrinths with "Path of Thunder"* (New York: Africana Publishing Corporation, 1971), 25–26. See Romanus Egudu, "Ezra Pound in African Poetry: Chistopher Okigbo," in *Critical Perspectives on Christopher Okigbo*, ed. Donatus Ibe Nwoga (Washington, DC: Three Continents Press, 1984), 337–48.

24. Whitelaw, "Interview with Christopher Okigbo," 55.

25. M. M. Bakhtin, *The Dialogic Imagination: Four Essays*, ed. Michael Holquist, trans. Caryl Emerson and Michael Holquist (Austin: University of Texas Press, 1981), 258–62. Bakhtin associates all artistic hybridization with the "intentional" mode.

26. Derek Walcott, *Omeros* (New York: Farrar, Straus and Giroux, 1990), 1.9.3, pages 51–54.

27. T. S. Eliot, "*Ulysses*, Order and Myth," *Selected Prose of T. S. Eliot*, ed. Frank Kermode (New York: Farrar, Straus and Giroux, 1975), 177–78.

28. Agha Shahid Ali, "Ghazal," *The Country without a Post Office* (New York: Norton, 1997), 40.

29. Agha Shahid Ali, *T. S. Eliot as Editor* (Ann Arbor: University of Michigan Press, 1986), 1. T. S. Eliot, *The Waste Land: A Norton Critical Edition*, ed. Michael North (New York: Norton, 2001), line 430, page 20. Ali discusses the ghazal as a form in his introduction to *Ravishing DisUnities*, ed. Ali (Hanover, NH: Wesleyan University Press,

2000), 1–14. See also David Caplan, *Questions of Possibility: Contemporary Poetry and Poetic Form* (New York: Oxford University Press, 2005), 53–59, and Malcolm Woodland, "Memory's Homeland: Agha Shahid Ali and the Hybrid Ghazal," *English Studies in Canada* 31, nos. 2–3 (2005): 249–72.

30. Michael North, *The Dialect of Modernism* (Oxford: Oxford University Press, 1994), 77–99.

31. Brathwaite, *History of the Voice,* 275–77.

32. Edward [Kamau] Brathwaite, "Calypso," *The Arrivants* (New York: Oxford University Press, 1973), 48–50; Eliot, *The Waste Land,* lines 200–201, page 12.

33. Eliot, *The Waste Land,* line 308, page 15.

34. Edward Kamau Brathwaite, "Dies Irie," *X/Self* (New York: Oxford University Press, 1987), 37–39; "Irae," *Middle Passages* (Newcastle upon Tyne: Bloodaxe Books, 1992), 90. (Brathwaite again revised the poem in the American edition of *Middle Passages* [New York: New Directions, 1993], 117–20.) See also Keith Tuma, *Fishing by Obstinate Isles* (Evanston: Northwestern University Press, 1998), 256–58.

35. Brathwaite, "Irae," 90.

36. Okigbo, "Come Thunder," *Labyrinths*, 66. Ellipsis in original.

37. Stephen Spender, *The Thirties and After* (New York: Random House, 1978), 13.

38. Neil Lazarus, "'Unsystematic Fingers at the Conditions of the Times': Afropop and the Paradoxes of Imperialism," in *Recasting the World: Writing after Colonialism*, ed. Jonathan White (Baltimore: Johns Hopkins University Press, 1993), 137–60.

39. Paul Douglass, "Reading the Wreckage: De-Encrypting Eliot's Aesthetics of Empire," *Twentieth-Century Literature* 43, no. 1 (1997), 1–26.

40. Harish Trivedi, "'Ganga Was Sunken': T. S. Eliot's Use of India," in *The Fire and the Rose: New Essays on T. S. Eliot*, ed. Vinod Sena and Rajiva Verma (Delhi: Oxford University Press, 1992), 44–62.

41. Trivedi, "'Ganga Was Sunken,'" 56.

42. W. B. Yeats, *The Poems*, rev. ed., ed. Richard J. Finneran, vol. 1 of *The Collected Works of W. B. Yeats*, ed. *Finneran and George Mills Harper* (New York: Macmillan, 1989), 295.

43. Edward Said, *Orientalism* (New York: Pantheon, 1978), 3.

44. W. B. Yeats, *Letters on Poetry from W. B. Yeats to Dorothy Wellesley* (New York: Oxford University Press, 1940), 8–9.

45. Ezra Pound, *Lustra* (1916; New York: Knopf, 1917), 53.

46. Pound, *Gaudier-Brzeska*, 89.

47. Among recent books on the impact of East Asian culture on modernism, see Josephine Nock-Hee Park, *Apparitions of Asia: Modernist Form and Asian American Poetics* (New York: Oxford University Press, 2008); Zhaoming Qian, *The Modernist Response to Chinese Art* (Charlottesville: University of Virginia Press, 2003), *Orientalism and Modernism* (Durham: Duke University Press, 1995), and his edited collection *Ezra Pound and China* (Ann Arbor: University of Michigan Press, 2003); Yunte Huang, *Transpacific Displacement* (Berkeley: University of California Press, 2002); Ming Xie, *Ezra Pound and the Appropriation of Chinese Poetry* (New York: Garland, 1999); and

Robert Kern, *Orientalism, Modernism, and the American Poem* (Cambridge: Cambridge University Press, 1996). See also Eric Hayot's useful overview in "Critical Dreams: Orientalism, Modernism, and the Meaning of Pound's China," *Twentieth-Century Literature* 45, no. 4 (1999): 511–33.

48. On the poem and haiku, see Jyan-Lung Lin, "Pound's 'In A Station of the Metro' as a Yugen Haiku," *Paideuma* 21, nos. 1–2 (1992): 175–83.

49. W. H. Auden, "In Memory of W. B. Yeats," *Selected Poems: New Edition*, ed. Edward Mendelson (New York: Random House, 1979), 81.

50. Marjorie Perloff, *21st-Century Modernism* (Oxford: Blackwell, 2002), 1–14, 154–200.

51. Andreas Huyssen, "Geographies of Modernism in a Globalising World," in *Geographies of Modernism: Literatures, Cultures, Spaces*, ed. Peter Brooker and Andrew Thacker (New York: Routledge, 2005), 9.

52. A. K. Ramanujan, "Where Mirrors Are Windows: Towards an Anthology of Reflections" (1989), in *The Collected Essays of A. K. Ramanujan*, ed. Vinay Dharwadker (Delhi: Oxford University Press, 1999), 8–9.

6. Caliban's Modernities, Postcolonial Poetries

1. Andreas Huyssen, "Geographies of Modernism in a Globalising World," in *Geographies of Modernism: Literatures, Cultures, Spaces*, ed. Peter Brooker and Andrew Thacker (New York: Routledge, 2005), 15.

2. See Kwame Anthony Appiah, "The Postcolonial and the Postmodern," *In My Father's House: Africa in the Philosophy of Culture* (New York: Oxford University Press, 1992), 137–57; Linda Hutcheon, "Circling the Downspout of Empire," in *Past the Last Post: Theorizing Post-Colonialism and Post-Modernism*, ed. Ian Adam and Helen Tiffin (Calgary: University of Calgary Press, 1990), 167–89; and Fredric Jameson, *Postmodernism; or, The Cultural Logic of Late Capitalism* (Durham: Duke University Press, 1991). On modernity and postcolonialism, see Simon Gikandi, *Writing in Limbo: Modernism and Caribbean Literature* (Ithaca: Cornell University Press, 1992).

3. "Long Live the Vortex," ed. Wyndham Lewis, *Blast* 1 (1914), n.p.

4. W. B. Yeats, "Introduction," *Later Essays*, ed. William H. O'Donnell (New York: Charles Scribner's Sons, 1994), 215.

5. Ezra Pound, *Hugh Selwyn Mauberley*, III, in *Poems 1918–1921, including Three Portraits and Four Cantos* (New York: Boni and Liveright Publishers, 1921), 54.

6. T. S. Eliot, *The Waste Land: A Norton Critical Edition*, ed. Michael North (New York: Norton, 2001), III, lines 223, 255–56, pages 13, 14.

7. W. H. Auden, *Selected Poems: New Edition*, ed. Edward Mendelson (New York: Vintage–Random House, 1979), 300.

8. Hart Crane, *The Bridge* [1930], *The Complete Poems of Hart Crane*, ed. Marc Simon (New York: Liveright, 2000), IV, lines 75–76, page 78.

9. Marshall Berman, *All That Is Solid Melts into Air: The Experience of Modernity* (London: Verso, 1983), 13.

10. Jean Toomer, "Her Lips Are Copper Wire," *Cane* (1923; New York: Norton, 1988), 57. On this poem, "Gum," and "Reapers," see Michael North's readings in *The Dialect of Modernism: Race, Language, and Twentieth-Century Literature* (New York: Oxford University Press, 1994), 169–72.

11. Toomer, *Cane,* 5.

12. Toomer, *Cane,* 14.

13. Sterling Brown, "Slim in Atlanta," *The Collected Poems of Sterling A. Brown*, ed. Michael S. Harper (Evanston, IL: Triquarterly Books, 1996), 81–82.

14. Claude McKay, "The White City," *Complete Poems*, ed. William J. D. Maxwell (Urbana: University of Illinois Press, 2004), 162.

15. McKay, *Complete Poems,* 154, 163.

16. See Berman, *All That Is Solid,* 15.

17. Kofi Awoonor, "Songs of Sorrow," rpt. in *The Penguin Book of Modern African Poetry*, 4th ed., ed. Gerald Moore and Ulli Beier (Harmondsworth, UK: Penguin, 1998), 103–4.

18. Lenrie Peters, "Parachute Men," *Selected Poetry* (London: Heinemann, 1981), 25–26.

19. Agha Shahid Ali, "The Dacca Gauzes," *The Half-Inch Himalayas* (Middletown, CT.: Wesleyan University Press, 1987), 15–16.

20. Derek Walcott, "The Fortunate Traveller," *Collected Poems, 1948–1984* (New York: Noonday–Farrar, Straus and Giroux, 1986), 461.

21. Okot p'Bitek, *"Song of Lawino" and "Song of Ocol"* (London: Heinemann, 1984), 126.

22. Okot p'Bitek, *"Song of Ocol,"* 129.

23. Frantz Fanon, *The Wretched of the Earth*, trans. Constance Farrington (New York: Grove, 1963), 43.

24. Wole Soyinka, "Around Us, Dawning," *"Idanre" and Other Poems* (New York: Hill and Wang, 1967), 12.

25. Soyinka, "Death in the Dawn," *"Idanre" and Other Poems,* 10–11.

26. Edward Kamau Brathwaite, "X/Self's Xth Letters from the Thirteen Provinces," *X/Self* (Oxford: Oxford University Press, 1987), 80. (Ensuing references appear in text.) See Keith Tuma's reading of this poem in *Fishing by Obstinate Isles* (Evanston: Northwestern University Press, 1998), 244–49.

27. Louise Bennett, "Country Bwoy," *Selected Poems*, ed. Mervyn Morris (Kingston: Sangster's Book Stores, 1983), 11–13, 125. (Ensuing references appear in text.)

28. See Appiah, "Tropologies of Nativism," *In My Father's House,* 47–72.

29. Raymond Williams, "Metropolitan Perceptions and the Emergence of Modernism," *The Politics of Modernism: Against the New Conformists* (London: Verso, 1989), 45.

30. Langston Hughes, "The Negro Speaks of Rivers," *The Collected Poems of Langston Hughes*, ed. Arnold Rampersad and David Roessel (New York: Vintage Classics–Random House, 1995), 23.

31. W. B. Yeats, "Adam's Curse," *The Poems*, rev. ed., ed. Richard J. Finneran, vol. 1 of

The Collected Works of W. B. Yeats, ed. Finneran and George Mills Harper (New York: Macmillan, 1989), 80.

32. Ezra Pound, Canto 14, *The Cantos of Ezra Pound* (New York: New Directions, 1972), 63.

33. See David Chinitz, *T. S. Eliot and the Cultural Divide* (Chicago: University of Chicago Press, 2003), and North, *Dialect of Modernism*.

34. Hughes, "The Weary Blues," *Collected Poems*, 50. I offer a fuller reading of the poem along these lines in my *Poetry of Mourning: The Modern Elegy from Hardy to Heaney* (Chicago: University of Chicago Press, 1994), 144–47.

35. Langston Hughes, "The Negro Artist and the Racial Mountain," *The Nation* 12.2, no. 3181 (1926): 693.

36. Appiah, *In My Father's House*, 149.

37. Christopher Okigbo, "Fragments out of the Deluge," VI, *Labyrinths, with Path of Thunder* (London: Heinemann, 1971), 29. (Ensuing references appear in text.)

38. Kofi Anyidoho, "Hero and Thief," in *Penguin Book of Modern African Poetry*, 130.

39. Syl Cheney-Coker, "On Being a Poet in Sierra Leone," in *Penguin Book of Modern African Poetry*, 339.

40. Linton Kwesi Johnson, "New Craas Massakah," *Mi Revalueshanary Fren: Selected Poems* (London: Penguin, 2002), 55.

41. Johnson, "New Craas Massakah," *Mi Revalueshanary Fren*, 54–55.

42. Okigbo, "Hurrah for Thunder," *Labyrinths*, 67; Johnson, "If I Woz a Tap-Natch Poet," *Mi Revalueshanary Fren*, 95, 96, 97.

43. Bennett, *Selected Poems*, iv–v.

44. Carolyn Cooper, *Noises in the Blood: Orality, Gender and the "Vulgar" Body of Jamaican Popular Culture,* Warwick University Caribbean Studies (London: Macmillan Caribbean, 1993), 40.

45. Ben Okri, "On Edge of Time Future," in *Penguin Book of Modern African Poetry*, 302.

46. Okri, "On Edge of Time Future," 304.

47. Walcott, "The Schooner *Flight*," *Collected Poems,* 350.

48. Walcott, "The Schooner *Flight*," 347.

49. Derek Walcott, "The Light of the World," *The Arkansas Testament* (New York: Farrar, Straus and Giroux, 1987), 48, 50.

50. Agha Shahid Ali, "The Country without a Post Office," *The Country without a Post Office* (New York: Norton, 1997), 48–51.

51. Lorna Goodison, "Island Aubade," *Controlling the Silver* (Urbana: University of Illinois Press, 2005), 2.

52. Goodison, "Island Aubade," 3. Cf. the Pauline epistle in Philippians 4:12, "I know both how to be abased, and I know how to abound."

53. Goodison, "Ode to the Watchman," *Controlling the Silver*, 8–9.

54. Edward W. Said, "Reflections on Exile," *Reflections on Exile and Other Essays* (Cambridge, MA: Harvard University Press, 2000), 186.

55. Johnson, "If I Woz a Tap-Natch Poet," *Mi Revalueshanary Fren*, 94.

56. Kamau Brathwaite, *History of the Voice: The Development of Nation Language in Anglophone Caribbean Poetry* (1984), rev. and rpt. in *Roots* (Ann Arbor: University of Michigan Press, 1993), 297 n. 46.

7. Poetry and Decolonization

1. Edward W. Said, *Culture and Imperialism* (New York: Knopf, 1993), xii.

2. Said, *Culture and Imperialism*, 8.

3. United Nations, Decolonization Unit (2000–2006), "History," "The United Nations and Decolonization," http://www.un.org/Depts/dpi/decolonization/main.htm (accessed January 20, 2006).

4. *Oxford English Dictionary*, 2nd ed. (1989), qv "Colonization" and "Decolonization."

5. Said, *Culture and Imperialism*, xxii. On the history of decolonization, see Raymond F. Betts, *Decolonization*, 2nd ed. (New York: Routledge, 2004); James D. Le Sueur, *The Decolonization Reader* (New York: Routledge, 2003); Neil Lazarus, "The Global Dispensation since 1945," in *The Cambridge Companion to Postcolonial Literary Studies*, ed. Lazarus (Cambridge: Cambridge University Press, 2003); and Robert Young, *Postcolonialism: An Historical Introduction* (Oxford: Blackwell, 2001).

6. Kwame Anthony Appiah, *In My Father's House: Africa in the Philosophy of Culture* (New York: Oxford University Press, 1992); Homi K. Bhabha, *The Location of Culture* (London: Routledge, 1994); Gayatri Chakravorty Spivak, *A Critique of Postcolonial Reason* (Cambridge, MA: Harvard University Press, 1999)

7. Derek Walcott, *Another Life* (London: Jonathan Cape, 1973), 152.

8. United Nations, Resolution 1514 of the General Assembly, "Declaration on the Granting of Independence to Colonial Countries and Peoples" (December 14, 1960), 66, http://www.un.org/Depts/dpi/decolonization/declaration.htm (accessed January 20, 2006).

9. United Nations, "Declaration," 67.

10. "Catalog," in *The New Princeton Encyclopedia of Poetry and Poetics*, 2nd ed., ed. Alex Preminger and T. V. F. Brogan (Princeton: Princeton University Press, 1993), 74.

11. United Nations (2000–2006), "History."

12. Immanuel Kant, *Critique of Judgment*, trans. J. H. Bernard (London: Hafner-Macmillan, 1951), 90–91.

13. Said, *Culture and Imperialism*, 226.

14. Derek Walcott, "A Sea-Chantey," *Collected Poems, 1948–1984* (New York: Farrar, Straus and Giroux, 1986), 46.

15. Edward [Kamau] Brathwaite, "Calypso," *The Arrivants: A New World Trilogy* (Oxford: Oxford University Press, 1973), 48.

16. Lorna Goodison, "To Us, All Flowers Are Roses," *Selected Poems* (Ann Arbor: University of Michigan Press, 1992), 1.

17. James Anthony Froude, *The English in the West Indies; or, The Bow of Ulysses* (New York: Charles Scribner's Sons, 1897), 347.

18. Goodison, "To Us, All Flowers Are Roses," 1.

19. Kant, *Critique of Judgment*, 99-101.

20. *The Independence Anthology of Jamaican Literature*, ed. Arthur Lemiere Hendriks and Cedric Lindo ([Kingston,] Jamaica: Arts Celebration Committee of the Ministry of Development and Welfare, 1962).

21. John McLeod, *Postcolonial London: Rewriting the Metropolis* (London: Routledge, 2004), 102.

22. Linton Kwesi Johnson, "Inglan Is a Bitch," *Mi Revalueshanary Fren: Selected Poems* (London: Penguin, 2002), 39.

23. "It was a sight to cure sore eyes, a time to live to see."

24. Louise Bennett, "Independence Dignity," *Selected Poems*, ed. Mervyn Morris (Kingston: Sangster's Book Stores, 1983), 117.

25. Bennett, "Independence Dignity," 116.

26. Okot p'Bitek, *"Song of Lawino" and "Song of Ocol"* (London: Heinemann, 1984), 107.

27. Frantz Fanon, *The Wretched of the Earth*, trans. Constance Farrington (New York: Grove, 1963), 148-205.

28. Okot p'Bitek, *"Song of Lawino,"* 110.

29. Walcott, "The Sea Is History," *Collected Poems*, 367. (Ensuing references appear in text.)

30. Philip Larkin, "Homage to a Government," *Collected Poems*, ed. Anthony Thwaite (New York: Farrar, Straus and Giroux, 1989), 171.

31. Noël Coward, "Mad Dogs and Englishmen," *The Lyrics of Noël Coward* (London: Methuen, 1983), 122.

32. Tony Harrison, "On Not Being Milton" (1978), *Selected Poems*, 2nd ed. (London: Penguin, 1987), 112.

33. Harrison, "On Not Being Milton," 112.

34. Quoted in Edward W. Said, "On Mahmoud Darwish," *Grand Street* 12.48 (1993): 115. (Ensuing references to this essay appear in text.)

35. Edward W. Said, *On Late Style: Music and Literature against the Grain* (New York: Pantheon, 2006), 148.

36. Edward W. Said, *Orientalism* (New York: Pantheon, 1978), 5, 3.

37. Said, *Culture and Imperialism*, xii.

38. Gertrude Stein, *Everybody's Autobiography* (1937; New York: Cooper Square Publishers, 1971), 289.

39. Said, *Culture and Imperialism*, 221. (Ensuing references appear in text.)

40. W. B. Yeats, "Man and the Echo," *The Poems*, rev. ed., ed. Richard J. Finneran, vol. 1 of *The Collected Works of W. B. Yeats*, ed. Finneran and George Mills Harper (New York: Macmillan, 1989), 345.

41. Frantz Fanon, "Concerning Violence," *Wretched of the Earth*, 35-106.

42. In Fanon's words, colonialism "turns to the past of the oppressed people, and distorts, disfigures, and destroys it" (*Wretched of the Earth*, 210).

43. Lorna Goodison, "Guinea Woman," *Selected Poems*, 64. See A. K. Ramanujan's "Elements of Composition" and "Small-Scale Reflections on a Great House" in *The Collected Poems of A. K. Ramanujan*, ed. Vinay Dharwadker (Delhi: Oxford University Press, 1995), 96–99, 121–23.

44. Edward W. Said, "The Politics of Knowledge," *Reflections on Exile and Other Essays* (Cambridge, MA: Harvard University Press, 2000), 378–79.

45. Derek Walcott, "An Interview with Derek Walcott," conducted in 1977 by Edward Hirsch, *Contemporary Literature* 20, no. 3 (1979): 288; Roddy Doyle, *The Barrytown Trilogy: The Commitments / The Snapper / The Van* (London: Penguin, 1995), 13. See also Walcott, "Leaving School" (1965), in *Critical Perspectives on Derek Walcott*, ed. Robert D. Hamner (Washington, DC: Three Continents Press, 1993), 32.

46. See, e.g., Lorna Goodison, "Bedspread," *Selected Poems*, 67–68, and Agha Shahid Ali, "I See Chile in My Rearview Mirror," *A Nostalgist's Map of America* (New York: Norton, 1991), 96–97.

47. See my Yeats chapter in *The Hybrid Muse: Postcolonial Poetry in English* (Chicago: University of Chicago Press, 2001).

48. Chinweizu, Onwuchekwa Jemie, and Ihechukwu Madubuike, *Toward the Decolonization of African Literature* (1980; Washington, DC: Howard University Press, 1983), 1. (Ensuing references appear in text.)

49. Said, *Culture and Imperialism*, 212.

50. Said, *Culture and Imperialism*, 214.

51. Edward Kamau Brathwaite, *History of the Voice: The Development of Nation Language in Anglophone Caribbean Poetry* (1984), rev. and rpt. in *Roots* (Ann Arbor: University of Michigan Press, 1993), 275, 278, 291.

52. Brathwaite, *History of the Voice*, 286–87.

53. Said, *Culture and Imperialism*, xx.

54. Walcott, "Ruins of a Great House," *Collected Poems*, 20.

55. Felix Mnthali, *Echoes from Ibadan* (Ibadan, privately printed, 1961), rpt. in *The Penguin Book of Modern African Poetry*, 4th ed., ed. Gerald Moore and Ulli Beier (London: Penguin, 1998), 172–73.

56. Ezra Pound, "A Pact" (1909), rpt. in *Personae* (New York: New Directions, 1949), 91.

57. Edward W. Said, as quoted on the back cover of Agha Shahid Ali, *The Country without a Post Office* (1997; New York: Norton, 1998).

58. Agha Shahid Ali, "By Exiles," *Call Me Ishmael Tonight: A Book of Ghazals* (New York: Norton, 2003), 28–29. On Ali's "tangled literary and cultural loyalties" in this and other ghazals, including his echo of "exiled by exiles" from Said's essay on exile, see David Caplan, *Questions of Possibility: Contemporary Poetry and Poetic Form* (New York: Oxford University Press, 2005), 53–59. On Ali's hybridizing use of refrain and return, including a reading of this ghazal, see Malcolm Woodland, "Memory's Home-

land: Agha Shahid Ali and the Hybrid Ghazal," *English Studies in Canada* 31, nos. 2–3 (2005): 249–72.

59. Agha Shahid Ali, "Lenox Hill," *The Rooms Are Never Finished* (New York: Norton, 2002), 17–19.

60. Said, *Culture and Imperialism*, xviii–xix.

61. Edward W. Said, *Humanism and Democratic Criticism* (New York: Columbia University Press, 2004), 36. See also his more extended discussion of Cavafy in *Late Style*, 142–48.

62. Chinweizu, Jemie, and Madubuike, *Toward the Decolonization*, 1.

63. Ngũgĩ wa Thiong'o, *Decolonising the Mind: The Politics of Language in African Literature* (Portsmouth, NH: Heinemann, 1986).

8. Poetry and the Translocal: Blackening Britain

1. Grace Nichols, "Wherever I Hang," *Lazy Thoughts of a Lazy Woman* (London: Virago, 1989), 10.

2. Stuart Hall, "Cultural Identity and Diaspora," in *Identity, Community, Culture, Difference*, ed. Jonathan Rutherford (London: Lawrence and Wishart, 1990), 222, 226.

3. James Clifford, *Routes: Travel and Translation in the Late Twentieth Century* (Cambridge, MA: Harvard University Press, 1997), 254. Clifford's book develops the concept of the translocal (7).

4. Homi K. Bhabha, *The Location of Culture* (London: Routledge, 1994), 6.

5. This historical information is drawn from Peter Fryer, *Staying Power: The History of Black People in Britain* (London: Pluto Press, 1984), 373–99; Paul Gilroy, *"There Ain't No Black in the Union Jack": The Cultural Politics of Race and Nation* (Chicago: University of Chicago Press, 1987); Kathleen Paul, *Whitewashing Britain: Race and Citizenship in the Postwar Era* (Ithaca: Cornell University Press, 1997); and Bruce King, *The Internationalization of English Literature,* vol. 13 of the Oxford English Literary History (Oxford: Oxford University Press, 2004). See also Ashley Dawson, *Mongrel Nation* (Ann Arbor: University of Michigan Press, 2007).

6. On black British poetry, see Fred D'Aguiar, "Have You Been Here Long? Black Poetry in Britain," in *New British Poetries*, ed. Robert Hampson and Peter Barry (Manchester: Manchester University Press, 1993), 51–71; Romana Huk, "In An-Other's Pocket: The Address of the 'Pocket Epic' in Postmodern Black British Poetry," *Yale Journal of Criticism* 13, no. 1 (2000): 23–47; King, *Internationalization*; Nicky Marsh, "'Peddlin Noh Puerile Parchment of Ethnicity': Questioning Performance in New Black British Poetry," *Wasafiri* 45 (2005): 46–51; *Write Black, Write British: From Post Colonial to Black British Literature*, ed. Kadija Sesay (Hertford, UK: Hansib Publications, 2005).

7. On postcolonial representations of London, including some of the works discussed here, see John McLeod, *Postcolonial London: Rewriting the Metropolis* (London: Routledge, 2004). See also Ian Baucom, *Out of Place* (Princeton: Princeton University Press, 1999).

8. Hall, "Cultural Identity," 226, 235.

9. Claude McKay, "Old England," *Complete Poems*, ed. William J. Maxwell (Urbana: University of Illinois Press, 2004), 45–46.

10. Paul Gilroy, *The Black Atlantic* (Cambridge, MA: Harvard University Press, 1993).

11. Kamau Brathwaite, *History of the Voice: The Development of Nation Language in Anglophone Caribbean Poetry* (1984), rev. and rpt. in *Roots* (Ann Arbor: University of Michigan Press, 1993), 275, n.17. For an ingenious reading of the poem's ambivalences, see Charles Bernstein, "Poetics of the Americas," *Modernism/Modernity* 3, no. 3 (1996): 13–14.

12. Paul, *Whitewashing Britain*, 132.

13. Louise Bennett, "Colonization in Reverse," *Selected Poems*, ed. Mervyn Morris (Kingston: Sangster's Book Stores, 1983), 106–7.

14. Louise Bennett, "Colonization in Reverse," *Yes M'Dear: Miss Lou Live* (Island Records, 1983).

15. Stuart Hall, "Calypso Kings," *Guardian,* June 28, 2002.

16. Brathwaite, *History of the Voice,* 279, 281.

17. The following calypso transcriptions are mine, from *London Is the Place for Me: Trinidadian Calypso in London, 1950–56,* compact disc (Honest Jons Records, 2002).

18. Bhabha, *Location of Culture*, 86.

19. The National Archives (UK), "Bound for Britain: Experiences of Migration to the UK," 2000, http://www.learningcurve.gov.uk/snapshots/snapshot11/snapshot11 .htm (accessed April 11, 2006). These signs often also excluded the Irish.

20. Wole Soyinka, "Telephone Conversation," *Times Literary Supplement*, August 10, 1962, 569.

21. Linton Kwesi Johnson, "Inglan Is a Bitch," *Mi Revalueshanary Fren: Selected Poems* (London: Penguin, 2002), 39–41.

22. John Agard, *Mangoes and Bullets: Selected and New Poems, 1972–84* (London: Pluto Press, 1985), 44.

23. Johnson, "New Craas Massakah," *Mi Revalueshanary Fren*, 54–59.

24. Fryer, *Staying Power,* 398–99.

25. Johnson, "New Craas Massakah," 54.

26. Grace Nichols, "Beauty," *The Fat Black Woman's Poems* (London: Virago, 1984), 7.

27. Nichols, "The Fat Black Woman Goes Shopping," *Fat Black*, 11.

28. Nichols, "Island Man," *Fat Black*, 29.

29. Nichols, "Tropical Death," *Fat Black*, 19.

30. Homi K. Bhabha, "The Vernacular Cosmopolitan," *Voices of the Crossing,* ed. Ferdinand Dennis and Naseem Khan (London: Serpent's Tail, 2000), 141.

31. Bhabha, "Vernacular Cosmopolitan," 140.

32. Bernardine Evaristo, *The Emperor's Babe* (London: Penguin, 2001). (Ensuing references appear in text.)

33. Derek Walcott, "Ruins of a Great House," *Collected Poems, 1948–1984* (New York: Farrar, Straus and Giroux, 1986), 20.

34. Evaristo, *Emperor's Babe*, 41, 42. (Ensuing references appear in text.)

35. Paul Gilroy, *Against Race* (Cambridge, MA: Harvard University Press, 2000), 252.

36. Evaristo, *Emperor's Babe*, 195. (Ensuing references appear in text.)

37. Walcott, "A Far Cry from Africa" and "The Schooner *Flight*," *Collected Poems*, 17–18, 346.

38. Evaristo, *Emperor's Babe*, 201. (Ensuing references appear in text.)

INDEX

Abu-Lughod, Janet, 9
Achebe, Chinua, 117, 156
    Things Fall Apart, 53, 110
Agard, John, 164
    "Listen Mr Oxford don," 172
Agbabi, Patience, 164
Aldington, Richard, 34
Alexie, Sherman
    "Crow Testament," 58, 59
Ali, Agha Shahid, 3, 12
    and alienation, 136, 137–38, 139
    and elegy, 72, 90, 160
    and Eliot, xii, 104, 105, 160
    and ghazals, 56, 104–5, 160
    influence of non-English languages
        on, 19
    and migration, 140, 160
    and modernism, xii, 104–5, 115, 117,
        118, 157
    and modernity, 124–25, 129, 130
    Said on, 159–60
    South America compared to Kash-
        mir, 157
    and syncretism, 104–5
    and translation, 39
    works: "By Exiles," 160; *The Coun-
        try without a Post Office,* 137, 159–
        60; "The Dacca Gauzes," 124–25;
        "Ghazal," 104–5; "Lenox Hill," 72,
        90, 160; *T. S. Eliot as Editor,* 105

alienation, 130–40
Allen, Donald, 38
American poetry, 38–39
Anderson, Benedict, 24, 75–76, 78, 79,
    92
    Imagined Communities, 73
anthologies, national. *See* national an-
    thologies
antinationalism, xi, 77–82
Anyidoho, Kofi, 134
apocalypticism, 106–8, 157
Appadurai, Arjun, xi, 9, 26, 28, 43, 54, 63
Appiah, Kwame Anthony, xi, 10, 132, 142
Arac, Jonathan, 19
art, transnational, 11
Ashbery, John, 38, 39, 52
    "The Instruction Manual," 54
Ashcroft, Bill, 96
Auden, W. H., 52, 114
    and elegy, xii, 77, 82–85
    influence of Yeats on, 85
    influence on American poets, 38
    influence on Heaney, 85
    influence on Plath, 85
    influence on Walcott, 85
    and locality, 3, 20
    and migration, 140
    and modernism, 2, 119
    and modernity, 121
    national identity of, 24, 25, 34

Auden, W. H. (*cont.*)
    works: "Chinese Soldier," 121; "In
        Memory of Sigmund Freud," 84–
        85; "In Memory of W. B. Yeats,"
        34, 82–84; "Prologue at Sixty," 16,
        34; "The Unknown Citizen," 121
Austen, Jane, 159
Awoonor, Kofi, 124, 130, 158

Baker, Houston, 96
Bakhtin, Mikhail, 3–4, 61, 103, 106
Balibar, Étienne, 24
Baraka, Amiri, 33, 43, 97–98
    "A Poem for Black Hearts," 74
Baudelaire, Charles, 19, 85
Beginner, Lord
    "Mix Up Matrimony," 170
Bennett, Louise, 16, 43
    and alienation, 135, 139
    Braithwaite on, 158
    and Britain, 164, 167–68
    and decolonization, xii, 146–47, 149,
        161
    influence of McKay on, 36
    and modernism, 117, 119
    and modernity, xii, 128–29, 130
    popularity of, 134, 135
    use of Creole, 12, 14–15, 19, 42
    works: "Bans a Killin," 42; "Census,"
        128; "Colonization in Reverse,"
        167, 177; "Country Bwoy," 128; "In-
        dependance," 147; "Independence
        Dignity," 147; "Jamaica Elevate,"
        147; "Jamaica Oman," 128–29;
        "Rough-Ridin Tram," 128; "Sarah
        Chice," 128; "South Parade Ped-
        dler," 14–15
Berman, Marshall, 121
Bernstein, Charles, 29, 44, 46
Bhabha, Homi, 8, 142, 164, 169, 175
Bible, 142
    Song of Solomon, 10
Bion, 72
Bishop, Elizabeth, 2
    influence of Auden on, 38

"In the Waiting Room," 14, 63–68,
    69–70
and traveling poetry, xi, 39, 52, 63–68,
    69–70
black British poetry, xiii, 163–80
Blake, William, 114
Blasing, Mutlu Konuk, 63
blues, 43, 119
Bly, Robert, 39
Boland, Eavan, 39
    "Anorexic," 41
    "Mise Eire," 41
Bradstreet, Anne, 71
Brathwaite, Kamau, 4
    and apocalypticism, 107
    and Britain, 164
    on calypso, 168
    and decolonization, 151, 155
    and elegy, xii, 87–88
    and heteroglossia, 106
    influence of Eliot on, 10, 97–98, 105,
        106, 115, 158
    the local and the global, 12
    on McKay, 30, 106, 166
    and migration, 39, 140
    and modernism, xii, 97–99, 105, 106,
        107, 115, 157
    and modernity, 127, 129, 130
    and multi-locational poetry, 58
    and place-names, 144
    works: "Calypso," 106, 144; "Hawk,"
        87–88; *History of the Voice,* 97, 158;
        "Irae," 107; "Wings of a Dove," 107
Breeze, Jean Binta, 164
British poetry, black, xiii, 163–80
Brodsky, Joseph, 39
Brooke, Rupert
    "The Soldier," 56, 73–74
Brooks, Gwendolyn, 43, 46
    "The Rites for Cousin Vit," 56
    "A Song in the Front Yard," 56
Brown, Richard Danson, 197n23
Brown, Sterling, 4, 42, 43, 114, 119, 126, 131
    "Memphis Blues," 58
    "Slim in Atlanta," 122–23

Brown, Terence, 39
Bryher, 34
Burns, Robert, 29
Butler, Judith, 78–79, 82, 83, 85, 86,
    92–93
Byron, Lord, 53

calypso, 168–70
Campbell, George, 15
Carson, Anne
    "The Glass Essay," 58
Casanova, Pascale, 12
catalog verse, 142–45, 147, 150
Cavafy, Constantin, 152–53
    "Waiting for the Barbarians," 161
Cervantes, Lorna Dee, 18–19, 46
Césaire, Aimé, 151, 156, 157, 158
Cézanne, Paul, 36
Chaucer, Geoffrey, 40, 142
Cheney-Coker, Syl, 134
Chin, Marilyn, xi, 6, 17, 46
    "Chinese Quatrains (The Woman in
        Tomb 44)," 90
    "How I Got That Name," 2
Chinweizu, 158, 183n33, 199n4, 207n48,
    208n62
Churchill, Winston, 30
citizenship. See national identity
Clampitt, Amy
    "A Procession at Candlemas," 57, 59, 72
Clark, J. P., 158
Claudel, Paul, 34
Clifford, James, xi, 17, 28, 43, 51–52, 100,
    163
collectivity, 134–35
colonialism
    and the English language, 19
    and globalization, 13–15
    and modernity, 123–26
    vs. local culture, 29–30
    See also decolonization; post-
        colonialism
compound characters, 1–2
computers, 127
confessionalism, 38, 46

Conrad, Joseph, 125
Cooper, Carolyn, 135
Costello, Bonnie, 57
Coward, Noël, 150
Crane, Hart, xii, 121
    The Bridge, 54–55, 126
Crawford, Robert, 26–28, 188n18
Creeley, Robert, 33, 39, 97–98
    "I Know a Man," 43
Creole
    use of by Claude McKay, 19, 29–30,
        106
    use of by Derek Walcott, 136
    use of by Linton Kwesi Johnson, 19,
        172
    use of by Lord Kitchener, 169
    use of by Louise Bennett, 12, 14–15,
        19, 42
creolization, 3, 10, 28, 47
Cullen, Countee, 42
cultural identity, 59–60, 134–39
culture-of-birth determinism, 35–37

Dabydeen, David, 30, 164
D'Aguiar, Fred, 164
Dante, 40
Darwish, Mahmoud, 152–53, 157, 160
Davie, Donald, 38
Day Lewis, C., 25
decolonization, xii, 141–62
    and communal history, 155
    and national anthologies, 145–46
    and national identity, 12–13, 154–58
    and place-names, 142–45, 146, 150,
        154–55
    and Said, xii, 11, 13, 141, 152–61
    and sublimity, 142–49
    See also colonialism; postcolonialism
de Man, Paul, 67
Dickinson, Emily, 1
Dimock, Wai Chee, 20
displacement. See migration
Donne, John, 53, 81, 114
Douglas, Ann, 35
Douglass, Paul, 109

Dove, Rita, 43
"The Great Palaces of Versailles," 58
Doyle, Laura, 185n57
Doyle, Roddy, 156
Duchamp, Marcel, 35
Dulac, Edmund, 111
Duncan, Robert
"An African Elegy," 60

Eagleton, Terry, 25
East Asian influences, 10, 27–28, 109
Edelman, Lee, 63, 65
Edwards, Brent Hayes, 61
elegy, 71–93
and epitaphs, 88–89
and migration, 86–90
and nationalism, xii, 34, 72–82
and transnationalism, xi–xii, 71–72,
81–93, 160
Eliot, T. S., xi, 4, 17, 29, 47, 159
and Agha Shahid Ali, 104, 105
and alienation, 131
antimodernity of, 121
and apocalypticism, 106–7, 108
compared to Langston Hughes, 61–62
compared to McKay, 32
and compound characters, 2
criticized by William Carlos Williams, 35
and elegy, 89
and Europe, 20, 27, 115
and heteroglossia, 105–6
influence of Donne on, 114
influence on Auden circle, 46
influence on Braithwaite, 10, 97–98,
105, 106, 115
influence on Okigbo, 133, 158
influence on Walcott, 98–99
and Larkin, 37, 38, 98
the local and the global, 3, 14
and migration, 140
national identity of, ix, 24, 25, 27–28,
36
and syncretism, 104, 105
and traveling poetry, 52, 61–62

use of alien cultural materials, 11, 28,
109–11
use of non-English languages, 18–19
works: "East Coker," 32; "The Fire
Sermon," 106–7; "Little Gidding,"
2; The Waste Land, 14, 28, 89, 98,
105, 106, 108, 109–11, 113, 121, 160
Ellmann, Richard, 44
Empson, William, 25
English language
and alienation, 137
and colonialism, 19
dominance of, 18–20
epitaphs, 88–89
ethnic identity. See racial/ethnic identity
Evaristo, Bernardine, 3, 17
and Britain, xiii, 146, 164, 175–80
and compound characters, 2
The Emperor's Babe, 2, 175–80
the local and the global, 14

Fanon, Frantz, 126, 148, 155, 156, 158
Featherstone, Mike, 16
Fenollosa, Ernest, 27
Ford, Ford Madox, 27
formalism, 38–39, 43
Freud, Sigmund, 41, 84–85
Friel, Brian, 143
Frost, Robert, 118
Froude, James Anthony, 1

Gaudier-Brzeska, Henri, 27
gender and dialect, 29–31
ghazals, 56, 104–5, 160
Giddens, Anthony, 6, 13, 59, 64
Gikandi, Simon, 13, 96
Gilroy, Paul, 166, 178
Ginsberg, Allen, 11, 46, 97–98, 152, 153
"Kaddish," 43, 90
Glissant, Édouard, 10, 30, 96
globalization, xi
and colonialism, 13–15
and homogenization, 6–10
and locality, 3–18

and modernity, 4, 5–15, 26–28, 31, 35,
    189n23
and technology, 25–26
and transportation, 25–26
Gonne, Maud, 78, 79
Goodison, Lorna, 3, 12
    and alienation, 136, 138, 139
    and decolonization, 151, 155
    and heteroglossia, 106
    influence of Yeats on, 95–96, 115
    the local and the global, 14
    and migration, 39, 52, 140
    and modernism, xii, 95–96, 101, 102,
        105, 106, 115, 118, 157
    and place-names, 144–45
    and South African feminism, 156–57
    works: *Controlling the Silver*, 138;
        "Country, Sligoville," 95–96;
        "Guinea Woman," 155; "Island
        Aubade," 138; "Ode to the Watch-
        man," 138; "To Us, All Flowers Are
        Roses," 144–45
Graham, Jorie, 39
Graves, Robert, 25
Gray, Jeffrey, 52
Gunn, Thom, 38

Hacker, Marilyn, 39
Hafez, 19
haikus, 56, 113
Hall, Stuart, 9, 163, 165, 168
Hannerz, Ulf, 9
Hardy, Thomas, 37, 55–56, 60
Harjo, Joy, 11, 46
Harper, Michael S.
    "Nightmare Begins Responsibil-
        ity," 72
Harrison, Tony, xiii, 2, 11, 157
    "On Not Being Milton," 151
    "The School of Eloquence," 151
Hass, Robert, 39
Hayden, Robert, 38, 43
H.D., xi, 25, 34, 140
    "Oread," 45
    The Walls Do Not Fall, 34

Heaney, Seamus, 2
    and elegy, 71–72
    influence of Auden on, 85
    the local and the global, 14, 39–40,
        191n55
    on Plath, 57
    and traveling poetry, 60
    works: "Alphabets," 16–17, 40;
        "Anything Can Happen," 40;
        "Bogland," 39–40; "Electric
        Light," 40; "Station Island," 40
Hejinian, Lyn, 19, 39
Held, David, 183n34
heterogenization, 9–10, 144
heteroglossia, 105–6, 157, 175
Hill, Geoffrey, 38, 39
    "September Song," 86
Homer, 53, 142
    The Odyssey, 1
homogenization, 6–10
Hopkins, Gerard Manley, 39
Horace, 19, 40
Housman, A. E., 35, 37
Howe, Susan, 58–59, 60
    "Rückengifur," 58–59, 70
Hughes, Langston, 17
    and alienation, 131–32
    compared to D. H. Lawrence, 33
    compared to Eliot, 61–62
    and compound characters, 2
    as an indigenous poet, 42, 43
    influence of Whitman on, 33, 114
    and jazz and blues, 119
    and modernism, 26, 118
    and modernity, xii, 122–23, 126
    national identity of, 25, 33
    and traveling poetry, xi, 52, 60–63, 67,
        68, 69–70
    works: *Fine Clothes to the Jew*, 122; "I,
        Too," 33; "The Negro Artist and
        the Racial Mountain," 131–32;
        "The Negro Speaks of Rivers," 14,
        33, 60–63, 131; "Theme for English
        B," 2, 15–16; "The Weary Blues,"
        131

Hughes, Ted, 39, 40
  "Out," 58
Hulme, T. E., 27
Huntington, Samuel, 12
Huyssen, Andreas, 8, 115, 119
hybridization, 3, 28, 47

identity, national. *See* national identity
identity, racial/ethnic. *See* racial/ethnic
    identity
imagism, 45
imperialism. *See* colonialism
*Independence Anthology of Jamaican Liter-
    ature, The,* 144–45
Irish poetry, 39–41

Jakobson, Roman, 76
James, C. L. R., 157
James, Henry, 27
Jameson, Fredric, 8, 13–14, 96
jazz, 37–38, 43, 97–98, 119
Jekyll, Walter, 29–30
Jemie, Onwuchekwa, 183n33, 199n4,
    207n48, 208n62
Jewish poets, 44, 46, 114
Johnson, James Weldon, 131
Johnson, Linton Kwesi, 3, 46
  and alienation, 139
  and Britain, xiii, 164, 172–74
  and collectivity, 134–35
  and decolonization, 146, 149, 161
  influence of Okigbo on, 85
  and modernity, 127
  use of Creole, 19, 172
  works: "Inglan is a Bitch," 146, 172;
    "New Craas Massakah," 134, 172–
    74
Johnson, Osa and Martin, 63, 64, 65, 67
Jonson, Ben, 81
  "On My First Son," 72
Jordan, June
  "Poem about My Rights," 60

Karadzic, Radovan, 74
Kay, Jackie, 164

Kearney, Richard, 40
Kenner, Hugh, 44
Kipling, Rudyard, 34, 92
  "Epitaphs of the War," 88–89
Kitchener, Lord, xiii, 15, 164, 168–70
  "If You're Not White You're Black,"
    169–70
  "London is the Place for Me," 168–
    69
  "My Landlady's Too Rude," 169
Koch, Kenneth, 143
Krishnaswamy, Revathi, 9–10

Larkin, Philip, xii, 37–38, 98, 151
  "Homage to a Government," 38,
    149–50
Lawrence, D. H., 25, 33
Lazarus, Neil, 109
Ledwidge, Francis, 40
Lee, Li-Young, 3, 18–19, 39, 46
  "Persimmons," 18
Levertov, Denise, xii, 24, 33, 37
  "Olga Poems," 87
Lévi-Strauss, Claude, 100
Lewis, Wyndham, 27, 121, 126
Lindsay, Vachel, 27
lineation, 53–54, 61, 69
Lipking, Lawrence, 74
lists. *See* catalog verse
Livingston, Robert Eric, 182n13
Lloyd, David, 39
locality, 3–18, 39–40
Longfellow, Henry Wadsworth
  Song of Hiawatha, 10
Lowell, Amy, 25
Lowell, Robert, 39, 114
Loy, Mina, 17
  "Anglo-Mongrels and the Rose," 2,
    32–33, 118
  compared to Yeats, 32–33
  and compound characters, 2
  and elegy, 86–87
  and migration, 6, 52, 140
  national identity of, 24, 25, 32–33, 36
  "Songs for Joannes," 36

MacDiarmid, Hugh, 118, 119, 126
MacLeish, Archibald
  "You, Andrew Marvell," 54
MacNeice, Louis, 25
Madubuike, Ihechukwu, 183n33, 199n4,
  207n48, 208n62
Mahon, Derek, 41
Marinetti, F. T., 121, 126
Markham, Edward, 164
Marson, Una, 164
Martínez, Dionisio D., xi, 2–3, 46
  "Hysteria," 14, 68–70
Masters, Edgar Lee, 27, 35
Maxwell, William J., 188n23
McGill, Meredith, 47–48
McGuckian, Medbh, 41
McKay, Claude, xi, 2
  Braithwaite on, 158, 166
  and Britain, xiii, 15, 164, 165–67
  communist activities of, 188n23
  compared to Eliot, 32
  Euro-American technique of, 42
  and form, 45
  influence of Robert Burns on, 29
  and migration, 52, 140
  and modernism, 119
  and modernity, xii, 123
  national identity of, 25, 29–31, 36
  use of Creole, 19, 29–30, 106
  works: Constab Ballads, 165; Harlem
    Shadows, 29; "If We Must Die,"
    30–31; A Long Way from Home,
    166; "A Midnight Woman to the
    Bobby," 29–30; "Old England,"
    165; "Outcast," 32, 123; Songs of
    Jamaica, 165; "The Tropics in New
    York," 123; "The White City," 123
McLeod, John, 146
Merrill, James, 38, 52
Merwin, W. S., 19, 39
metaphors, 57
Michaels, Walter Benn, 61, 188n17
migration, xi, 24–26, 31–37, 86–90, 136–
  37, 164–80
  See also traveling poetry

Milosz, Czeslaw, 39
Milton, John, 72, 143
  "Lycidas," 74
Mnthali, Felix
  "The Stranglehold of English Lit.,"
    159
modernism
  and alienation, 130–40
  and antimodernity, 121–30
  and apocalypticism, 106–8, 157
  and Asian influences, 10, 109–14
  Euromodernism vs. non-Western
    modernism, 47, 96–97
  heteroglossia, 105–6, 157
  and migration, 25
  and postcolonialism, xii, 47, 95–115,
    117–40
  syncretism, 102–5, 157
  translocalism, 101–2, 157
modernity, xi
  and colonialism, 123–26
  and computers, 127
  and globalization, 4, 5–15, 26–28, 31,
    35, 189n23
  and postcolonialism, xii, 119–40
  and transportation, 126–27
  vs. tradition, 120–30
Moore, Marianne, 35, 38, 119, 143
Moretti, Franco, 88
Morris, Mervyn, 128, 135
Moschus, 72
mourning. See elegy
Muldoon, Paul, 2, 4, 39, 40–41, 52, 58
  "The Grand Conversation," 41
  "7, Middagh Street," 40–41
Murray, Les
  "The Powerline Incarnation," 14

Naipaul, V. S., 117
names, places. See place-names
Narayan, Kirin, 28
national anthems, 81
national anthologies, 145–46
national identity, ix–x, 23–31, 34, 43–49
  culture-of-birth determinism, 35–37

national identity (*cont.*)
    and decolonization, 154–58
    and national anthologies, 145–46
    and place-names, 144–45
    See also racial/ethnic identity
nationalism and elegy, xi–xii, 34, 72–82
nationalist poetry, 34–35, 37–38
Neruda, Pablo, 157
Ngũgĩ wa Thiong'o, 48
Nichols, Grace, 4, 15, 146, 163, 164,
    174–75
    The Fat Black Woman's Poems, 174–75
    "Wherever I Hang," 163, 175
North, Michael, 26, 29, 106, 189n24
Nussbaum, Martha, 182n11

O'Hara, Frank, xi, 38
    "The Day Lady Died," 54
Okigbo, Christopher, xi
    and African models, 42, 158
    and alienation, 132–33, 136, 137
    and apocalypticism, 107–8
    and European models, 158
    the global and the local, 4–6, 15
    and heterogenization, 9
    influence of Eliot on, 133
    influence of Pound on, 103, 133
    influence of Yeats on, 85, 102–3, 108, 133
    influence on Linton Kwesi John-
      son, 85
    and modernism, xii, 42, 98–99,
      102–3, 105, 107–8, 115, 118, 157
    and modernity, 6, 9
    and syncretism, 102–3
    and traveling poetry, 60
    works: "Come Thunder," 107–8;
      "Distances," 133; *Heavensgate,* 4–6,
      12, 110, 133; "Hurrah for Thunder,"
      133; "Initiations," 133; "Lament of
      the Masks," 72, 102–3; "Lament
      of the Silent Sisters," 133; "New-
      comer," 133
Okot p'Bitek
    and alienation, 139
    and catalog verse, 143

and decolonization, xii, 147–48, 149,
    151, 161
and heterogenization, 9
as an indigenous poet, 42, 43, 158
influence of Longfellow and the
    Bible on, 10
influence of non-English languages
    on, 19
the local and the global, 12
and migration, 52
and modernism, 98–99
and modernity, 125–26, 129, 130
popularity of, 134
works: *Song of Lawino,* 6–8, 9, 10,
    65–66, 67, 70, 134, 147–48; *Song of
    Ocol,* 125–26
Okri, Ben, 139
    "On Edge of Time Future," 135
Olson, Charles, 33
    "Projective Verse," 33, 98
Ong, Aihwa, 31
Oppen, George, 44, 46, 114
orientalism, 11, 109–14, 153–54
otherness, 63–68
Owen, Stephen, 9
Owen, Wilfred, xii, 72, 84, 92, 93, 118
    "Strange Meeting," 85–86

Pease, Donald, 37
Perloff, Marjorie, 114
Peters, Lenrie, 124
Petrone, Beth, 88
Picasso, Pablo, 27, 36
    Les Demoiselles d'Avignon, 11
place-names, 39, 40, 41, 95, 142–45, 146,
    150, 154–55
planetary poetry, 16–17
Plath, Sylvia, 1, 2
    and elegy, 89–90
    influence of Auden on, 85
    influence on Eavan Boland, 41
    national identity of, 24, 38
    and traveling poetry, xi, 57, 59, 60
    works: "Cut," 57, 59; "Daddy," 89–90;
      "Lady Lazarus," 40

Porter, Dennis, 11
postcolonialism
    and alienation, 130–40
    and cultural identity, 134–39
    and modernism, xii, 95–115, 117–40
    and modernity, xii, 119–40
    and postmodernity, 119–20
    See also colonialism; decolonization
postmodernity, 119–20
Pound, Ezra, 2, 29, 32, 119
    and alienation, 131
    antimodernity of, 121
    criticized by William Carlos Wil-
        liams, 35
    and East Asian poetry, 10, 27–28
    and elegy, 89
    and heteroglossia, 105–6
    on importation of models, 25
    influence on Jewish poets, 46, 114
    influence on Okigbo, xii, 103, 115, 133
    and Larkin, 38, 98
    and migration, 6, 140
    national identity of, 25, 27–28
    and translocalism, 101
    and traveling poetry, 6, 51, 52–54, 58,
        59, 60
    use of alien cultural materials, 11, 28,
        109, 113–14
    use of non-English languages, 18–19
    works: *The Cantos,* 27, 51, 52–54, 70,
        103, 109, 118; *Cathay,* 113–14; "Hell
        Cantos," 131; *Hugh Selwyn Mau-*
        berley, 89, 131; "In a Station of the
        Metro," 45, 113; "A Pact," 159
Pratt, Mary Louise, 54
prose fiction, 3, 53
Purohit Swami, Shri, 32

racial/ethnic identity, 24, 43–47, 61–63
    See also national identity
Ramanujan, A. K., 98–99, 105, 115, 117,
        118, 140, 155
    "Chicago Zen," 101–2
Reznikoff, Charles, 46, 114
    Holocaust, 46

rhyme, 55–56
rhythm, 55, 56
Rich, Adrienne, 38, 41, 44
Riding, Laura, 25, 34
Rimbaud, Arthur, 67
Ríos, Alberto, 19, 46
Robbins, Bruce, 15, 17
Robinson, E. A., 35, 42
Roethke, Theodore, 39
Rukeyser, Muriel, 44
Rushdie, Salman, 47, 102

Said, Edward, xii, 11, 13, 24, 49, 51, 112,
        138, 141, 152–61
    Culture and Imperialism, 143, 153–61
    Humanism and Democratic Criticism,
        161
    Orientalism, 153
Salter, John, 96
Sandburg, Carl, 35, 36, 42, 68
Senghor, Léopold, 36, 157
Sexton, Anne, 72
Shakespeare, William, 143
Shelley, Percy Bysshe, 81, 92, 114
Simic, Charles, 39, 52
Simon, Paul, 109
Smith, Zadie, 176
Snyder, Gary, 39
Sollors, Werner, 24
Song of Solomon, 10
South Asian influences, 109–10
Soyinka, Wole, 3
    and Britain, 15, 164, 171–72
    and decolonization, 155
    and European models, 42, 158
    and migration, 39, 140
    and modernism, 98–99, 117, 118, 157
    and modernity, xii, 126–27, 129, 130
    works: "Around Us, Dawning," 126;
        "Death in the Dawn," 126–27;
        "Idanre" and Other Poems, 102, 126;
        "Telephone Conversation," 171
Spender, Stephen, 108
Spenser, Edmund, 81
Spivak, Gayatri, 17, 19, 64, 67, 142

Stafford, William
  "Report to Crazy Horse," 60
stanzas, 54–55
Stein, Gertrude, 29, 32, 126, 153
  and migration, 140
  national identity of, ix, 23, 25
  polylingualism of, 36
  Tender Buttons, 118
Stevens, Wallace, xii, 35, 38, 60, 119
  "Bantams in Pine-Woods," 55, 59, 70
  "The Death of a Soldier," 90–91
  "To an Old Philosopher in Rome,"
    91–92
Stewart, Susan, 25
sublimity and decolonization, 142–49
Swinburne, Algernon Charles, 81, 85
syncretism, 102–5, 157

Tagore, Rabindranath, 32, 119, 157
Tate, Allen, 38
technology, global, 25–26
Tennyson, Alfred Lord, 81, 92
  In Memoriam, 71, 72, 81
  "Ode on the Death of the Duke of
    Wellington," 76–77, 81
Tiger, Young. *See* Young Tiger
Tolson, Melvin, 58
  Harlem Gallery, ix, x, 42–43, 55
Tomlinson, Charles, 38
Toomer, Jean, xii, 2, 12, 26, 42, 46
  "Gum," 122
  "Her Lips Are Copper Wire," 122
  "Portrait in Georgia," 45
  "Reapers," 122
  "Song of the Son," 122
*Towards the Decolonization of African
    Literature* (Chinweizu, Jemie, and
    Madubuike), 9, 96, 157–58, 162
tradition *vs.* modernity, 120–30
translocalism, xiii, 13, 15–16, 43, 101–2,
  157, 163–80
transnationalism
  use of term, 13, 31, 47, 181n5
transportation, 25–26, 126–27

traveling poetry, xi, 51–70
  and cultural identity, 59–60
  lineation, 53–54, 61, 69
  metaphors, 57
  and otherness, 63–68
  rhyme, 55–56
  rhythm, 55, 56
  stanzas, 54–55
  See also migration
Trivedi, Harish, 109, 110

United Nations
  Declaration on the Granting of In-
    dependence to Colonial Countries
    and Peoples, 142–43, 161

Virgil, 81
Volkan, Vamik, 74–75
von Hallberg, Robert, 52

Walcott, Derek, xi, 17, 101
  and alienation, 136, 137, 139
  and Britain, 164
  compared to Louise Bennett, 42
  and compound characters, 1–2
  Darwish compared to, 152, 153
  and decolonization, xii, 148–49, 151,
    154–55, 161
  and globalization, 8
  and heteroglossia, 106
  influence of Auden on, 85
  influence of Eliot on, 98–99
  on the Irish, 156
  and migration, 39, 140
  and modernism, 98–99, 103–4, 106,
    117, 118
  and modernity, 6, 129
  and place-names, 142, 144
  and syncretism, 103–4
  and traveling poetry, 53, 55, 58, 60
  use of Creole, 136
  works: "Eulogy to W. H. Auden,"
    72; "A Far Cry from Africa," 103,
    178; "The Fortunate Traveller," 16,

53, 125; "The Light of the World,"
136; *Omeros*, 8, 42, 55, 103–4; "Pre-
lude," *Collected Poems*, 98–99; "Ru-
ins of a Great House," 159, 176;
"The Schooner *Flight*," 1–2, 3, 5, 12,
106, 136, 178; "A Sea-Chantey," 144;
"The Sea Is History," 58, 148–49
Weber, Max, 128
Westover, Jeff, 61
Whistler, James, 27
Whitman, Walt, 26, 27, 33, 42, 72, 114,
143
Wilbur, Richard, 114
Wilde, Oscar, 175
Williams, Raymond, 25, 26, 130
Williams, William Carlos, 26, 35, 38, 39
Al Que Quiere!, 35
"Death," 72
"The Kermess," 56
Kora in Hell, 35
Winkiel, Laura, 185n57
Winters, Yvor, 38
Wolfe, Charles
"The Burial of Sir John Moore," 76
Wordsworth, William, 39
Wright, James, 88

Yeats, W. B., 2, 11, 118, 159
and alienation, 131
antimodernity of, 121, 126
and apocalypticism, 108
compared to Mina Loy, 32–33
Darwish compared to, 152, 153
and decolonization, 12, 13, 154–55, 157
and elegy, xii, 77–85, 92
influence of Blake on, 114

influence of Shelley on, 81, 114
influence of Spenser on, 81
influence of Swinburne on, 81, 85
influence on Auden, 85
influence on Auden circle, 46
influence on Lorna Goodison, 95–
96, 115
influence on Okigbo, 85, 102–3, 108,
133
and Larkin, 37, 38
national identity of, ix–x, 25, 32–33,
119
Said on, 157
and syncretism, 102–3
and traveling poetry, 52, 54
use of alien cultural materials, 11, 109,
111–12
works: "Easter, 1916," 32, 77–80, 81;
"In Memory of Eva Gore-Booth
and Con Markievicz," 80–81, 83;
"In Memory of Major Robert
Gregory," 80; "An Irish Airman
Foresees His Death," 80; "Lapis
Lazuli," 32, 54, 111–12, 113; "Man
and the Echo," 154; "Mourn — and
Then Onward," 77; "Sailing to Byzantium," 32; "The Second Coming," 108; "Under Ben Bulben," 83;
"Vacillation," 54
Young Tiger
"I Was There (At the Coronation),"
170

Zephaniah, Benjamin, 164
Zukofsky, Louis, 36, 46, 114
"Poem Beginning 'The,'" 46